SCOTTISH WRITERS TALKING 2

Scottish Writers Talking 2

IAIN BANKS
BERNARD MACLAVERTY
NAOMI MITCHISON
IAIN CRICHTON SMITH
ALAN SPENCE

in interview

Edited by Isobel Murray

TUCKWELL PRESS

First published in Great Britain in 2002 by
Tuckwell Press Ltd
The Mill House
Phantassie
East Linton
East Lothian, EH40 3DG

ISBN 1 86232 280 5

The publishers acknowledge subsidy
from the Scottish Arts Council
towards the publication of this volume

Scottish
Arts Council

Typeset by Hewer Text Ltd, Edinburgh
Printed and bound by Bell and Bain Ltd, Glasgow

CONTENTS

ACKNOWLEDGEMENTS

The editor is forever grateful to all her victims in this volume. The earlier parts of these interviews could not have been completed without the financial help of the University of Aberdeen Development Trust, and the book was completed with help from the University Arts and Divinity Research Committee. Bob Tait was endlessly helpful, especially when he intervened in the relevant sessions.

Other help is gratefully acknowledged: from Aberdeen's Queen Mother Library, and from colleagues and friends, especially Nancy Robertson, Fiona Insch, Paul Bohan, Thomas Wratten, Donalda Crichton Smith, Dr Barbara Fennell, Professor David Hewitt, Dr Alison Lumsden, Mig and Frank Brangwin, Laurence Graham, and Sheriff Richard Scott.

Isobel Murray
May 2002

INTRODUCTION
Isobel Murray

THE FIVE LENGTHY interviews presented here are in no sense presented as topical. They are in-depth interviews, in which Isobel Murray, sometimes in tandem with Bob Tait, encouraged individual writers to talk at length about their work, their early lives, and what was of importance to them. The idea is to illuminate their work and our idea of the authors. They will not go out of date if an author publishes another book. So the earliest of these is our interviews with Naomi Mitchison, in 1984, and the most recently completed was the one with Alan Spence, the second part of which was recorded in 2000. What matters is not how recently the interview took place, although it is always very important that the reader knows when that was, at what stage in the writer's career.

The brief Preface to the first volume in this series, *Scottish Writers Talking* (1996), explains that one main negative impetus for starting our series was the omission of any Scottish writers at all from the collections of *Paris Review* interviews, the first series of which began volume publication in 1958 in the series entitled *Writers at Work*, published by Penguin. The interviews are ongoing, and publication continues, in a rather diffuse way. Once started, however, we felt we could improve a bit on the *Paris Review* model. Their interviews, begun in 1953, cover writers from every continent, and are typically 20–25 pages long, whereas ours are much more discursive. In our approach, a great deal of preparatory work has to be done by the interviewer, reading or re-reading as much as possible of the writer's *oeuvre*. Then, unrestrained by the limitations of periodical pages, I like to let our writers talk at leisure, revealing themselves and their preoccupations generously to interested readers. One hope here is that we may occasionally ask questions or elicit answers that future readers would want to ask. If I could call back Grassic Gibbon, I'd ask whether the reader was to suppose Chris dead at the end of *Grey Granite*, and whether if he'd had time for second thoughts he wouldn't have liked to excise Ewan's saying, 'suddenly and queerly *The Last Supper, Chris*'. But eager interviewers also fall on any unexpected titbit: some future researcher of *To the Chapel Perilous* will seize with interest, as both of us did, the moment when Mitchison let fall that one of its characters was based on that great journalist James Cameron (p. 100).

The sustained length of the interview allows time to venture beyond prepared material, or the set of unconsciously prepared responses we have found most writers in the public eye have developed through brief newspaper or radio interviews. They are not savagely cropped, although 'sort of's' and 'well's' are edited out, and almost nothing is added except the indication that irony, sarcasm or humour was being adopted – (L). Notes added in parenthesis in italic are mine, intended to explain references and elucidate contexts.

The Paris Review has used anonymous interviewers, while we are clear who was there and who said what. All our interviews are with a writer plus Bob Tait and myself, or with myself only. I think it is important to explain in each case whether we knew the writer in advance, and in what capacity. This is done before each interview here. In the first volume we spoke to George Mackay Brown and Norman MacCaig, both old friends, to William McIlvanney who was not only friend but at the time Writer in Residence at Aberdeen University, and to Jessie Kesson and John Reid, 'David Toulmin', neither of whom we knew before their respective interviews, but both of whom became friends thenceforth. In this volume, Iain Crichton Smith was a very old friend, Bernard MacLaverty and Alan Spence became our good friends through serving as Writers in Residence, Iain Banks was a very approachable visiting speaker, and Naomi Mitchison was a rather daunting unknown, who in fact became not just a friend but a collaborator in various literary enterprises.

So – what is the status of such an interview? I would always warn my students that a writer cannot change what s/he has written elsewhere by a statement in interview of what s/he was trying to do: this is self-evident. But we have perhaps got beyond the heated critical debate over the Intentional Fallacy, which was begun in 1946 by W K Wimsatt and Monroe C Beardsley. Interview material cannot of course change achieved works of art, but it can illuminate, inform or offer annotation. The various celebrated guest editors of the *Writers at Work* series have offered alternative visions. Wilfred Sheed has an interesting Introduction to the Fourth Series. He had previously been sceptical about the value of such interviews, but offered big claims in reparation here (1976), even asking: 'Can the interview as a form pass beyond the realm of necessary small talk into art itself?' and answering himself: 'Perhaps. Whenever a good writer uses words, literature is a possibility'. But his basic claim is less lofty:

> The interviews represent the authors' contributions to their own gossip. These are their own fair copies of themselves, and this is the way they would like to be talked about. . . . One senses a continuity of self-creation that would reveal itself equally in small or large matters. . . . The interviews tell stories that even the watchful subjects may not have wanted told; but also, and really more valuably, they tell each subject's favorite story about him or herself.

Alfred Kazin proposed a rather different view in the Third Series (1967). He praises the contents of that volume as 'unusually sensitive and adroit exercises in getting contemporary writers to reveal themselves'. He goes on, stressing his view that an interview is an attempt to understand the fame, or 'exceptionality', of the writer:

> The biographical art of the profile. . . . A profile . . . is a sketch. . . . It is not an intellectual biography. . . . it is a close-up, a startlingly informative glance – usually sympathetic. . . . The interview becomes a way of getting the writer to document this exceptionality himself. . . . The modern writer is likely to feel that his life and work speak for each other; when an interviewer gently presses him to tell more, he will gladly try, for in the writer's own mind clarity about a seemingly personal matter seems to advance that moral clarity which is tantamount to literary power. . . . There is always something professional and impersonal in a writer's concern with his own experience.

I would agree in part with both, to different extents in different interviews, and would go on to make larger claims for the volumes that can result. Sheed said that 'Literature is a battleground of conflicting faiths', and suggested that this in part constituted 'the value of a collection of discordant voices, each hawking its own dogmas'. In our case, both volumes of interviews are connected by a common label –

'Scottish'. At a time when Scottish critics are intently re-examining questions of Scottish identity, the larger picture, discordant or not, has a particular interest when we put together a collection of 'Scottish Writers Talking'.

IAIN BANKS

I FIRST MET Iain Banks when I was invited to chair a Meet the Author session at the Edinburgh Book Festival in 1987. He was one of three relatively new arrivals on the Scottish fiction scene, the other two being Ronald Frame and Frederic Lindsay. It was a successful session, and I was happy, in my capacity as potential future interviewer, to make preliminary contact with all three. But I had already made another kind of contact with all three, as a fiction reviewer. Luckily I had had no problems in praising their exciting new work. I missed out on Banks's notorious debut with *The Wasp Factory*, but reviewed *Walking on Glass* in 1985 – 'strong meat' – and *The Bridge* in 1986 – 'he has made a giant stride'.

Banks was articulate and unaffected, and so when he was invited to read and talk to the Aberdeen Literary Society in 1988, it seemed an opportune moment at least to begin an in-depth interview – before the unusually prolific writer produced more than could reasonably be tackled in the format! I had enjoyed the science fiction novel *Consider Phlebas* (1987), and would go on to read Banks's SF with pleasure because I find his prose compelling, but I was and am far from experienced in criticism or discussion of SF, and was a little worried about that. Luckily, because of the way the interview went, this was of minor importance. It turned into an interview about the early life and times, of interest to any curious reader of Banks. Opportunities to continue it have not been obvious, and it seems to me that it stands free on that basis, and will be enjoyed as such.

29th November 1988, 14 Devanha Terrace, Aberdeen
Present: Iain Banks and Isobel Murray

IM I am going to start by asking Iain in a very straightforward and obvious way to tell us something about his childhood and his upbringing and when the book thing first took hold of him.

IB Well I come from two fairly large families. I think my dad has got about seven or eight brothers and sisters and my mother has round about the same. Although I am an only child myself, I've got scads and scads of cousins. I had a very small individual sort of family with the three of us, so that I guess it was something obvious like the cliché about the only child who retreats into their own little private world. I imagine that there probably is a higher preponderance of only children who become writers, because it is a more reasonably solitary profession than even the other narrative arts.

IM   Can I intervene for a minute and ask the Scottish question, which is: does this huge family background mean it was a Catholic family?

IB   Funnily enough, no. They are both Prods actually, although my paternal grandfather is an atheist and my dad is and I've since become one as well.

IM   But a Protestant atheist?

IB   Yes, aha, yes . . . starting from Protestant, yes. (L) I had that sort of only child upbringing but at the same time I had this extended family of loads of cousins which I've kept in touch with. I was brought up in North Queensferry – born in Dunfermline! – and a lot of them ended up down in England. But I think that even when I was living in Fife it wasn't as broad a Fifer accent as it might have been, so I always had to remain intelligible to my cousins. They'd come up here and I'd go down there, you know.

    When I was nine, my dad was working in the Admiralty – he started out as an able seaman on defence boats working out of Rosyth. In 1963 when I was nine, we moved to Gourock and my dad was working out of Greenock. He eventually ended up as a First Officer, you know, a mate. He's retired now.

IM   Does that mean he was away from home a lot?

IB   Not really. Occasionally. I think the most he ever went away as a rule was about two weeks or so. It wasn't exactly a nine to five job, although on some days it could be. If they were just working on something in the Clyde estuary the boat would just be out for a few hours and come back to port, you know. But sometimes I might go with him. One time I went away down to Great Yarmouth. The particular boat my dad was on specialised in recovering crashed military jets. If one went down in the sea, then they were often called out to do it. They had quite a good team of divers and the sort of specialist equipment and all the rest of it for picking up the wreckage to look for whatever had gone wrong, you know. So that was about the most that he went away for. It was about two weeks at a time. It wasn't like it was the deep sea or whatever. It did mean that my poor long-suffering mother had to look after me quite a lot of the time. I was sort of, you know, waiting for him. 'Where's my daddy?' 'SHUT UP!' (L)

IM Did you find it difficult to move your world when you were about nine?

IB Well, not too much actually. I was sorry to leave the Ferry. North Queensferry was a fabulous place to grow up for a wean. It had everything in terms of what you looked for as a child. There is coastline on three sides for a start, and a sort of neck of land joining it to Inverkeithing. It had loads and loads of the old gun placements. The old barracks used to be down at Port Lane and it was a fabulous place to play. There were loads and loads of old tunnels and bunkers and gun emplacements – all that sort of stuff from the war. They had gun batteries to protect the bridge – mostly anti-air guns. And there were the Ferry Hills which are just up from the higher part of the peninsula which has its own wee loch with the wee island in the middle. I mean, it was Swallows and Amazons stuff. Fascinating place! A whole microcosm. Well, not of Scotland but in terms of various landscape it was a great place. I was sorry to leave there. I was sorry to leave my friends as well obviously, but we still have relations living in the Ferry. I still have an aunt and uncle who live there at the moment in fact. [*Banks moved back to North Queensferry to make his home there in 1991.*] So they were always coming through. Gourock is not that far in the car, well the van, and they would come through every weekend, or second weekend, whatever. Often enough. So it wasn't too terrible. I think also because I was or could be quite solitary sometimes, just retreating into myself, I suppose that made it a bit easier. *That* much was going with me, so I wasn't really missing too much. But yes, I missed a lot of my 'wee pals' and my first girlfriend who I had at the age of five. (L)

IM Were you enjoying school in North Queensferry?

IB Apart from the fact that I ran away once, I did actually, yes. I can't remember why I ran away. It was not that very far away to run, mind you. It was only over the wall into the house from the schoolyard – the playground. Yes, I did enjoy it actually. I always liked doing essays, that was the thing, right from the start. In fact I was a very slow reader at first, but then between six and seven I went straight from 'The cat sat on the mat' to reading the *Reader's Digest* at the age of seven! You know I think I suffered for that. (L)

IM Would you say this is evidence of an early love of literature? (L)

IB No! (L) Addicted to condensed books – my God! No, it was slightly more complicated than the stuff my contemporaries were reading, I think. But I was very slow to start. Once I did get going I was reading fairly sophisticated stuff for a wean.

IM And you were already enjoying writing things before you moved schools?

IB Oh yes. I was nine when I moved and by that time I was quite aware that English was my best subject. It was the only one that I really, really enjoyed. The rest were all right, but English was the one that I really looked forward to. It was just a joy. I really didn't feel that I could do anything wrong. It was almost irrelevant that you were being tested for it every now and again. So I came to regard the English prize and coming first in English as almost a right. But especially when it came to writing essays. If there was a choice of doing fiction I always, always took it. I always thought, 'To Hell with "What you did in your summer holidays?" or "Write a newspaper article about a bank robbery"', or something boring. I suppose I could have joined *The Sun* or something, and pretended to write facts – in fact writing fiction, but I wasn't prescient enough to think of that at the time.

IM You wanted to tell stories even at that age?

IB Yes, that's right.

IM That's good. Before we leave North Queensferry, were you conscious then or are you conscious now – looking back – of belonging to a particular class in society?

IB Not really. It is something I have thought about. It was strange. When we started out we were fairly sort of, if not incredibly poor then certainly not particularly well off. Mind you, we were the first family in the street to have a television. That was one thing that had a definite effect. I was raised a child of the television age in a lot of ways. Because my dad was away fairly often – and you know, poor mum was stuck in the house carrying me – we actually had a television before I was born which in 1954 was pretty early. Mum still talks about me lying on my back on her lap looking upside down at the newsreader on the television with a little mouth going 'Ba, ba, ba', laughing away trying to impersonate this upside down person in tones of grey in the corner. (L) Yes, that was one thing we had and I suppose we had a sort of car. It was actually a succession of old vans we tended to have. But apart from that, there was not a vast amount of money. But because we were living in the Ferry with a lot of relations around the place, you had that sort of closeness of the family. It didn't really matter too much. I suppose we were in a sense upwardly mobile because we went from my dad being an able seaman to eventually becoming an officer. You know, one of the officer classes! I have always been a bit dubious about my ever claiming to be any particular class at all really. My working-class credentials don't bear very close scrutiny, I don't think. (L)

IM But you were, for example, the first generation of your family to get higher education?

IB Yes. Well I was just the first Banks to have letters rather than numbers after my name, you know. It sounded good but I never actually discovered anyone who did go to prison.

IM OK, well tell me about moving to Gourock.

IB It wasn't particularly traumatic. It wasn't very far. It wasn't like moving to Australia or something. Much the same really except more of the same, in the sense that I was happiest doing English or whatever.

IM It's another very picturesque place to live.

IB Yes. We were always lucky in terms of having pleasant views. The view from the house in North Queensferry . . . my bedroom window looked slap onto the bridge. So that had a major effect on things. (L)

IM That's a tiny, simple thing I've learned about you this morning already. You lived in North Queensferry. It figures, doesn't it, with *The Bridge* coming up?

IB Oh absolutely! Not literally in the shadow but literally outside the bedroom window. There it was, you know, filling up half the view.

IM So if somebody else was using the Forth Bridge as a structural device in a novel it might be a fairly artificial thing to do, but for you to do it, it's like using the natural scenery.

IB Just about, yes. It also had a tremendous effect on me. I always did admire it. My dad used to tell me about times back. I suppose it must have been in the 30's when you would go to the Hawes Inn over in South Queensferry and walk back over the bridge, which you are not supposed to do, you know?

IM A lot of people did it. (L)

IB   It was a world symbol as well. You were used to seeing it in advertisements and on television now and again and in books and so on, with the result it was a sort of world symbol, especially with it being painted all the time and all the rest of it. Yes, you were conscious of living – you had a definite sort of pride. You know, 'This is my bridge!' So Gourock was not quite the same. We moved through there. Again, we had a fabulous view quite high up on the hill above Cardwell Bay, looking over Ben Lomond and the Cobbler and the Highlands in general, the start of them. When we first went we had lots and lots of river traffic as well. I remember I had a log of all the ships. I had an old copy of the Lloyd's List and I had this big sort of Admiralty chart book that my dad had got me, a log book sort of thing. I used to copy down all the ships that came up and take doodle drawings of them, and I had a thing that gave you all the shipping lines and the colours of their flags, funnel emblems and so on. I used to note all these down. It's died away. There isn't even a container terminal there now and also there is really more or less only the Cal Mac car ferries now. When we went through there, there must have been perhaps a dozen steamers tied up to the Gourock pier each night during the summer.

IM Did you ever harbour ambitions of going to sea?

IB   I did for a while actually. Yes. My pal at school at the time, his dad was on iron ore carriers, I think it was, in the proper Merchant Marine, you know? His dad was away for months at a time and I think yes, for a while I entertained visions of myself as a navigating officer or whatever. It turned out my eyesight wasn't good enough anyway, but I don't think my heart was really in it. It was a passing fancy more than anything else.

IM So in Gourock you would be moving before all that long to secondary school. Was that really more of the same? Good at English and quite enjoying the rest?

IB   Yes, I wasn't too bad at Physics either, funny enough. I quite enjoyed that, but that was more sort of the practical side. I could see the way the experiment made sense of the figures rather than the other way round. My pure mathematics wasn't particularly good. French, stuff like that, well, I was all right. I wasn't bad and ended up with three Highers or whatever – two 'A's and a 'B' or something – no, one 'A' and two 'B's. Oh, I can't remember!

IM You can't remember now, but did you take it seriously at the time?

IB Fairly so, yes. I wanted to get to university. That was the main thing.

IM You did?

IB Yes, I decided that fairly early on. It was a possibility and I think my
    dad quietly so, my mother a bit more, actually said, 'Look, you could
    go to the university. Wouldn't that be good?' 'Yes, OK. Fair enough!
    If you insist!' (L) It wasn't an expectation or anything. I think they
    thought it would be a good idea if I could. I think by that time I
    actually got into the idea that because I was in the 'A' stream, it was
    more or less expected. The only sort of real academic mistake I ever
    made was to do Latin instead of anything else. I hated Latin.
    Absolutely despised it. Not once did I find that it helped with
    my English. Always the other way round. Because I heard the word
    spelunking I guessed that spelunca meant a cave. It never worked the
    other way round. They said, 'Oh, it will help you with English',
    'Bugger off!'. (L) So, that was my only mistake. That really was a
    young form of snobbery I think. It was assumed that the smart kids
    who were going to go to university should do Latin. And fair enough,
    there were still places like that. St. Andrews, for example, which
    asked for Latin. You couldn't do English without it. I still find
    myself repulsified . . . anyway.

IM Anyway that's hopefully in the past everywhere now. So do you
    remember before you actually went to university, you were pretty
    much of a reader, yes?

IB Yes.

IM Was it just anything and everything? Were there special areas of
    things? Were you reading science fiction, for example?

IB I think I was round about . . . yes, when I was still in Junior High. I
    went to Gourock High to do up to 'O' Levels, and fifth and sixth
    year I went to Greenock High. That was in Port Glasgow and also in
    Greenock itself. So I was collected there to do Highers. I was still in
    Gourock High when I discovered science fiction. In the Gourock
    library there was an absolute mine of all those wonderful yellow
    Gollancz covers, and Ya-haa! I only realised years later that I'd read
    lots and lots of stories by people like Robert Heinlein, but I never
    bothered with the titles of the books, or the names of the authors. If
    it was a yellow Gollancz, it was an SF book. That was for me. I
    suppose, at the most, fifty percent of my reading at one point was
    science fiction. For the rest of it, I was reading just anything I could
    get my hands on. Anything: occasionally rather Boys' Own stuff like

the Conquest of Everest, that sort of stuff, and expeditions to the South Pole. I was still reading Biggles as well at that time.

IM   But it was mostly fiction?

IB   Almost all fiction, yes. I always feel a bit inadequate when it comes to biography. I just can't interest myself that much, that intensely, in somebody's life. A terrible thing to admit. I've never been a great fan of biography. I think it is probably something of a failing.

IM   Can you imagine ever writing an autobiography?

IB   Oh, I'd rather not. A terrible idea. (L) Having said this, thirty years later, you know! Not really. It is too much of a self-indulgence. I'm quite happy for other people to do it. That would be all right. But for me to do it? I think it would just be – ugh.

IM   I can imagine you enjoying hoodwinking the poor would-be biographer in all sorts of ways. (L)

IB   If everything goes on as it has so far, then I suppose that if I remained semi-fashionable or whatever, I might eventually attract the sort of people who could come along . . .

IM   It seems likely. We discovered last night, and may I remind the reader that we are talking in November '88, that one of my students is already working on Alasdair Gray and Iain Banks, when Iain is thirty-four. So if, as he says, he manages to stay fashionable for twenty years there will have been biographies, I'm sure. It's horrendous.

IB   It is actually. Frightening. (L) Frightens the hell out of me. Yes. It is a bit difficult trying to take a complete sort of purist attitude about it. I can understand why some writers, I think Thomas Pynchon is one, won't have anything to do with the whole publicity thing. The only thing you get is just the books and nothing else. There's no interviews or anything else, just what you choose to put out as your fiction or whatever. I can see there is definitely an argument for doing that, but at the same time it is good to be able to explain yourself sometimes. Quite often just because the way that a book is taken, it is not what you actually intended. It is almost a scientific experience to find out: even though you do find yourself saying, 'Well, actually what I meant was . . .' 'Ah, that's not good enough, I'm sorry'. If the consensus is the book is of a certain sort then you don't have too much leeway to say, 'Well, I know that it's not'.

IM   I suspect there's also the fact that when your books are selling well, it nourishes you in some way, the thought that people are wanting to read them and are enjoying them. Kilgore Trout had a very, very lonely life. It can't have been easy to persevere in that kind of situation: whoever wanted to interview Kilgore Trout? Not very many! (L)

IB Yes, it is a good feeling I suppose. That's one thing when we were talking yesterday about the *Paris Review* Interviews and all the rest. I was talking to one journalist who was asking a really basic question, 'Why do you write?' I blethered my way through an answer for a wee while. I think I gave it a reasonably cogent explanation. I can't remember what I said, mind you. (L) Never mind. He was saying that the best answer he had ever read was another *Paris Review* Interview, and I can't remember the actual author involved: I think it was a French author. There was a very long paragraph, more or less just the one sentence of very intellectually crafted argument about why one was driven to write. Then he just stopped and said to the interviewer, 'Well look, you can put all that in if you like, but the truth is you do it because you want to be loved'. That is why you write, and there's a lot to that. You just want to impress people. You just want people to come up and say, 'Really liked your book'. What you are hoping they are really saying is, 'I think you are a wonderful person'. (L) At that real basic level beyond or beneath the urge to communicate and to try and put your ideas across.

IM And to make money.

IB Well, yes. Need to keep the roof over my head. But it is just this thing, almost childish; it's rooted in childhood: you want to be liked. You want to be stroked on the head or whatever. That's very much why you are doing it and I think I'd be very suspicious of a writer who denied that there was that motive formed at least part of the overall drive to write.

IM Do you think if you stopped being 'fashionable' it would make a big difference to your literary output?

IB I don't think so. It's very difficult to tell. I keep waiting for this. In short-term matters I'm a terrible pessimist. I did use to conduct mind experiments, thinking, 'Supposing I did have it handed down on tablets of stone'. You know, the clouds part and the big hand comes down. The guy in the grey flowing beard, who says, 'You will never ever publish anything in your entire life. Forget it'. Would I still write? Yes I would. I even used to get a kick just from writing something for my friends and getting their criticism on books or whatever. And also, just a natural pleasure in simply writing, getting things sorted out in your own mind, which I find writing can actually do. It's not simply that you have an idea and you put it across to the best of your ability in a book and that's it, that sort of simple linear flow. The actual thinking involved and trying to work out how you are going to say what you are saying, actually alters what you are thinking in the first place. It's worth writing just for that internal pleasure, if you like. It sorts your own mind out.

IM You were suggesting yesterday, I think, that doing it on the word processor had a special sort of quality?

IB It takes a lot of the frustration out, apart from anything else. That's probably the main effect it has. Yes, the thing with word-processing, I think it does give a greater opportunity to write more idiosyn-cratically, if you like. Some writers use it to cram in every single possible idea, others use it to take everything out, completely to strip the narrative of every single word. You can fiddle around with it to your heart's content on a word processor the way you can't typing. In theory you can, by typing vast numbers of drafts and all the rest of it. In practice, I think you rapidly approach a point where you've got so many branching possibilities that you would lose track of the thing completely. I think for me, it is simply the frustration factor that matters. I don't really like going back to something. It would really annoy me if you had maybe five or six mistakes on a page or whatever, or you wanted to do something fairly simple, just move this sentence from the start or midway through a paragraph to the end or whatever. You have to retype the whole damn page when most of it was OK. I actually bore quite quickly. If I was reading an old bit that was all right, there's every chance it would suddenly develop a new mistake because I was so bored as I was doing it. I wasn't paying proper attention. The main thing is it takes the frustration out of it. That's what really matters.

IM Well, supposing we went back. We've got you at Greenock now – at school and still good at English, and quite interested in other things, especially Physics. What about things like games and activities and things? Were you a sporty type?

IB A bit, yes. I used to do quite a lot of badminton and tennis. I was never very good at fitba. Pretty awful in fact. (L) I didn't have the most important thing you can have in football – that sense of where everybody else is. I always had to look round to check and make sure they were wearing the right shirt or whatever before I passed the ball. (L) The only technique I ever developed was when I was going to tackle somebody, I sort of stamped my feet so they knew I was coming! (L) Try and intimidate them off the ball. Didn't work very often. So I wasn't terribly good at team games but things like, say, tennis and badminton, I was all right at. I used to really love, really look forward to doing PE at Gourock because we had a PE teacher there who was just a really good guy. We used to go in early for the period just after playtime or whatever. We would go in early. If it was after lunchtime or whatever, we would go straight into the gym. In Greenock they were much more sort of disciplined about it and it wasn't anything like as much fun. There was one classic occasion with one of the older PE teachers: this poor kid came in and said, 'Excuse me, Sir! I've got a broken leg'. He's got on plaster up to his thigh and the wee guy looked at him and said, 'Just keep your vest on and do what you can'. (L)

Yes, that was the difference, I suppose, just maybe the schools' approach to it. I wasn't weedy or anything. I was always sort of biggish for my age. I was reasonably good at games and stuff.

IM   As you said yesterday in another connection off the tape, you don't enjoy very much collaborating, working with people. In the same way, team games were not your bag. It's interesting.

IB   Again, that's got to do with being an only child or whatever.

IM   Could be.

IB   You're sort of used to getting your own way and doing it your way. The only time I've sort of collaborated with anyone was on the original draft of *The Wasp Factory* screenplay. I didn't enjoy that. I mean the lassie I was working with who was going to be the director of the film if it ever got made, I got on quite well with her, it was just the actual simply coping with somebody and collaborating with somebody else. I did not take to that at all. I always want to do it my way, you know. (L)

IM   Might be a pause for a refrain here. So you were going to go to university. What made you choose Stirling?

IB   Well, there was two slightly conflicting reasons. One was simply that Stirling did continuous assessment, and I didn't like exams. It was the only thing I didn't like. Apart from English – again that was dead easy. I used to get nervous before exams. No more than anybody else. I wasn't actually throwing up or anything. One or two of my schoolmates were. They were really nervous. I just didn't enjoy it and I thought if there was any way of not having to do exams, you know, why the hell? And you could still go to university and all the rest of it. Why not take that? So that's why Stirling attracted me. And in a way, it was all down to fate. (L) What happened was, you know you get that UCCA checkbook thing of responses that you send off. Well, I'd applied to Stirling and Glasgow, and I can't actually remember now which one was my first choice, but I remember I got a firm response, a firm 'yes' back from Stirling, and I was still thinking about perhaps going to Glasgow or Strathclyde or whatever it was. I thought I'd wait and see what they said. So I sent off a conditional acceptance of the Stirling offer, and before the thing came back from Strathcylde saying I could go there as well, a letter came from Stirling saying thank you for your firm acceptance. And I thought, 'What?' (L) And I looked back to the little book and I had sent off a conditional and not a firm acceptance, and I thought, 'Ah, what the hell!' (L) Looks like 'I am meant to go to Stirling'. Could just be pure laziness. I couldn't be bothered arguing about it.

IM Does this implied time sequence mean you did do a sixth year at school after you had done your Highers?

IB Yes. I re-did Physics. I changed my Physics grade from a 'C' to a 'B', I think. I resat Mathematics again and got a third or fourth 'O' Level or whatever! (L) I picked up another 'O' Level for French which already had two. I ended up with about fourteen 'O' Levels but four of them were Mathematics and three were French – something daft like that. (L) Yes, I did my dissertation in Sixth Year English. It was – what the hell was it now? It was about science fiction anyway. It was about non-realistic writing in science fiction. In an act of bravado, I was sort of shilly-shallying about. If I can backtrack a bit, to my sort of technique of doing an essay in exam conditions. I used to sit there and look at the paper for ages. If it was a two-hour exam, I would sit and look at it for about an hour. 'I haven't got any ideas', you know? In the absolute minimum time that I still had left, it was, 'Ah! I have ideas!'. You know, race through. It looked dead impressive. It looked incredibly cool. But I wasn't actually trying this, you know? (L) So as I was saying, something of the same sort happened with this dissertation. It was due in and due in and I was supposed to discuss it with my English teacher who has since become a good friend.

IM You are allowed to mention names in these situations.

IB Joan Lewis in fact. She's retired now. It's through Joan that I met
    Bernard MacLaverty. She was on at me one day saying, 'Come on.
    Have you got a proper plan of this together?' OK. So I went off and I
    wrote the whole thing that night. (L) 'There you are', next morning.
    I didn't get a particularly good grade but it was the sheer showman-
    ship of 'Na na, na, na na!' Yes, I wrote it all in one night. Ha, ha, ha!
    Slight sort of cutting off one's nose to spite one's face there, perhaps.

IM There was a sense in which you already weren't terribly seriously
    academically ambitious.

IB Not really.

IM You were going on because you enjoyed it, rather than because it was
    a particular academic height you wanted to scale?

IB Oh yes. Very much so.

IM So, you go to Stirling and you sign up to do English and Philosophy
    and Psychology.

IB Psychology, yes.

IM Have you any excuses?

IB I'd already decided I wanted to be a Writer with a capital W. So
    those seemed to be the things I should do. You know, obviously you
    should do English. Philosophy seemed to be the thing as well, if you
    are going to write any meaningful books. (L) So I had pretensions. I
    didn't always enjoy it, but I still went. I didn't want to turn out trash
    here, you know. So yes, Philosophy seemed to be a good thing for
    that. Actually not in the way I expected, but it did pay real dividends
    I think. Psychology? Well, you know. Obvious. There'll be char-
    acters in that. (L) I don't think it really did have much effect. I'm not
    sure that Psychology claims to be a science any more. Would I have
    written any less shakily if I had done Economics? Witch doctordom,
    whatever. Philosophy, yes. I actually got better grades in Philosophy
    than I did in English. We can waffle more in Philosophy. In terms of
    pure academic success, my English wasn't particularly good. For the
    first time, I was actually sharing a room, with this guy whose father
    was an English teacher from Cumbernauld. And this guy was really
    good – just looking at a piece of writing and spotting all the things
    that the writer had put in there or whatever. We compared essays
    afterwards. He got an 'A' and I got a 'C' or whatever. He would
    point these things out and I'd think, 'Oh yes. That should have been
    obvious. Of course'. I think we were doing *The Mayor of Caster-*

bridge at one time – about Hardy, and this guy spotted all these things I don't think anybody would have perhaps spotted at all. When things were pointed out, they did seem quite obvious and, 'Hardy must be making a point if he is comparing this particular character to this inn-sign because it was very flat and two-dimensional', and awesome stuff. Wow, yes! That's really neat! But it passed me by, damn it! (L)

IM   So, before you went to Stirling were you already writing for yourself?

IB   Yes. I was. In my early teens I think I started writing my first novel. I thought it was, actually, I thought it was a novel. It was about 10,000 words. A longish chapter! (L) Where a lot of it came from in fact was, it used to take me ages to get to sleep. My brain was spinning round for at least an hour after, you know, my tousled head hit the pillow. I used to make up these stories. Really they weren't literary-based stories. They were really based on television or whatever. I used to make up these adventure stories about secret agents and spies and all that sort of stuff. Later on, science fiction as well. I made these up, would think all these to myself and go through these stories at night. Eventually I would conk out. It originally came from that. One particular one I thought, 'That's quite a good story. I might actually write that'. But it was strange, there were different departments for these, which weren't talking to each other. The writing bit which was doing essays in school and all the rest of it, and this other, almost show-business based idea. You know, these Big Budget, Behind the Eyes, Inside the Brain a sort of a TV series in fact, having different adventures for the same people, effectively a series. The very first book, my first attempt at a book, had an incredibly snappy title, *The Hungarian Lift Jet*. A piece of technology! (L) I started trying to write that and I'd only written about 10,000 words and thought it was a novel. I tried it again when I was sixteen. By this time I had just gone up to Greenock High. I decided that one way to make myself write, I would tell everyone about it and say, 'I'm writing a book'. (L) If I don't say anything I can quietly give up. If I tell everyone they're all going to say, 'Na na na'. So I told everyone I was writing a book. That ended up about 140,000 words. It was quite a respectable length for a novel. Twice the length of *The Wasp Factory*. I was sixteen when I finished that. This one was written in pencil in longhand in a big Admiralty logbook that my dad brought back from the boat.

The next one was this incredible 400,000-word long mega blockbuster that wouldn't end. That was the first one I actually typed. That was when I was eighteen. I was just finishing that when I went to Stirling. I wrote another one when I was at Stirling. My first science fiction.

IM Did you ever send that one to a publisher?

IB I actually had a good mind to send the second one – the blockbuster! Oh God! (L) It was written, no margins, written in foolscap, not A4 paper, single spaced. The other thing is, the only crime I didn't commit was typing on both sides of the paper. I only didn't do that because it was tissue thin. If I had, it would have gone right through to the second impression. I don't imagine anyone would want to look at the first page of that, why I didn't even finish reading that. A disaster. It was a complete first draft. No revision at all. I had this idea, and I didn't realise how publishing worked. I thought you could send something like this off and a publisher would say, 'Well, needs a lot of work but a definite rough diamond here'. Bullshit. It just doesn't work that way. You've got to present it as well as you possibly can because they do get so much stuff. They know that ninety per cent of the stuff they get – well more, ninety-nine per cent of the stuff that does come in goes over the transom onto the slush pile. Phrases that my editor told me never to use but that's the way they refer to it internally. Ninety-nine per cent of that is basically rubbish and unpublishable, so you do have to take care. The purist in me, part of me didn't want to sell out or whatever. You know, you shouldn't conform to this petty bourgeois ideal! It's got to be really well presented. Who cares?! That's not the point. I'm a Writer. Yes, you do have to present it as well as possible. And an absolutely flawless first page. You can have a few corrections halfway through or whatever. You've got to do everything you can to make it easy because some poor beggar's got to sit down in a publisher's office or at home with a pile of what they know is mostly going to be crap. You might make their job a little bit easier for them.

IM Did you get any helpful letters or just your actual straightforward rejection slips?

IB The only sort of variation I got – this was when it was all happening. I got a wonderful rejection slip. (L) Anyway, in retrospect, saying, 'Dear Mr Banks, we quite liked your book, but because of the current paper shortage –' (L) I thought it was great. I didn't at the

time. No, there weren't any helpful letters at all. Just can't fit this
into our current list or whatever.

IM It didn't really make any difference to your determination to carry
on?

IB Not really. I had a list of about eight dozens of publishers. I think I
always used to start with Jonathan Cape.

IM Not Gollancz?

IB Not Gollancz. Well, I did the science fiction, yes. That was with
Gollancz, I think. I can't remember. I'm sure I've got a list
somewhere in one of my old notebooks of who I sent it to. Once
a book had come back about a dozen times, I sort of went, 'Ach well'.
It always takes about a month or so at least. I think three weeks was
the absolute minimum turn round. And again, once they had looked
at it and thrown it back into the Return to Sender pile. By that time I
usually had a plan or idea for the next book anyway. After being
totally committed to the book you were sending off, you suddenly
thought. 'Ach well, it's not that good. I can do better the next time'.
So you lost enthusiasm for that and then went on to the next novel.
There's that constant thing of, 'Well, this one will be the one'.

IM So, when you were a student at Stirling, you were attempting poetry
as well as prose?

IB Yeah. It's funny the way it started as well. I don't think I was making
any great effort to get anything published. It means a lot more to me
than it's going to mean in terms of the art of poesy or whatever. I was
always a great fan of *The Waste Land*, as I still am. Not that I liked
very much of what Eliot actually stood for but I still absolutely love
The Waste Land. It's my favourite poem. (L) I think Eliot's my
favourite poet in fact. Second only to Uncle Bill himself. Although I
liked *The Waste Land* immensely; I could go on reading it for ever, at
the same time I sort of thought, this recalcitrant bit of me thought,
'Nice to take the piss out of this somewhere'. I wrote this poem
called 'Damage' which was meant to be a sort of a mickey-take of *The
Waste Land*. Gradually, as I was writing it, I thought, 'Actually, this
isn't too bad. It could stand on its own. Ach, to hell with it'. (L) So I
finished it as a proper poem. And I thought, I've used words in
different ways. Much more sort of compressed and there's a bit more
leeway than you can in prose. So I started writing poems. I haven't
done any poems for about ten, twelve years I think. It's just a phase I
was going through. Honest! (L)

IM Can you imagine, though, going back to it, having discovered a different kind of thing that one can do in poetry? You might at some stage?

IB I can imagine, but I'd have to change a good bit from where I am at the moment. I found that in bits of *The Bridge* I was using a language in an almost poetic sort of level of complexity and density in particular. I think that it is almost more of a challenge to use language in that way within prose and get away with it and make it work, than it is in poetry: poetry can almost be sort of self-indulgent in that way. The way I do it, it can be! (L) I can imagine going back to that but I don't think for a while yet. I did one long, long narrative poem which I've had occasional thoughts that I might turn into a story in fact. Although the same sort of impetus or impulse is still occasionally there. It's just that it lends to come out as an instant scene in a novel or a short story rather than into a poem. It's possible that I might go back to it. I short of missed it for quite a while as well. I used to get a real sort of immediate kick out of writing a poem. You could do it and half an hour later that was it, it was effectively finished. You might go back to it a few days later and tinker with it. You got a much more immediate benefit from writing it than writing a novel. It's not as if you're going back over months of work

Tape Two of the Iain Banks Interview
29th November 1988

IM At the end of the last tape, Iain was talking about a phase – a relatively short phase in his life, when he wrote poetry. He was also saying to me yesterday off tape that when he was an undergraduate he was more of a lone wolf than he had been before or since. I was trying to work out whether these two things had anything in common. You had to have a solitary phase to do something with your introspection or something?

IB That hadn't actually occurred to me. That these two things were sort of concurrent. Yes. I think there probably was an element of that. I think also simply the fact I was going through my youth anyway, starting from when I was sixteen, seventeen. Damn! I can't remember. Anyway eighteen I suppose when I actually went. I was trying to get my own ideas together and get my head together, man! (L) So I suppose I was going through that sort of self-analysis and trying to work out what my own particular views were and all the rest of it. Poetry was probably a part of that. And also I think simply experimenting. Trying to find out different ways of using words. At that point I hadn't written any short stories at all. I had written about two, and when I was there the third novel. Straight into the deep end and disappeared! (L) So I hadn't done anything that was shorter than that, apart from essays obviously, which by the time you have to do them in tend to be very short. If they're done under exam conditions, obviously they are very short and they won't let you do fiction – you know, fictional essays – at university apart from the creative writing group perhaps! (L) So I think yes. Part of it was experiment and I suppose there was an element of here I was closeted away by myself, and although I was keeping in touch with people through in Greenock – I was going through there every second weekend and doing the traditional thing of taking my mum my dirty washing! I was also keeping in touch with people I knew from school there. There were people at Paisley Tech, people at Strathclyde and Glasgow and all the rest of it. One guy lived in Paisley, a couple of the guys lived in Paisley. But most of the people who were going to Glasgow, at least initially for the first year, were staying at home and travelling. So Greenock was still the focal point for all of us and I was deliberately keeping in touch with them. As I say, a lot of the other weekends I would be coming through to North Queensferry to see my relations through that way. So I wasn't really entering fully into university life.

IM   Can I ask, because you threw that remark away which immediately became interesting to me. Did you join a creative writing group?

IB   Yes I did actually. At Stirling, yes.

IM   Tell me about that.

IB   I remember I actually wrote a sonnet once. (L) It wasn't very good because Norman MacCaig said so!

IM   MacCaig was running the writing group?

IB   Well he was one of them, yes. I think it was Rory Watson was in it as well, and Martin Gray and yes, I think they were the leading lights. I think Norman came in particularly for the poetry part of it. I wasn't particularly good at it. I don't think I amazed everyone by my brilliance. Because I was so used to writing novels, you can't sort of distribute a dozen copies of that to your chums in Creative Writing. (L) So I was concentrating more on the poetry I suppose. I suppose I was still a bit shy about actually showing too much to anyone.

IM Were you caring what they thought about it?

IB Yes.

IM Really vulnerable?

IB I was quite defensive as well, I think. I shied away a bit from anything too experimental or whatever. I was trying to keep fairly safe about what I was showing to my friends, especially as poetry really is about unbaring your soul – more so than a novel. Just by being larger a novel has a disguise about it. It is fiction and it is not autobiographical. You consider yourself more in poetry as opening up. I enjoyed doing it. I probably enjoyed it more from just the sociability of it, and that's one way that I was – you know, getting on with people, I suppose. I was socialising probably more with like minds. It was probably more rewarding than any actual benefit I might have got from useful, constructive criticism. You know, then as now I don't take well to criticism! 'What do you know?' (L)

IM Let me ask you about that in brackets because again that's something that we might not get back to and it's interesting. How important are reviews or criticisms of your work? Are you really positively impressed by, you know, positive reviews, and do you manage to shake off if you get any negative ones?

IB Oh yes, especially *The Wasp Factory*.

IM There was something very flattering about most of those unfavourable ones!

IB There are different categories of reviews. There's good good reviews, good bad reviews, bad good reviews and bad bad reviews. That's just the start of it! (L)

IM Do you keep them all?

IB Well they send me them, and it seems a bit wrong to chuck them all out. I keep a file on each book, which actually starts with initials and notes. The only thing it doesn't contain is the manuscript itself, which I keep locked safely away. (L). Occasionally if I've had to do some research or other – I think the file on *Espedair Street* has the relevant British Rail timetable! That's where all the reviews go as well. I do keep them: I don't tend to take much notice of them, to be perfectly honest.

IM Are you actually nervous when the book's coming out?

IB Not really. I got such a flying start with *The Wasp Factory*. I'd assumed that after maybe five or six years, if I was able to write a book a year, if I was able to get the damned things published, I might just be able to scrape by and make a living, and give up my day job. But because *The Wasp Factory* was so sudden and Macmillan published it, and people began talking about television interviews, setting up interview after interview with papers and all the rest. And people were sending in reviews in advance, it doesn't actually happen often at all, people sending a photocopy of reviews they'd sent to a magazine. I thought, wait a minute! This doesn't happen to everybody! (L) What people were saying time and time again is true, a review's a review, and it doesn't matter if it's a bad review, you got mentioned! Some writers would give their right arm to get half a dozen reviews. And I really had more than I could cope with over *The Wasp Factory*. So I'd got that established – me as a name you could recognise. People were looking for the next book, no matter what I'd done with it.

IM   Fay Weldon famously called you 'the Great White Hope of British Literature'. I was interested that she used the word British, where most English writers would use the word English.

IB   I suppose, if she'd just read *The Bridge*, she would be aware that it was much more of a Scottish novel in a lot of ways. The actual experience of the guy, upwardly mobile from working to middle class as a background, that probably was transferable from university to university, probably fairly similar in a lot of big cities. Even so, I think there is a very definite Scottish atmosphere to *The Bridge*.

IM   It's much more memorably Scottish than for example *The Wasp Factory*, although I faintly affronted you yesterday by not remembering that as being all that Scottish. (L) I remember the isolation of the setting, rather than it being a Scottish isolation.

Well, let's get this poor guy out of university. You decided not to do Honours.

IB   Yes.

IM   Because you thought it was about time you moved on?

IB   I liked university. I thought, it looks like quite a good life, actually. (L) I could just about imagine myself, if I applied myself and worked hard, there might be a possibility of becoming a lecturer, and it was quite tempting. But being offered a job somewhere was by no means a foregone conclusion; as I say, I wasn't particularly good in the fundamental academic sense, and my grades were not brilliant, but I thought, if I really put my mind to it, I could fit in here, or if not here somewhere. But I do remember thinking, well, this probably isn't going to be good for you as a writer, Banksie. At the back of my mind was the fear of ending up as one of these campus writers that only writes novels about campus life, and I did want to get out of that and not be stuck in any particular groove, and I did want to get into the rest of the world, and see a bit more. I already had plans to go on a mega hitching trip. At one stage I was going to go around the world, and go on the Trans-Siberian railroad. But that fell through and I just did Europe instead for about three months.

IM Was this after you left university?

IB Yes, in 1975. I think the furthest north I got was Bergen in Norway, the furthest East was either Berlin or Venice, because it was the same sort of longitude, and the furthest south was Rabat in Morocco, and I was all over the place in between.

IM This is supposed to be a question which you answer with due care and attention (L): I'm interested in whether you were on your own all this time.

IB Yes. You travel fastest by yourself for a start. And you're more exposed to what you're doing. I love hitching in France: I could hitch round France for ever. And for some reason I always got lifts. I managed to get away unmolested, and un-knocked over the head. But I was aware of the dangers, not paranoid, but always thinking it could be dangerous. You are more open to the actual place, much more involved in the place around you: you haven't got someone else to talk to in your own language. Obviously you might meet people in youth hostels, but it does expose you more to the country: it's a comprehensive experience of the foreignness of a place, if you're by yourself. And also I decided where I wanted to go, and wasn't trailing around with someone who wanted to go and see yet another bloody cathedral. (L)

IM Being Banksie wanting to do Banksie things! Okay, so you finish at university and you have this splendid three months. Then am I right in saying you set about seeing how you could most easily or simply earn some kind of living until – and you were always fairly sure there was going to be an until – you were supporting yourself by your writing.

IB And it worked quite well for a few years in fact. The plan was I used to find some work somehow, through the Greenock Labour Exchange, for about six months, and then take the next six months off, and live off my savings. Because I was still living at home with my parents, I could live fairly cheaply. I'd still got to give my mum – I can't remember what it was, £20 or £30 quid a week for my keep, but it was still a hell of a lot cheaper than actually trying to set up home by myself.

IM   And also you didn't have to worry about your laundry. (L)

IB   So that was the scheme, and in the six months when I wasn't actually working I'd either be off travelling somewhere or actually writing. One thing I did have and still have is I can write quite quickly. When I'm really on song I can do about 5,000 words a day, and shouldn't need *too* much revision. It needs revision, but at work on the word processor I won't change more than maybe about a quarter of the actual stuff you end up with. Obviously you have to change 100 per cent when you're doing a second draft if you're just doing it on a typewriter. So I learned to write quickly, which is a great benefit. My editor said, 'Banksie, how fast do you actually write?' I said, 'Well once I get going if I'm really enjoying myself and it's a good bit of the book I can do about 5,000 words a day, 1,000 words an hour, at the real top rate'. He didn't actually blanch, but, 'Don't tell that to the magazines and news magazines'. 'Why not?' It's meant to be sheer hell. I sweat the words out, you know! I've worked for the last three days and there's one sentence! Oh God, yes! And I live in a garret, you know. Having said that, it sounds great – 5,000 words a day. It's like writing the Bible every year. But it doesn't really work that way. And the months you aren't writing you're still thinking about it. And quite often books have been lying around for years and years and years, either as a first draft already done or the idea, even though you haven't actually written it. It is always at the back of your mind somewhere, and you are thinking about it even if you don't know you're thinking about it. I have had a few experiences where I've had some sort of technical problem in a book or I needed something for that book, and suddenly the idea occurs to you, perhaps only a day or two later – maybe months later, maybe years later – and you suddenly think, 'That's the solution!' I don't believe in Muses or anything like that. It is purely some little sub-programme in the back of your mind sort of sifting through all the possibilities. Perhaps it's like the computer in a way. Most of it is garbage, most of it doesn't work and suddenly you think, 'Ah! This is what we need!' That does happen – that you are working on it even when you don't know you are, when you are doing other things. It can take years and years and years before the idea finally comes to a head. When it is finally written, it is written very very quickly.

IM Last night you were reading stories to the Aberdeen Literary Society that you said you actually first conceived in '78/79.

IB That's when the first drafts of those were written.

IM That is a good instance of what you are talking about really.

   It sounds to me as if your parents must be remarkably laid back, that they weren't sort of biting their nails and saying, 'For goodness' sake Iain, where's your career?' or whatever. (L)

IB My mum always said, 'You should always go and do teacher training. It will always stand you in good stead', which is quite true. I can see the sense of that. The trouble was, my heart wasn't really in teaching and I'm convinced I had teachers at school whose hearts weren't in teaching, that they had gone into teaching because they had the academic background and they were capable of doing it, but it's a real gift to be able to teach properly in that way. Not simply to have the enthusiasm, but to be able to put that enthusiasm across to other people. I'm sure I had teachers who had just drifted into it. It wasn't a real vocation. I would be like that if I did it and I didn't want to use it as some sort of fallback position and inflict myself upon generations of kids. They would be better off without a teacher whose heart wasn't in the teaching as well as in the subject itself. So I decided not to do that. I suppose it was also a bit of bloodymindedness. It did seem the sensible thing to do in a lot of ways but to hell with that.

IM There is a strong Scottish tradition that would have the parents in this situation saying, 'Look Iain, you've had a year to try and make it. It's down to you now'. Were they very long-suffering?

IB Yes. One thing was that my mum was delighted that I had simply got a degree. I think I was the first of these two extended families to actually have a degree. It was a great thing. My dad's attitude always has been the more laid back of the two. As long as the bairn is happy, you know. (L) My dad was a very, very able – able seaman! – able man – very, very intelligent, but he never really got on in the Admiralty in the way he could have. This is not me indulging in hero worship of my dad. I've heard this from loads of people – officers above him in the Admiralty and all the rest of it. If only he had kept his mouth shut at certain points, you know, been prepared to get his nose dirty. Then he could have really got on in the Admiralty. Some of the tales he used to come back and tell about the inefficiency and stupidity of the Admiralty, and some of these absolute dingbats who were in charge. It always made my blood boil. He just wasn't prepared to suffer these upper-class idiots in silence, and if he thought someone was being stupid or making the wrong decision, he would tell them! It cost him a really high-flying career but it didn't matter. He was happy. That was the only thing he actually liked, the almost hands-on experience of actually working these ships. He really enjoyed that. In the later years as the job changed a bit, it's become nothing like as much fun as it used to be.

I suppose all my dad was concerned about was, 'Was I happy?', and that's why it didn't matter. He was delighted that I had got a degree and all the rest of it. He didn't have any of the classic thing. You know, 'I want my son to have all the things that I didn't have', and all the rest of it. I was to be happy, and that was the main thing. He hadn't a tremendous career and all the rest of it, but he had his own sort of pride that he never kowtowed or got his nose browned! (L) That was good enough. That was my dad's attitude and very, very laid back. In that sense in a very quiet and understated way, very supportive in fact. And also very generous. I don't think he would ever see me collapse into destitution.

My mum was always a bit more 'Oh, he's got to make his own living', and all the rest of it. Mum was a bit more concerned that I should have a proper career. I just seemed to get away with it somehow. To this day I don't know how! (L) I think I just convinced them I did want to be a writer and it was the one thing I wanted to do. The more I think about it, they must have been quite indulgent of me. My mum never made that big a fuss. No-one really tried to shove me into doing anything else.

IM There is a sense in which one can imagine that life pattern going on for ages and ages and ages, but you certainly ended up in London and in Kent. Was that your own impulsion that took you down there?

IB That was lack of jobs in Greenock! (L) Jobs gradually dried up. This was a long time ago – back in '79, you know. This is when the Tories could still actually have those posters for the '79 election campaign saying Labour Isn't Working. Remember that? When unemployment was almost a million! Jobs in Greenock started to dry up even then – even before the depredations of the Thatcherites. One of my pals was down in London so I just did the standard Scottish thing of moving down to London. I wasn't like some poor kids from Glasgow that arrived at a platform at Euston with ten bob in their pocket who usually become rent boys or something! When I went down I had a place to stay at my pal's flat. This guy had been one of my best friends in Greenock. There were three of us that were really close. The other one ended up down there eventually as well. I went down in December '79. I think it was February 1980 when I got this job with the firm of lawyers. It was purely because I didn't completely want to go down to London, but I quite liked London. There was a girl that I was seeing down there quite often but I didn't go down there because of her, even. I didn't particularly want to go to London. I like it to visit but not to stay in and living there for four years only confirmed this. But it was the standard Scottish thing because I couldn't find any work up here, so I had to 'head south, young man'.

There was some idea of being closer to publishers.

IM I was going to ask about that.

IB It didn't make any difference. The only difference that it made was I saved on postage on the outward journey! When I worked for this firm in Chancery Lane – well, Gray's Inn and then Chancery Lane – both had offices within a half-hour radius of all the main publishers. That was the only thing that made any difference. I never did have any contacts with anyone in publishing at all.

IM So you stayed four years in London. Always at this job in the lawyer's office?

IB Yes.

IM What was it you were doing there?

IB I was a Law Costs Draftperson or a Costing Clerk.

IM Could you explain that?!

IB Well simply, if you had a big file and the lawyers themselves didn't want to do the bill for it, then they passed it to me. I had to write the narrative for the bill, which could involve a bit of fiction in itself, I tell you! But there were formal aspects of it where if someone's awarded costs in a court case, they've got to pay your costs. Obviously an unscrupulous lawyer might just pile everything in there and charge vast amounts of money, so it's got to be 'taxed', as it's called. For Taxing Masters – more or less a small court in itself.

It can in fact go before a judge to have the bill taxed. You simply present your bill and somebody doing the same job comes along and argues against it. It does actually involve certainly very boring stuff like counting every letter and timing every phone call, and if the lawyers have done their job properly and left good file notes and all the rest of it it's OK. It's actually quite a good job because in the firm I was working for, there wasn't too much of that formal side of it. Most of it was just doing the narratives for big bills that lawyers didn't have the time to do themselves. It was always cost effective for them to get on and make their – you know, whatever it is – £2 a minute they were charging. That would involve me spending a week doing mega bills.

Anyway, because the firm had a few famous name clients – it didn't do any criminal work, just civil stuff – they also had some big corporate clients like Columbia, EMI and Warner, the film distributors, and Total Oil and Marks and Spencers. Some of the film files in particular were fascinating. Also two of the lawyers specialised: one guy specialised in divorce and the other guy specialised in adoption, and they were both very, very good at their jobs. The guy who did adoption had virtually never lost a case. In concession to decency, the firm actually charged his time out at half the rate it should have been because usually, although he was technically instructed by the prospective parents, he was actually paid by the local authority. Some of the divorce files. You often got quite interesting details – love letters and stuff like this. Technically, they didn't have to read the whole thing, but some of them were a damn sight better than novels. And some of the adoption cases. You saw kids in really terrible states – perhaps battered and abused and all the rest of it, and they finally end up with parents who really did love them. It was really quite heartwarming. The guy always asked for a picture of the kids at the end with their parents. It warmed your wee heart. (L)

IM   It sounds like a tailor-made job for the novelist in the making. It gave you all sorts of insight into business and all the rest of it.

IB   It was an overview: it wasn't the whole of society but quite an overview of a fair amount. I haven't used anything directly from that but the overall experience of finding out how people work and the way things happen was very, very useful. Again, it was pure luck that I fell on my feet in that respect in that job. It wasn't particularly well paid. That was when it came to it quite a good thing. If say it was really good fun and I would think about studying Law, I suppose it's possible that in those four years I might have become an Articled Clerk or whatever, with prospects of making mega bucks as a lawyer. I think when the prospect of making not that much more money initially on books had come along, I might not have taken it, but because I was on £10,000 or £11,000 a year at the time as a Costing Clerk and when the paperback deal in particular came along, I knew I could survive the next couple of years just on that. I thought I might as well go for it.

IM You didn't really stop at any stage the scribbling?

IB Not really. There might have been a couple of years between books – between about '72 and 1980 there were about six books. I suppose only about a year to eighteen months at the most between novels. It's actually less now because I'm working harder, I suppose.

IM Certainly your publishing record since *The Wasp Factory* has been very quick.

IB It looks very prolific actually but I feel dead, dead lazy. It's terrible. I'd really need to check back in my diary. Certainly since I moved to Edinburgh in January this year, I didn't really do any work until about just over a month ago. I suppose I was always half thinking or planning my book. I felt really bad. Part of it was the unsettling of actually moving and secondly I had just split up with my girlfriend at the time. That was after about seven or eight years together, so that was quite a traumatic event. Whether that is an excuse for that, I don't know. It did take me a long time to start on this book.

IM Well, we have you there in London and writing away. Incidentally, can I ask you in brackets because again I thought about this, not with reference to the next few years, but where are all these unpublished books? Have you still got them all, or have they been destroyed one way or the other?

IB I would never destroy them.

IM Sacred books!

IB Well, that's my babies! (L) The one before *The Wasp Factory* was *The Player of Games*, the last one that I've actually published. They were getting better all the time. *The Wasp Factory* was the best of the lot in as much as it was finished. It actually went to a second draft and was a much more competent piece of work. *The Player of Games* came very, very close to being published in its original draft. It still was effectively a first draft. The first draft was written in incredibly quick time. It was written over three weeks. It was actually written on seventeen writing days. I look back at the diary I was keeping then and I can't believe it. I was still going out and partying and getting drunk with my pals, going out with my mum to go shopping – you know, carrying her shopping bag and all the rest of it. I must have been doing about twenty pages a day. I can't do that nowadays. It's a bit more of an effort. My God! That was some work rate. When I look back at that first draft and it's pretty good actually! Having had time to think about it, I went back to re-write it last year. The book is far, far better now. There is a lot more going on, more sort of strands go through and gradually gel and come together. The first part of the book is quite profoundly different from what used to be the first quarter. That was the easiest one to go back and re-do. As I was saying, to my great disappointment it actually takes more time to re-do an old book than it does to do a new one from scratch. That's another thing where my editor was saying, 'You shouldn't mention these old books'.

IM   They were old books. By the time they come to print, they are not old books any more.

IB   And often, even though it is a brand new book, it is actually an old idea, so it is not as simple as it appears. I do have plans to re-do the two previous science fiction books before *The Player of Games*. One is called *Against a Dark Background*, and the other one is called *Use of Weapons*. Both are going to need a lot more work than *The Player of Games* needed. In a way, I'm not looking forward to it. In a way I am, because I like the stories and they have become part of almost my personal mythology in a way. These stories are like old friends in a way and I really think they are good stories. The way they are written isn't particularly good. The actual stories really work. I want to see them out there as part of the canon, as it were, but they are going to take a lot of work. [*Against a Dark Background was published by Iain M Banks in 1993, and The Use of Weapons by Iain M Banks in 1990.*]

IM   Can you give me a brief rundown about how you broke through with *The Wasp Factory*, and can we actually get the name of this long-suffering editor of yours who has obviously put in so much work, Iain.

IB   Well, his name is James Hale. The guy was my editor and still is. *The Wasp Factory*? Well, I wrote it in this wee flat I was sharing in

Islington. That was in the summer of 1980. I think it took about ten weeks altogether. I was just doing it weekends and evenings. I had hoped I might get it done in about six weeks but it took ten. People kept on dragging me out for a pint – well, not dragging, knocking on the door and saying, 'Coming for a pint, Banksie?' That to me is dragging. (L) So I had it done in about ten weeks and I gave it round to my friends. I had already decided I was going to do a second draft for the first time. I had deliberately turned away from science fiction, thinking I had a better chance – you've got more publishers to send the book to, if it's not science fiction. I had to wrestle with my conscience about that. Am I selling out? In a way I had quite deliberately chosen a book which still had a setting and a character that gave you some of the freedoms you have in science fiction, making up your own society and religion and whatever. Frank does that. He actually makes up his own religion. There is some feeling of remoteness of the island almost being like another planet. So I had done that and I said that I was going to do a second draft. I gave the first draft round to all my pals. At least a dozen, maybe fifteen people read the book. I didn't actually take very much notice of what they said, but it was nice to have them commenting. (L) Then I re-did it. I did a full second draft and sent it off.

I think Macmillan must have been about the seventh publisher I took it to: and it just kept coming back. I found out from a chap called Martin Edwards (he wasn't there at the time but he is now a Managing Editor) at Gollancz, for the science fiction part in particular. He said he actually found the reader's report from *The Wasp Factory* when it came into Gollancz. The reader's report said it was quite well written but far too weird ever to get published. I fell on the floor when he told me that. It was really strange when I took *The Wasp Factory* into Macmillan's offices. I met this lassie I was going out with, we met in the lawyer's office. And I hadn't actually realised Macmillan published fiction at all because they just weren't that well-known. I was looking through the records in a yearbook and I noticed it said Macmillan Fiction. If it had been that much further away I wouldn't have taken it. It was only five minutes' walk away and I thought that's only five minutes there and five minutes back and fifteen minutes for a pint! Or two! (L) So we toddled down to Little Essex Street. The firm was in Chancery Lane at the time so you went down Chancery Lane, across Fleet

Street and down to the very start of the Strand, Essex Street and
Little Essex Street. So it was literally a five-minute walk. Annie and
I went in, and there was this very forbidding receptionist. I'm now
great friends with the real receptionist, but this was the one who was
standing in at lunchtime. She said, 'Yes, what is it?', and I said, 'Can
I just leave this book?' and she asked who it was going to. I said
someone in the Editorial Department. 'Yes, but who?' 'I don't
know!' (L) I wasn't in tears, but I felt really depressed. So depressed
that when Annie suggested that we go for a pint, 'No, I don't feel like
having a drink'. She nearly collapsed in the gutter when I said that,
you know, 'What?!' So I felt really bad about that and I thought,
that's it: no way.

I think someone must have read the first page and saw that there
was a policeman mentioned. They gave it to a chap called Lord
Harding who at the time was in the crime line of Macmillans. They
were very, very big on detective stories. He'd read it, and to this day
I don't know what he really thought of it, but . . . he handed it to
James Hale. I always imagine him handing it with his fingers at the
very edges of the book. Apparently he said something like, 'I think
you might find this interesting'. James read it on the Sunday and as
he said, 'I felt the hairs on the back of my neck stand on end'. This is
good! He rang me up on the Monday morning. I was sitting there
quite happily at my desk when the phone rang. I found out later
from James's secretary. He'd read the book. I don't know *what* sort
of mental image he had. I suspect what a lot of people had when they
had read *The Wasp Factory* and hadn't heard or seen me, was a cross
between Rob Roy and Rasputin. (L) This is definitely the image that
James had of me, his secretary told me later. He was sitting there
nervous about ringing up, and finally he dialled this number which
in fact was only about a quarter of a mile away in Chancery Lane,
and he got the office switchboard, 'Denton, Hall and Burgin. Can I
help you?' He put the phone down! He had to be persuaded to ring
back. 'Is Mr Banks there?' 'Oh yes, we'll put you through'. And that
was it.

It was a bit like winning the pools. Because I didn't have any
contact – I didn't know anybody in publishing or in the media at
all – I'd no experience whatsoever of anything like that. Suddenly
in this instant, this guy went, 'Yes. My name's James Hale. I'm
from Macmillans'. 'Aaaaaaah!' (L) 'I'd like to talk to you about it'.

'GREAT!' It is almost an anti-climax because I had been preparing myself for it for years and years and years. I remember
when I wrote the very, very first novel I actually sent away to
anyone. I sent it to the first publisher and I was thinking they
would think, 'Yes, good, we'll have this'. I was already rehearsing
the answers to the questions on the Parkinson Show and the Nobel
Prize acceptance speech! (L) You do rehearse all that sort of stuff.
I thought they would write a letter first but there was this phone
call. I met James that lunchtime and found out that it was only up
to him. It wasn't some sort of committee decision. Are you going
to publish? Oh yes, I think so. (L) Oh, Happy Day! I then rang
round all my friends.

IM   Did you find yourself talking money early in this or were you so
interested in getting published, that money took a back seat?

IB   I was getting published, by far the most important thing. They just
said the book won't actually give you any money, and I just said OK.
The actual advance wasn't much. It was about £2,500, I think –
£1250 on signature and £1250 on publication, which was reasonable.
Initially they were thinking of maybe 2,000 in hardback or whatever.

IM   Do we know in fact what they have sold?

IB   I'm not sure. They claim they actually printed 10,000 for the first
run. I don't think they actually did somehow. James gets very cagey
about this when questioned closely. I think they probably sold
something like 5,000 in hardback. That's a guess. In paperback I
think it is getting on for 150,000 or something like that over the
years.

IM   That's in the English version?

IB   Yes.

IM   Not to mention, she said importantly to the microphone, the
Japanese and the Hebrew.

IB   Hebrew, yes. I think it's been sold to about ten countries. I think
we've got a clean sweep of Scandinavia now – Denmark, Holland. I
think we've got Germany – I'm not sure. The States certainly, and
Japan and Israel. Where else? I think that's about it. Oh, and France.

IM   Was it after *The Wasp Factory* was accepted that you left the law
firm fairly quickly?

IB   Yes it was. This was in '83 when James rang up. I knew I was going
to be published in eleven months. I knew it was going to be some
time in February '84 and it had to be a Thursday because books are

always published on a Thursday. Daft idea – you can't have a publishing party on a Thursday night.

IM Presumably it's to catch the Sunday papers?

IB Well, a lot of papers have book reviews on Fridays as well. I still think it's a daft idea but never mind. All my friends used to complain – Why do it on a Thursday? I've got to go to work the next day, dammit! Anyway, I knew it would have to be some Thursday in February '84 and I happened to mention that my birthday would fall on a Thursday on the 16th February. And they said, 'Oh, what age are you?' 'Twenty-nine?' 'No, thirty'. Right, right! What was strange – I'd feel a bit uncomfortable about putting a coincidence like this into a novel, I did come down to London thinking that if I hadn't managed to get anything underway by the time I was thirty, I would just give up. I would just go up to the north of Scotland, up to the wild west coast somewhere and do anything, become a fisherman or something and still keep on writing in my spare time. It was very sort of neat in a way. It was bang on my thirtieth birthday when the book actually came out. I must admit I had known eleven months beforehand that it was all underway but that was very nice. I had a sort of combined birthday party and book launch at James and his wife Hilary's flat in the Barbican. A good laugh.

IM So, then you moved down to Kent?

IB Annie's parents live in Canterbury. We wanted to get out of the city, so we went to Faversham. It is the first in the line of where you can go. You can go to Canterbury but you change at Faversham. We were both still commuting at this stage. We were actually living in London together for two or three years and then we moved to Faversham. I was commuting for about a year. Faversham was quite close to Canterbury – about ten miles, not too far from Annie's parents. It was handy for commuting and we could afford a house as well. It cost about £20,000 or £19,500, which we could sort of afford. Mind you James was appalled when I said I was going to give my job up. He said 'Oh, don't do that!' He said, 'How much do you need to live on?', and I said, 'I can get by on about £10,000 a year'. I don't know what sort of money I was making at the lawyers round about that time. That was me down in Faversham after that point.

The other neat thing was my dad retired from the Admiralty within about a month of me, not retiring, but taking up my chosen profession as a writer. These things seemed to dovetail nicely and they went together. After my mum and dad no longer having Dad going out to work and all the rest of it, that would keep their interest up or whatever. They still had me to think about. I think my mum was a wee bit concerned about some aspects of *The Wasp Factory*. But the great thing was the fact that her son had actually got a book published.

Books published by Iain Banks by the time of the interview, plus the two he mentioned on page 28 as existing in draft, later published. He uses the name Iain M Banks for his science fiction novels.

Iain Banks, *The Wasp Factory*, 1984
Iain Banks, *Walking on Glass*, 1985
Iain Banks, *The Bridge*, 1986
Iain M Banks, *Consider Phlebas*, 1987
Iain Banks, *Espedair Street*, 1987
Iain M Banks, *The Player of Games*, 1988
Iain M Banks, *The Use of Weapons*, 1990
Iain M Banks, *Against a Dark Background*, 1993

BERNARD MACLAVERTY

BERNARD MACLAVERTY CAME to the University of Aberdeen in 1983, for a two-year stint as part-time Writer in Residence. He had moved to Scotland from Northern Ireland some time before, and was living with his family on Islay. They moved to Glasgow after Bernard left us, and have settled there.

When Bernard was in Aberdeen, we generally entertained him to a meal on Sunday evenings – or rather, he entertained us! He is a born talker and storyteller: it is no accident that this interview more than any other includes the code '(L)'. Frequently the tapes deteriorated into a chorus of laughter, the writer enjoying it as much as his audience. In this way we became fairly well acquainted. He was slightly daunted, at first, at the idea of the eavesdropping tape recorder, but soon got used to it, or forgot its presence.

Tape number one 24 April 1984.
Present: Bernard MacLaverty, Bob Tait, Isobel Murray.

IM I want to start gently, talking about biographical facts, Bernard's youth, his childhood, whether he lived in the kind of house with books in it, what it was like growing up in Belfast in – when?

BM Early fifties. Where do I begin with all that?

IM Any topic that takes your fancy.

BM Well, we lived in a big kind of Victorian terraced house, three floors, surrounded by old people. My father brought in extra oldies to live with him, and I think that that was one of the saintly qualities that he had. We brought in an aunt – a great aunt, a grandmother, and a grandfather, and in the same house there was my mother and my father, myself and my brother. Now directly across the street there was what we called Auntie Cissie's, and there was a grandfather there, Auntie Cissie, Uncle Jim and two cousins. So it was almost like a wee community.

IM A late and splendid experience of the extended family?

BM Yeah. So if you had a row in your own home, you could run out across the road; get in a row in that house and you could run back home. And I have most fond memories of all that older generation. I don't want to sound nostalgic, but it was, it was great. The grand-father across the street, he was MacLaverty, and he was a huge man, about 6′ 2″, and always had his white head of hair, and a bowler hat, and he actually worked as a wood-turner until he was 83 – I just told you off-tape there about making a platter or a bread board. He worked until he was 83, and then his firm was taken over by somebody else, and he was given the sack.

IM At 83!

BM At 83. (L) And he died within a fortnight. He didn't die *of* anything: he died.

IM He came to an end.

BM And he had some lovely stories. I think it was this finger –

IM The third finger of the right hand, interjects helpful interviewer.

BM (L) It was all crooked. He used to tell us about that, and he'd say that he was just cutting up wood one day in a bandsaw, and he just 'took the top of her right off'; so he says, 'and I reeshled round in the sawdust for her' (L) 'and I got her out and I stuck her back on and put a bit of insulating tape round her, and that's why it's that way the days, boy'. (L) And he also – a blade out of a saw, one of the circular saws, actually flew out and hit him in the head, and made a quite deep cut. And he said the cut wasn't too bad, it was the wee girl in the office poured iodine into it (L) and that was the worst. He was a marvellous character.

IM This early family experience does seem to have been important to you. Are you conscious in any way of having used it in your writing?

BM Oh yes. There are a number of stories that use that kind of material, not necessarily what I've just been saying to you, but the others, the grandmother and the great aunt. The great aunt, Aunt Mary, was a monitress, a school teacher, and she was the supposed educated one, and would read to us; most nights she would read. But it wasn't anything great: it was things like *The Coral Island* and who's the other woman? – Enid Blyton. And would read us a chapter of that every night before we'd go off to bed. And it didn't matter the quality of the writing, that was a great experience, in that you got your chapter. We didn't have TV, but that was something to look forward to at night, to get your chapter.

IM Did the other people in the house read much?

BM Not at all, I would think. Auntie Mary had a number of books. We'd one bookcase, a glass one, about the size of that one over there. The helpful interviewer will now point out what size it is. (L)

IM And that it's a china cabinet . . . (L)

BM And they were mostly religious books, you know, like H V Morton *In the Steps of St Paul*, and what was that Evelyn Waugh – *Helena* – and stuff like that. D K Broster, A J Cronin, stuff like that, all in this one book shelf. My father didn't read much; he read I suppose a wee bit. He listened to music, and made his own gramophone. (L)

IM Made his own gramophone!

BM He had a big set that actually played with wooden needles, pine needles. And we had two wee cups beside the deck, one was unused needles and then you put them over, but we always got them mixed up, so that you never knew what was what. (L) And he would play sentimental things like 'Whispering Hope' and some operatic stuff, John McCormack and a few things like Schubert's 'Unfinished', a wee bit of Beethoven, some piano stuff – that was the extent of the culture in the house. But he was a painter. We've talked about the music, and we've talked about the books, but he was a commercial artist who had I think a very nice water colour technique when he started, but he didn't do an awful lot. His main job, I think, was painting cinema posters. And then towards the end of his life he set up in business for himself as an advertising agency and did a number of contracts or whatever you call them for chick-hatcheries, the YP Pools, Kennedy's milk. I can actually visualise it now: the Kennedy's milk advert was a baby with a nappy on it running round with the milk bottle. (L)

IM The first time you told me about your father doing the cinema posters, I was being sympathetic, feeling that perhaps a great artist was feeling very cramped doing this, but if he voluntarily went into an advertising agency, he must have been at least fairly shrewd about where the money was, and the possibilities of earning a living.

BM Well, there wasn't really much money about in our house: we weren't poor by any means, but I suppose we had enough.

IM Would you say middle class?

BM Yes, I think that. It's always a very difficult term to use, that, you know.

IM   I know, but it's even harder when we don't try and use those terms at all. It wasn't a housing-scheme, for example?

BM   No. We were in process of buying our own home as a sitting tenant, and I can remember always going down to pay the mortgage, which was three pounds one and eight a month. (L) So that was the kind of riches it was. And then after he died, there is no doubt that there were hard times. My mother went out and worked in a shop, a hobbies shop, which was really great for me just at that age.

IM   Your father died when you were quite young?

BM   Yes, twelve. And then after that my mother had to keep us going in shoes.

IM   And all these old people as well?

BM   Yes. Presumably they were getting pensions. I mean, I never enquired into the finances of the house. Auntie Mary was the financier, and she had a big box, and she kept ledgers of the housekeeping, and would write in, you know, packet of Daz 12 pence or whatever it was. And she put sixpence away every week towards the Christmas turkey. She had this box with all the wee bits and pieces in wee alcoves, and she would put the money into it and write this whole thing up. She made it her job, to do the finances of the house.

IM   I suppose it's odd that we've taken so long getting to it, talking about a Belfast childhood in the late forties and fifties, but perhaps just from the book titles you gave us one could jalouse that it was a Roman Catholic household. Was religion a big item?

BM   Yes, very big, almost all-pervading, in that this particular house backed on to the church, so that the church really was only about 100 yards away. Which meant you couldn't use the excuse that it was raining or snowing, you know, that it was too far away for wee legs like mine to walk. (L) My father was a religious man who was in a lot of vague organisations like the St Vincent de Paul, and charitable things like that. The Young Philanthropists. (L) And my mother was totally bound up in it as well, and all the elders. I myself was an altar boy, and it was just the complete and total Catholic household. All the pictures, apart from my dad's water-colours, were religious pictures, Sacred Heart above the mantelpiece, and holding a big football in his hand with his eyes cast up to heaven. (L) As one of my mates said – he came in one night and said, 'Jesus, boys, the game's off!' (L)

IM Now you say it was a Catholic atmosphere at home, but were the neighbours Catholics? Was it an all-Catholic kind of area, or a mixed one?

BM It was a fairly mixed one.

IM And did you tend to be conscious always when you knew people, what they were?

BM Yes, there was a sense of survival, in that I suppose the street that you lived in and the streets surrounding it, you knew the people there, and could in some way trust them, but there was an area about quarter of a mile down the road called Tigers Bay, where James Galway came from, and they were the enemy. You were frightened to go through there, you would never come home that way.

IM They were by definition Protestants, whether they were or not, as it were?

BM Yes, and you avoided that area.

IM And did you know anything about Protestants? Apart from the fact that they were the enemy, in the same way that Joan Lingard, for example, draws wonderful pictures of what all Protestant children thought that Catholics were, apart from black and dirty: did you have any notion about what the difference was?

BM No. Well, the only difference was they might thump you, (L) and I don't think – it may be smug to say this, but I mean – I don't think that there was very much bigotry.

IM That's interesting.

BM Especially on our side. (L)

IM Now, presumably you went to a Catholic school?

BM The school was behind the house as well. And then later on I went to St Malachy's College, which was about a mile down the road.

IM And did this mean some of your friends didn't go to the same school as you?

BM No, because I didn't have any Protestant friends.

IM Not bigotry – just no Protestant friends.

BM Yes, but it was just the nature of the thing. I suppose if we put it numerically I think there would have been about five to ten Protestant families, childless families, in and around the street of different age groups. Maybe they would have had some children, but they wouldn't have been our age group. We formed football teams, we played cricket, we played soccer – which was very non-Gaelic, you know, so that we weren't prejudiced with regard to games. We

formed a skiffle group. Oh gosh! That was when the close friendships started to be formed.

IM These are close friendships which you still enjoy.

BM Yes, any time I go back. And we write to each other, and phone each
other up and that kind of thing, but it all began in and around that
age of what? – sixteen I think, or even earlier – fourteen? And we
formed a skiffle group. There was the time of the sport of football, of
cricket, and that was in a wider circle of people. And then that
gradually narrowed down to people who were interested in for want
of a better word arty things like skiffle groups, like music, like books,
like sitting talking in coffee bars and things like that.

IM And by the time you were fourteen, fifteen, sixteen, whenever it was,
were you at all thinking about becoming a writer?

BM Not at all, no. No, it was just something I didn't understand: I don't
think I'd read any books at that stage. (L)

IM Except for Enid Blyton and H V Morton.

BM Yes, well, at school I had read one novel, which was *The Wood-
landers*, I think [*by Thomas Hardy*], and I'd forgotten *Moonfleet [a
children's historical novel by J Meade Falkner, first published in 1898*].
I did read Biggles and things like that – Jennings and Derbyshire
and *Just William*, and then I made that jump from Biggles to
Dostoevsky. (L)

IM Were you ever a comics man?

BM Yes, oh yes, very much so. *The Wizard* . . .

BT That's reassuring.

BM Well certainly I remember running home from school to get them.
Was it Tuesdays and Thursdays it came out? And loving what was it,
V For Vengeance.

IM On the whole, Bernard, did you enjoy school?

BM Yes. I don't think I enjoyed Primary school. I just have bad
memories of it, bad smells and beatings and things like that, and
I was never really very happy except with this one particular teacher,
Gerry Tracey, who taught our qualifying class. It was the time of the
Eleven-Plus, though he couldn't have been an awful good teacher,
because there were fifty of us in the class and two of us passed.

IM Well I think if he had fifty of them in a class he was maybe doing not
badly. It's not an ideal number, is it? (L)

BT Doing all right just keeping you there.

BM One of the things he used to do, did I ever tell you this? He used to sit on the top desk and ask us to tear a wee feathery strip off the edge of your jotter, and then go up. And he would sit there, and if you could make him laugh, or make his face flinch by tickling him round the nostrils and the mouth and all that, he would give you a prize. So when you went up and tickled him with this wee feather round the face, he would sit there like a sphinx, impassive. The Secondary school was a lot better.

BT This was the what did you call it?

BM St Malachy's College, yes. It was run by diocesan priests and lay teachers; it wasn't run by an Order.

BT It was a Catholic school in the sense that it was financed by the church, was it? Or was it a state school?

BM The way it worked there, that the state financed Catholic schools.

IM As in Scotland.

BM I think there was an 80–90% grant or something.

BT Okay, but there wasn't any kind of independent –

BM Oh no, no, and you got into it by passing your Eleven-Plus. I went along on the first day in my new blazer and all the rest of it. The President whittled everybody in the room down to send them off to their classes except me, and I was left with this man. He says, 'What are you doing here?' And I told him my name, and he says, 'Oh, you've come here straight from the cradle: away back home, son, and come back next year'. But I didn't even get away like that, because I was on the way out of the school in my new blazer, and seniors saw me, and thought I was a first year, and then stuck me under the tap and ducked me. I went up the road like a drowned rat, you know, and went in to my mother and said 'I'm not allowed to go for another year'. But my dad negotiated at that point, and got me back in, and that was the year he died.

IM That must have been a terrific shock: was it sudden?

BM It was sudden to me, because I didn't know.

IM That's what I meant.

BM Nobody told me about it, I suppose, no I don't even think that in some senses I knew about it, but it was, it was a shock. I should have been able to put two and two together, because I think the previous summer he had gone to Lourdes, and I thought, he's away for a holiday to Lourdes, you know.

IM Well, any good Catholic doesn't have to be after a cure to go to Lourdes.

BM It was a parochial trip, and he went along. And then when he died all that financial thing changed: my mother had to go to work in the shop. Then she eventually got a job as a secretary in a school. And when I got round to failing those A levels, it meant something like £50 for another year. And at that time that was extremely steep, and there was much crying and bashing heads off walls and things to actually go back and do another year at A level.

IM Had you actually worked for that lot, or had you been playing around, as lads of that age very often do?

BM It's difficult to say: I think I worked the night before the exam. (L)

IM And did you have any preferred subjects at school? Was it always the arty subjects, as you called them, that took your fancy?

BM No, I liked bits of everything. I liked Science, what little bit of Art I did – I did Art in first year – this was the kind of careers guidance we got. I did Art in first year, and loved it, and thought in some senses of my father as being an artist, and that I'd like to carry on with Art. And you had to make your choice, I think it was second year, and I told the President that I was going to do Art. And he says, 'you'll do Science, or I'll hit you a kick in the arse'. (L) And that was careers guidance: I'd just lost my father and here was somebody who could advise you. So I gave up Art and then did Science.

IM Did you do a Science A level at the same time as your first sad attempt at English?

BM I passed my Chemistry.

IM You passed your Chemistry A level.

BM Failed my Physics A level. I can remember I was always borderline, you see. I remember doing Physics, and it was the last exam, and I was sitting in the study hall, and the sun was beaming in, and you know June, it was a hot, beautiful day, it was the last exam and I was struggling. I can remember the question on submarines and immersion, and I said 'drat!' (L) and walked out, and I failed that exam by one mark, so you know it caught up with me.

IM So you went back to school and you did English and –

BM Sorry! See footnote: for drat read something else.

IM Well I think that was almost to be taken for granted. You went back to school to do English, just English?

BM No, I did the whole gamut again – Chemistry and Physics.

IM Did you have to do Chemistry again although you had passed it? Seems hard.

BM I can't remember.

IM Anyway, you were back doing a full year, so I'm wondering when it came to jobs, was it simply what came up that meant your first job was on scientific lines?

BM I came out of school and was looking for a job, because that's the way the world works. I went down to a youth employment officer, and we talked about Forestry, and we talked about journalism and all the rest of it, for quite a long, long time. And then he said, 'Would you be interested in a job in science in the meantime?' And I said 'surely', so he pulled this piece of paper out of the desk and it was a job in the Anatomy Department at Queen's University, so I went up there, and 'in the meantime' lasted for ten years.

IM Does that mean you enjoyed it?

BM Yes – I seemed to enjoy everything, yes. (L)

IM I'm working on a complex diagnosis of whether you are too lazy to change to other things, or you're positively enjoying what you're doing.

BM Well, a bit of both. I mean it was enjoyable because I had good mates there: there was a good lad there called George Bryan, and he and I got on very well together, lots of jokes, a good view of life. It was an interesting place to be, surrounded as it was by dead bodies, and interesting work. You know, cutting sections, Histopathology, and at the same time I was doing night classes in medical lab technology.

IM With a view to improvement, or better job opportunities in that line?

BM Or promotion. When you got certain exams then you were in line for promotion and more money.

IM So for quite some time you saw yourself as making your career in that kind of line.

BM Oh yes, very much so.

IM So where did you go wrong? (L)

BM I suppose half way through the ten years, after about five years, it kind of changed. I went and worked on chromosomes, which at that time was a new technique, and you cultured blood and skin, and it was a real challenge. A sort of scientific challenge to get this thing to work every time: we were only getting it to work about 20% of the time at the beginning, and over the next five years we got that technique up to well over 90%. That meant because the technique was working I was sitting counting chromosomes down the microscope most of the day with a wee clicker. And there were interesting things in that too, the different abnormalities that were discovered, and we published papers on those. I think my first scientific paper I published was 'On the effect of phytohaemagluttinin, a chemical in the bone marrow of young rats', and there was another one, about the 'Ring G chromosome', and that was interesting. But certainly the counting of chromosomes wasn't. I also felt that I needed to do something else. All that time in the lab, the earlier years you weren't just as hard worked as you should have been, (L) and I read quite a lot of novels and books of poetry, and stuff like that, and it was at that time that I really became infected and affected by reading. That was the big Russian period, reading all these Russian books, not remembering any of them, but just really enjoying them. So when the crunch came, it was a kind of a dawning. When you say, did you envisage yourself in that forever, that's what frightened me, the thought of being 65, pottering about the lab counting chromosomes. So I went along to the Dean of the Faculty of Arts and asked him, you know, would I have to do A levels or what, and after an interview he asked me to come on in, come on in. (L) Then I went back home and told Madeline: we thought about our financial situation and all the rest of it. We actually took a fortnight's holiday in Donegal to try to think the whole thing out, and at the end of that fortnight had come down very firmly on the side of me staying in the lab, and trying to do what writing I was doing, and all the rest of it. I went back in on the Monday morning and saw the same people, the same job, the same smells, and said fuck it − (L)

BT Or drat?

BM Or drat, and I went over and put in my application for Queen's, so that a fortnight's rationalising was overturned by a smell. (L)

IM Now there's another force working here, that crept in without our duly acknowledging it. At the beginning of these ten years at the lab, you were a bachelor: by the time you were making these decisions you were married to Madeline. Did you have any family when you were being 'rational' about this?

BM Three.

IM Three of a family! So we can see why perhaps the rational view said go on earning money. Right, so there you were, making this rational decision. How did Madeline take it when you came home and said, 'You know that rational decision I made?' (L)

BM She has always been 100% behind me. She's a ministering angel!

But no, she's great, and has gone along with any decision. We've tried to come to decisions together, but obviously that decision would finally have been up to me, but she goes along with that, and the same with the one of giving up teaching to try and write.

IM Well, the one of going to university and becoming a student is obviously one that impressed her in the long term for the good, because I believe she's now herself an Open University student, as well as being a housewife, a mother and all that.

BM She was at Queen's before me. She was very bright at school, and went straight into university at age 17 and managed to fail her French, I think it was, three or four times on the trot, and had to leave. Hers was the source of that story, 'The Miraculous Candidate'.

IM This is a story which appeared in *Secrets*, wasn't it?

BM Yes. She was doing her Celtic exams, and they came and flicked out various papers, and they inadvertently gave her the Honours paper. And she was just doing Ordinary Celtic, and so she broke down in tears, and the guy helped her outside and brought her back in again, and she dried the tears and actually passed it. (L) So that was one of the sources of that story.

IM So when you decided at this stage that you would after all go to Queen's and study English, and she backed you in it, was it more a question of those years as a student, doing the reading and all the rest of it, or did you have a specific career with a degree in mind?

BM No, I think it was – sounds like a Hollywood movie – a question of proving something to yourself. Because over those ten years other friends of mine had gone through and got degrees, and you'd be sitting in conversation with them and you'd think why; is there a difference between us in some way – am I really so stupid? I just wanted to test that out, because you know I didn't feel I was stupid, but I felt I was just a bit ordinary and average, and I wanted to test that theory.

IM And you wanted out of the lab because you were a bit bored with it.

BM Yes, and I felt the whole thing, like medicine, would be good for me you know, and it was.

IM Was there ever any question that it was English you were going to study?

BM Yes, at one stage I felt I might go and do science, do a BSc, and then I would have technical qualifications plus an academic qualification

in a scientific subject, but . . . it was like Paul on the road to
Damascus – I can actually do what I want! Even right up to the last
minute in the Faculty of Arts you could do English and Zoology
under the one umbrella, you know, and I was going to try and do
that, so I ended up doing Philosophy and English and Russian
Studies. (L)

IM   And you enjoyed your time as an undergraduate?

BM   Yes, again. I seem to have enjoyed everything. (L)

IM   Don't knock it.

BM   It was great, cycling down the road in the morning, whistling your
head off, doing something you liked doing, making a lot of new
friends – and at the same time having that home thing to go back to,
which was great, rather than being a morose and footloose student.
So you were combining two things.

IM   You said earlier off-tape that you were finding it interesting now
making friends with students so much your junior. Did you find it
easy to get on with the undergraduates who were just a bit younger
than yourself?

BM   Yes, that was easy as well. Plus the mature students. I mean there
was a group of about five of us formed, not a gang (L) – a gang of
academics, walking up the street swinging their rulers. (L) There
were about five or six of us who got on very well together, and they
were a completely mixed age group. There was Ann Tannahill, who
was the same age as me, myself, a young fellow Gerry who was
straight from school, and a couple of other girls straight from school,
and we just had shared interests, like a sense of humour.

IM   So did you consort, as they say, with other people who were wanting
or hoping to write?

BM   Oh not – no.

IM   Or did you start this a while back?

BM   Yes, that's a while back: we'll have to wind the whole tape back now,
start again in the midst. (L)

IM   Pretend it's a word processor, and just put it in now.

BM   In the mid-sixties, that would have happened. When I was working
in the lab, there was a big fellow called Peter Paisley, of all things,
who was a BSc student. And I was helping him, and he was an odd
medical student, in that he was interested in literature and music and
things like that, and he ran the medical students' magazine, called
Snakes Alive. And there was a week we sat down and wrote the whole

magazine between us. I did the art criticism and wrote a short story, and he did the cinema criticisms and wrote a couple of articles, and I drew the cartoons. We generally got the whole magazine together between the two of us. And then I had a wee note from Philip Hobsbaum, who was lecturing in English at the time in Belfast. He said that he had read the story; somebody had brought it to his attention, and would I like to come along to the Creative Writing Group. Of course I was delighted, that was great, you know, to get, however mild, recognition like that. And I went along to this creative writing group, which at the time had nobody published in it, and it now looks kind of amazing when you rhyme off the names of the people who were in it; you know, there was Seamus Heaney and Michael Longley, Paul Muldoon, Frank Ormsby, I suppose myself now that I'm published.

IM I think you can suppose that. (L)

BM Jimmy Simmons was there for a time; Stewart Parker the play-wright, Hobsbaum himself, and I'm sure I've left a couple out, but they were all gathered in the same room. And what would happen would be, on Monday nights it was, you'd come along, and a couple of weeks beforehand you would hand in your stuff, then it would be typed out and run off, and everybody would get a copy through the post; and then you would turn up on the Monday night and the author would read his stuff. An example would be, say Heaney would read maybe six, seven poems, and people then would criticise and tear them apart gently, and put them back together again, and then you would have coffee. There was no drink allowed, because Hobsbaum felt that it would come to blows if there was drink, (L) people criticising your writing; and then after the coffee break thing people would bring a book along if they felt like it and read a passage, or a poem, or something that had impressed them over the past couple of weeks; and then everybody would abandon ship. That went on for perhaps four or five years, and even went on when Hobsbaum left: there was a guy called Michael Allen who ran it, sometimes in Heaney's house, sometimes in the pub.

IM It went downhill after Hobsbaum left, with that pub.

BM Yes, that was when Paul Muldoon came along. I remember well the night that he came. He was literally a wee fella out of school, but he looked even younger than a wee fella out of school, in his wee glasses. And he came in with his batch of poems that were – well, they weren't quite as good as John Donne's stuff, you know. (L) But they were measuring up there. And this wee lad of seventeen, eighteen, coming in and he knew what he was doing; that was quite remarkable. Heaney's jaw fell open. (L)

So that was a valuable time. I wouldn't like to put too much value on it, but it was a valuable time, in that it gave you something to do. You knew you could go along there every Monday night, and you knew that say in eight weeks' time it would come round to you again, and that you'd better have something or you'd miss your shot. So in those early days it forced you to write some stuff. The stuff I was writing at that time was all derivative; I didn't know where I was going. And the more I think about it, the more kind they were in that group to tiptoe round stories like that rather than hammer them. It was after that, 1970, that I got the first thing published, which was 'The Exercise' on radio [*later the first story in Secrets, 1977*]. I must have been married, oh yes. (L)

BT Was this Radio Ulster?

BM No; it was just BBC, BBC Morning Story.

BT Oh, BBC Morning Story, what's now Radio 4 Home Service.

BM But the regions opted in and out, you know.

BT Like the Scottish system at the time, yes.

BM I wrote this story and it looked about the right length. I wasn't even aiming for that, you know, it just came out about six pages typed, and somebody suggested to me that I send it off. And I did, and he wrote to me and said, come down and see me.

BT Who was this?

BM Sorry, a man called John Boyd, who was a playwright and a BBC producer. He was near the end of his career at that stage, and he just made one or two very small suggestions, and I carried those out, and he put it on the radio. And flushed with enthusiasm and success, I went home and wrote two more. (L) Both of which he accepted too.

IM If this geometric progression can keep up . . . (L)

BM And I think it was after about three of those that he said to me, don't always be writing stuff like this. (L) Go a bit higher, a bit more, a bit broader; which was good advice.

IM Which leads me to the whole business of the effect of studying English at university. There are all sorts of myths about it, and one of them is that people who want to write shouldn't study literature of the past, or that literary critics are the kiss of death. Did you get anything out of your undergraduate study of English?

BM Not a lot, not in those terms; not with regard to anything to do with
the writing. But one of the people who went along to the writing
group was Michael Allen, a lecturer in American literature, and he
was probably at that time the man who taught me most about
writing.

IM Did writing student essays seem anything like the same kind of
activity as writing stories?

BM Not at all, no: it was so much more difficult. (L) I'm serious. I think
it was like blood from a stone; it was really terrible.

Tape number two. 24 April 1984:
ongoing interview with Bernard MacLaverty.

BM I was just thinking there was someone in there whom I haven't
mentioned, who was very good to me at that stage, the very, very
delicate stage when you actually just start to write. That was a
woman who lived two doors up from us, a Mrs McCrudden, who
was an English teacher in a secondary school, and was a good friend
of the family. And somehow I got to her, and would show her what
writing I was doing at that stage, when it must have been pretty
diabolical. But she encouraged me a lot, and would praise things
ecstatically, and say this is wonderful, this is great; and you went out
of there thinking, great! And without that I think it might have been
very hard to go on. Certainly it was very, very good: she was an
amazing kind of a woman.

IM I suspect this is the lady you told me about the other day, when we'd
all been out watching an illegal showing of your video copy of *My
Dear Palestrina* [*a story from A Time to Dance, which Bernard had
adapted for television*]. The students were asking you about the roots
of that story and what had particularly inspired it, and you came out
with a couple of things, like Elocution lessons and something else: do
you remember what it was?

BM Yes. I went to Elocution lessons as a child. My mother offered me
the chance of either the piano or Elocution, something to do, to boost
the middle-class nature of the home, and having no piano (L) I opted
for Elocution. At least I think we maybe did have a piano; aye, we *did*
have a piano, but none of the notes worked. And I went to Elocution
for – I can't remember how long it was, it might have been a year, it
might have been two years – and finally I skived it so much that my

mother found out, and then she took me away from it. But that kind of experience of a young boy with a female teacher, I can just remember – I remember bits of it.

IM   When the students asked you about that directly, about *Palestrina*, you remembered that, and then a couple of minutes later you came to Mrs McCrudden. And this was actually a deeper experience, less immediately obviously the same. But it seemed to me to be much more of a wellspring to the story.

BM   It was never, ever on the surface. I never even thought of her. But then you know, thinking back, maybe there were elements in it of that, the way she dressed about the house. She had feet on her like swing boats (L), I hope this will never get as far as Ireland: the biggest bunions I've ever seen, God love her, but she was always so perfect when she went out.

IM   Sure. When you had finished the degree, which as you say you were doing for its own sake and to prove things to yourself, you did decide to become an English teacher. Was that an easy decision?

BM   Yes.

IM   A positive one?

BM   No. It was easy and negative. Actually I went out on teaching practice, and came streaking back from teaching practice to ask were there any places in the Library School, (L) but there weren't, and I'd shot my bolt. But I gradually learned to like teaching. Somebody propounded the theory to me that a teacher should only teach for about five years, and I feel that's not bad advice actually, because the first couple of years you're struggling to know what your trade is, then you master it, and then you start going downhill and taking shortcuts after that. And I think teachers who have been teaching the same thing year in, year out, for forty years or something like that – they tend to lose their edge. (L)

IM   But that also sounds like a highly ingenious way of defending, even promulgating, your own career pattern, which is to do something different every few years anyway.

BM   Yes, I think it's interesting to do that: God knows what I'm going to do next. (L) I suppose maybe writing screenplays is different to writing prose [*he had been writing the screenplay for Cal*], but I would like to go back to writing prose. And doing the garden. That's going to be my career from now on.

IM   So you decided to do teaching really because there wasn't a lot of choice?

BM Yes. There seemed to be a kind of railway track running from English into teaching. And I was unable to get off it.

IM But once you got into it you really enjoyed quite a lot of it?

BM Yes, I did enjoy an awful lot of it. The first teaching job was in Edinburgh.

IM This was the first time you'd spent any length of time in Scotland?

BM Yes. Once I'd got the qualifications together I applied for various jobs in Scotland, and got one in Edinburgh.

IM Why Scotland?

BM Ah well, I think Madeline and I had decided during the year before, during the Ulster workers' strike when the sewers were about to come up into the streets, and the whole place was discontent and tense, and there was *that* element. There was also the element that I think we'd always wanted to go away somewhere just to see what somewhere else was like. Those two reasons, plus the third reason of actually having to apply for a job, and thinking, why should it be Belfast. It certainly wouldn't have been England. (L) So I suppose maybe the Celtic nature of Scotland or something like that was more appealing, and at the time there were plenty of jobs. I think I got offered something like six schools in Ayr – in that division – and went over to Edinburgh and there were two jobs on the go there, so I accepted the Edinburgh one because there was the idea of the Festival, and the culture.

IM The poets' pubs . . .

BM Well, I didn't know they were there, but the idea of culture and the Edinburgh Festival – in three years in Edinburgh I think I went to one thing, which was The Chieftains. (L)

IM Well, you just ruined my next question, which was about the cultural impact of Edinburgh.

BT Paddy Maloney strikes again [*Paddy Maloney plays in the Irish band The Chieftains*].

BM The cultural impact of Edinburgh was kind of zero.

IM But you weren't living in Edinburgh, were you? Let's be a little fair to Edinburgh, you were living in Ratho.

BM That's right, eight miles outside, without a car.

IM So in a sense you weren't giving Edinburgh a big chance, because in so far as it has got all this cultural nature, living eight miles outside without a car and with a young family you weren't just ideally placed. You did however meet some of the Scottish literati?

BM Yes.

BT I would like to interject here because I feel we're missing something very important, and its very absence is significant. One reason for your leaving Belfast was the Troubles, and specifically the time of the Protestant workers' strike, but before that you'd lived through the time of the whole period of the mounting Human Rights movement. How did you respond to that development? Because that was a very hopeful period.

BM Oh yes, och aye. I mean we were all on marches and things like that.

BT But you haven't mentioned it, you see, that's what strikes me suddenly.

BM Why would I not have mentioned it? Simply, there is an awful lot of things I haven't mentioned. It didn't seem – or it doesn't seem in retrospect – as important. It was something you were doing, and you were doing it, and you knew there was never any hope of achieving anything with it, you know.

BT Even then?

BM Aye. You knew that the Unionist government weren't going to pay any heed to it. So you just went, you walked on the marches and you did things like that, and you voted. I voted. I don't think I've ever won an election for the candidate that I voted for, so you just get used to that. And it was part of the fabric of living there at the time. I don't think there was a feeling of, we're winning, or this is a revolution, or certainly not for me.

BT Ah, but some people did feel like that. Eamon McGann felt like that, Bernadette Devlin felt like that, and quite a lot of other near-contemporaries did feel like that.

BM They were at Queen's when I was in the Lab, and therefore I never had anything to do with them, or was never in any company with them.

BT Yes. I'm probably mentioning those as obvious names. The point is rather that people who were about your age looked upon the whole thing as having more point to it.

BM Well, I would say that I wouldn't have been as politically aware as they were. I was more wrapped up in things like finding out about jazz, writing at the time, and arguing with friends: talking with friends but not being political. I don't know whether that answers your question or not.

BT Yes it does. The question was not anything more complicated than just how did you feel about it, and that explains and describes exactly how you felt about it.

IM Are you more or less conscious of Northern Ireland and its difficulties and problems and so on, now that you've been away for a few years, and theoretically have had a chance to become more detached?

BM I think it's bound to happen. I don't want to be, but simply because you're not confronted by the Irish News and the Newsletter and Scene Around Six and all the minutiae of the thing that build up. All that gets filtered before it gets over here, but I have been back to Belfast within the last three or four weeks, and the atmosphere there is very much more relaxed than it was, even a year or two years ago. Maybe relaxed is the wrong word; just hardened, the people just don't seem to care. They just get into a track that will keep them out of trouble, and they keep on that track.

IM Your gradual approach to the notion of writing about something like the Troubles in your work only really happened with *Cal*, didn't it? [*1983*] And yet you said interestingly in an interview in *Cencrastus* magazine that what you were doing there wasn't actually specifically Irish: you'd like to think the same conflict situation, the same people could have happened in Poland or somewhere else, and that you were interested in the people rather than the politics.

BM Yes, I think that has to be, for fiction. Somehow it's the people and the characters involved in it, and you could manipulate the outward circumstances of the dilemma. It could be something else: it just happens to be the one I know about.

IM Is it one that you look like feeling compelled to write more about?

BM I don't think so. I would certainly want to continue to write about Northern Ireland, or using Northern Ireland as a background, but it certainly wouldn't be about the political violence of the present time. I think it's a kind of exorcism in a way; that you feel you can't have lived there through it and totally ignore it, because it's a very, very big thing, and this was an attempt in some way to face it. *Lamb* was an oblique attempt to face it, an extremely oblique way [*1980*].

IM Would you like to illustrate that a little?

BM Well, the man, Michael Lamb, who loves the boy, or has a misdirected love for him, ends up by destroying him. I felt in a way that that was an analogy for what certain people with Nationalist views are actually doing. That they are claiming to love something and yet they are destroying it at the same time. And it was there from the beginning, that idea, maybe it's not important to the book, but it was there.

IM Oh yes, I think it is. It has always impressed me the way in which the whole book is resonant of the Oscar Wilde line, how 'each man kills the thing he loves'.

BM The justification there would be Benedict's attitudes and his nationalism, his Republicanism, and at the end of the book both themes are brought together in that last paragraph.

IM That's very interesting. Meanwhile, we were in Edinburgh, weren't we? And I was looking for the story about the slap on the back.

BM I don't know that one.

IM Ah come on, you told me it. (L) About a man saying that you meet a lot of Scottish poets in pubs who'll clap you on the back, but just make sure they've taken the knife out of their hand first.

BM That was a man who was Prof of English in Belfast, John Braidwood, and he said, watch yourself when you go over there, he says, the poets all scratch each others' backs. With dirks. (L)

IM Well, did you experience anything either very constructive and vital, or anything particularly destructive in the Edinburgh literary scene in so far as you experienced it?

BM No, I found it difficult to meet people and that, and it took about a year or two before I was meeting people who were doing like things. The constructive thing in it was meeting Marilyn Ireland and Ishbel Maclean. Both worked at the BBC, and when I came to Scotland at first I had just done some schools radio, and therefore contacted them to see if there was anything on the go, and they gave me some work which I did. And Marilyn Ireland was then promoted and taken out of schools and put into drama. She approached me to write a radio play, which was 'My Dear Palestrina', and I think, you know, that's the positive side – that was the good side to come out of it. I can't think of many other people. Marcella Evaristi: meeting her, and her trying to write plays. We both won Arts Council Bursaries at the same time, which I suppose, looking at it objectively, must have caused a stir, to see that the Scottish Arts Council were awarding bursaries to Bernard MacLaverty and Marcella Evaristi!

IM So, apart from Marilyn Ireland and Marcella Evaristi, most of your friendships with Scottish writers were really formed after you left Edinburgh? On these rare forays to the mainland.

BM I met Liz Lochhead along with Marcella, and I think I met Jim
    Kelman very briefly once, at one of those launches of the Scottish
    short story book. John Herdman I met . . .

IM I'm sorry; I'm not trying to look for a social diary, but more whether
    it was easy for an 'outsider' to break in, and in general whether you
    find it helpful to be friendly with other writers, whether there are
    things you can discuss more easily with other writers about your
    work.

BM No, Edinburgh wouldn't have that effect at all.

IM Glasgow?

BM Yes, there's a disturbing element there of Jim Kelman and Alasdair
    Gray, trying to push techniques in different ways, which I don't
    think I would have done. Maybe in a small sense you'd just be highly
    conscious of the words that you're using and the way that you're
    writing: they are even more conscious I think in that way, and that
    would be I think a good influence. That makes you pay much more
    attention to what's going down on the page, but apart from that I
    don't think so.

IM Have you found the oft-repeated story of Scotland being a very small
    place where writers are all very jealous and envious of each other?

BM No, I haven't found that at all. For good writers. (L) Bad writers can
    be maybe a bit bitchy and jealous.

IM Right. Well, two or three years in Edinburgh?

BM Three.

IM And then MacLaverty wanted another change.

BM Yes, well, I was in Guidance teaching.

IM You kept very quiet about that.

BM Well, I taught for one year, and then I got promoted in Guidance.
    And I was very wary about the responsibility of it, because I did take
    it seriously. And the first day I got the job I was reasonably nervous
    about the whole thing. I got to my room and was sitting there waiting
    for, you know, some child to commit suicide or say that his father
    had wiped the family out with a shotgun or something (L), and you
    could look after him. And the door knocked, and this wee fella stuck
    his head in and I said, 'Yes?' He says, 'Sir, I put my banana in my
    bag and it's all squashed and gone all over me books.' And I gave him
    a tissue, and I was OK in the job for thereafter.

Bernard MacLaverty tape number three. 24 April 1984

IM I've asked Bernard about the times when he's conscious of things that have formed germs or ideas for stories or novels.

BM I suppose if we took the big ones first. *Lamb*. I knew I wanted to write either a very long short story or a novel – I wanted to call it a novel. At that time, I'd just read a piece in the paper about a case which ended in Edinburgh. I put it away for a couple of months, but it had really moved me when I read it in the paper. The judge said it was one of the most tragic cases he had ever had to preside over, and I began to think, and then added all my material to it; but it certainly did begin life as a case in a newspaper. The *Cal* thing –

IM Could you tell us what happened in the newspaper case?

BM Well, there was an Irish social worker whose name I can't recall.

IM That's all to the good.

BM He ran away with a boy, and gave him all the things that he didn't have. He took him to London, bought him presents, and gradually what money they had ran out, and all the hope ran out. They came as far as Edinburgh, and he drowned him in his bath in the North British Hotel, as he was washing his hair. An act of love like that finishing. Now for reasons of my own I wanted to change that ending, obviously, but that's where it began. And I think in plot it stayed fairly close to that. Well, I mean, it was several columns of newsprint, and I never actually looked back at it. The story was so vivid in my mind that it stuck with me. Maybe I should add that when it came to be published I panicked at the thought of libel, and asked Cape. I said that it began in a newspaper, and their legal department said that that was OK, because that was what was called something like common knowledge. Had I researched it in any way – I didn't – you know, had I gone and found out the backgrounds to both characters and written this book that way, it could certainly have been libellous. But I made no attempt – I mean, it was fiction for me.

IM Yes, Indeed! And very much a starting point. That's very interesting.

BM *Cal* was just a remark of Madeline's, that there must be a lot of boys knocking about Northern Ireland who'd done something in their adolescence which they would regret the rest of their lives; and at that point I started asking myself questions about it. The short stories, some of them, are –

IM Can you tell us a bit about how you got to the story of *Cal*?

BM Well, I suppose you know that in adolescence you do daft things.
The kind of daft things that I did would be reasonably harmless, I
suppose, like breaking into schools (L), but nowadays it can be that
you could become involved in violence and end up killing someone,
and have that on your conscience for the rest of your life. I also heard
a story of a family who were the last family on a big estate – the last
Catholic family there, and because they were under pressure they
were lent a gun. And because they were lent a gun to defend
themselves, the family felt obliged to help the organisation that
lent the gun, and that was a story by word of mouth, which is how
Cal becomes involved in it.

IM Is there any basis in fact or story for the Marcella character?

BM Not really. I suppose I wanted her to be an outsider of some sort,
which is why she is of Italian extraction, in order to be able to view
the thing from a distance and see it more ludicrously, although that
didn't really work out in the way that I wrote it. But I suppose it's
back to *Secrets* again: the idea really interested me of being close to
someone and having the one big thing that you can't tell them. And
that's the crux of the relationship between the boy and the woman.

And also I've been interested, and will be interested, in father/son
relationships. There was an uncle of mine who – he wasn't involved
in anything particular in the Troubles – but he became so affected by
them. He was a bright, sprightly man, who did the garden, and who
went fishing and all the rest of it. And what with the Troubles and
with the tension, he gradually went downhill, until he became a sort
of a mouse of a man, and almost total disintegration. There was a
period there that I didn't see him for some years, and he turned up at
a wedding; and you know he sat and he cried, and he wasn't the same
man at all. And I just thought of that as a kind of unknown casualty
of the Troubles, of what's happening there at the time. I mean,
people get shot and the like, and that's dramatic, but there are lots of
people who have gone like him. Although I believe he's OK now.

IM Good. While we're on *Cal*, there's a little footnote story, isn't there,
of your using an unfortunate kind of literal memory in the name of
your hero?

BM Ah, well yes! I think it may be that, as you grope back into your mind
for a name for a character, the ones that will ring true are the names
that you have maybe heard at one stage, and there was a guy who

lived in the same parish. I'd thought of lots of names, and Madeline had suggested names, and a prominent South Derry name was MacCrystal, and this had all the qualities that I wanted in the name. And I paired it up, I suppose, and felt the right ring of it with Cal MacCrystal. It also had the three letters – I wanted an individual as opposed to the groups of RUC, UDA, IRA, all that. And I also wanted a name which could help identify the Skeffington character, who is so precise that he calls him Cahal.

IM Yes, he's the IRA person.

BM Yes, the school teacher, whereas everybody else kind of slurs the name Cal. All those things I thought, yes, that's what I want, and I suppose somewhere at the back of my mind I realised that I'd heard this name before, about thirty years ago in Belfast when I was growing up. Four days before publication the phone rang, and it was Cal MacCrystal, who was a journalist in the *Sunday Times*. Certainly there was no maliciousness in it whatsoever, but he was disturbed by it. There was no way you could confuse a nineteen-year-old un-employed lad from County Down with a fifty-year-old journalist in London, working on the *Sunday Times*.

IM Though mind you, there were a few odd little coincidences, totally accidental, weren't there?

BM Total coincidence!

IM They both lost their mother when they were eight, and they both had an Auntie Molly, or whatever it was, and they both had a son called Cal.

BM Well no, they didn't – the father was called Shamie in the book: that was a little error on the part of whoever wrote that column, but –

IM It's understandable that the guy felt a little shaken.

BM Oh yes.

IM On one level, you're having very interesting conscious memories of things that you transmuted; and in a sense the Cal MacCrystal name wasn't sufficiently conscious in your mind for you to think of why you *were* conscious of it.

BM Well, I had known a Michael Lamb, and that didn't prevent me using that name, because it had all those elements that I wanted. The sacrificial thing in the Michael who is like God and all that, and Michael is a very common name, and it's good name, and it just feels right; and I was working along the same lines.

IM Now, can I ask a cheeky question? I gathered from a piece in a newspaper the other day that in the Penguin edition of *Cal* the name was going to be changed. I haven't counted, but am I right in jalousing that they started off by saying that it must be a name of so many letters, so that it will fit the space where MacCrystal was in the previous edition?

BM I was very generous, and I thought of that. (L)

IM What's it going to be now? McCluskey?

BM McCluskey. Which is also South Derry.

IM So – has he lost anything by being Cal McCluskey?

BM I suppose he's lost fractionally, but when you get into the dung that far up you want to get out of it fairly fast. (L)

IM As we heard today, *Cal* has been accepted for the Cannes Film Festival. So there's going to be a time quite soon when the film is the first knowledge that a lot of people will have of your work. In a class today one man said he couldn't read *The Great Gatsby* without seeing Robert Redford: will you mind when there are people who can't read *Cal* without seeing John Lynch?

BM I've never thought of that.

BT It's going to happen!

IM It will inevitably happen.

BM Yes, I would tend to work the other way round, in that for me the permanent thing is the novel. It was interesting to work on the film; it was interesting to work on a screenplay; it's a new world to be in again, doing new things, but I still feel that the novel –

IM The real *Cal* is the novel.

BM Yes. Oh, no doubt it's a version of it. I was going to make a very high-flown analogy there, but . . .

IM Go on! Go on!

BM Well, I mean you've got a symphony there, and it goes through so many performances, but the symphony is still there, you know: it's like a stage play too. But you've always got that base of the novel, which is for me the real thing.

IM And you don't think we're in danger of developing into a civilisation where people are so much more accustomed to visual images on screens than to reading books that the primary thing will eventually be the image?

BM No. I think people will continue to read books. But what I do think is that people are much more sophisticated visually than they are with words. I mean watching *Local Hero*, and I saw the last scene, and I thought immediately it came on the screen, that telephone is too close; and I knew he was going to phone that phone box, and it's a matter of inches, and visually you are that sophisticated, and I think a lot of people would have been. Even with ads. I showed my kids this ad, and it's Benson & Hedges, and what it is is a forge, with a whole lot of irons for heating in the fire. And there's a B, and there's an ampersand, and you know a few other letters scattered about, and I held it up to the kids, and I said, what's that an ad for? And they said Benson & Hedges. And you can put that visual information together, and how much more sophisticated that is than reading a sentence. Anyway, that's an aside.

IM You don't think that that will eventually in any way tarnish the effort people put into reading?

BM No, I don't! But I think it will go alongside that. I mean, I think that maybe writing a good film is as literary in some ways; it's a different way of telling a story. And cinema can be immensely powerful!

IM Is it an art form?

BM Yes!

IM But it's a corporate art form?

BM I suppose it becomes closer to a real art form when you get a director who has also written, like Bergman, who can control all the elements of it.

BT Could you direct?

BM I would love to try!

BT I thought so! (L) On the other side of the same coin, you've been fortunate in this case to be allowed to do the screenplay, which is quite unusual.

BM I think it is, yes.

BT Could you bring yourself to hand your novel, your short story, over to someone else?

BM Eh, I suppose it would depend on the money! (L) I've had advice on this, and I've heard people talking about it, and one guy that said this was a remarkably good Irish writer, the playwright Brian Friel; and he said, look, just let them take it and do what they like with it. You know that you have got the play, the story, the novel, and if they make a muck of it that's their fault, but the work is the thing that still stands. I don't know whether I agree fully with that. I really jumped at the opportunity of trying to write fiction in a different way.

BT You can really tell the story with images. It doesn't surprise me that you really feel that you would quite like to direct.

BM When *Lamb* was finished somebody bought up an option on it for a film. It was a guy called Ian Scorer, who was a freelance producer. And he asked me to come to London to meet the National Film Development Fund, who were going to try and fund me to write the script. And they talked to me and decided that I wasn't up to it, and they asked someone else to write it, a man called Brian Phelan. And he went away and wrote the script, but we have since not used that one. And I've written the script for it, which in all humility I think is better than Brian Phelan's.

BT And that's going to be done, then?

BM It's not certain yet. Because of what I was explaining to you yesterday: monies in films are going to be extremely difficult to come by.

BT This is the change in the law such that money invested in films is no longer tax-deductible, is it?

BM Yes, it's a very complex situation. But whether it'll affect *Lamb* or not, we've already submitted it to Channel 4. I would hope what we'll do is make a film of it and then we would hope to get it released in cinemas first for a couple of months, so that you can get reviews, and then have it shown on television. Once you've got those reviews then you can go to America, Australia, various places like that in order to sell your product, and get your money back, because there's an immense amount of money involved.

IM You mentioned Brian Friel, talking about writing for the theatre, and that's one thing we haven't mentioned, one thing which I don't know if you've done. Have you?

BM Just twice. I'll tell you about the first time. It was – I can't remember what age I was. I don't think it was so long out of school, and we'd joined St Malachy's College Old Boys Society, and decided that it needed some culture. It used to have a very thriving Dramatic Society which had gone defunct, and we decided that we'd put on some plays. I had written a play, and I wrote it, and directed it, I acted the lead, and – (L)

IM Modest with it!

BM And my mate acted the other male lead, and my cousin was the female in it. And we put it on the night of the worst fog ever in Belfast, and the audience consisted of my mother and me Auntie

Cissie and Mrs McCrudden. So I had put on a play, and I'd done all that, and there wasn't the slightest embarrassment. I kept forgetting my lines and saying, 'Sorry, Mother', so that you got away with that. (L)

The second occasion it was more professional, in that the story 'Phonefun Limited' [*published in A Time to Dance, 1982*] seemed to me to make a short piece for theatre, and we put it on in the Tron in Glasgow. It's a small place that has lunchtime plays, and you can come in, have a pint, watch a play and go back to your work with your head reeling. (L)

IM   And would you be interested at some stage in exploring further the possibilities of live theatre?

BM   Yes, I would. I think I would like to try that.

IM   Not a man sold on celluloid, then?

BM   I think that each of the media demands a different kind of response, and it is always interesting to try and cope with that in a kind of technical way.

IM   We were talking about conscious ways in which *Lamb* and *Cal* were inspired by things from real life. You were going to say a little likewise about any stories that had occurred to you.

BM   The stories that would be in *Secrets* – there's actually two: I came into the house and wrote them straight. There was 'A Rat and Some Renovations', which is a very light, silly story about discovering a rat in the house and trying to get rid of it, and a series of disasters actually occurred. The cat that we put after the rat was killed by a bus when it ran out of the house, and then my mother decided that we should put down phosphorus on bread, and we didn't know whether the rat was inside or outside, so we put bread in the yard and bread inside. And she was going to Mass next morning, and saw six wee birds lying with their feet up in the air. (L) So that was a cat and six birds, (L) and eventually we got the rat: and all this was for the American visitors coming, you see, so that the place would look nice for them.

IM   So it is actually a story that happened to your mother?

BM   And I was involved in it!

IM   – And to yourself, but neither of you is a character in the story as we have it, are you?

BM   Well, it's me and Peter, and Peter's named. It was just a straight writing down of what happened; and Gran was sitting in the corner, coming out in sympathy with the rat. (L)

IM That's magic. What's the other one?

BM The other one was a story called 'Where the Tides Meet', and it was an awful and nasty experience of going up towards Ballycastle and going out shooting one night. I'd never shot a gun in my life, and we were out with friends shooting, and he said, 'Do you want a shot of the gun?' They'd hit nothing, and he said, 'Aim at that fencepost there.' And I aimed at the fencepost – missed it, of course, but what we had forgotten was that we'd let the dog off the lead. And the dog was trained to run in the direction of the shot, and it just ran over the cliff. And it was the kind of story that grew out of that. Affection for my friend – I don't think it's a sentimental story – and how he was moved by the death of the dog. There are two stories just written down directly from experiences that happened.

IM Well, there are certainly some that one hopes do *not* come out of direct experiences. (L)

BM 'Phonefun Limited' I know you're talking about. Of the two prostitutes who make the obscene phone calls. In a way that was standing an idea on its head. There was a series of dirty phone calls that my Mother got, was subjected to, by some weird pervert. He must have been a baker of some sort – or even a master baker (L) – and he phoned up in the morning at three o'clock or five o'clock. This was when my poor grandmother was in hospital dying, so the phone had to be answered. My mother would run down in her nightdress and pick up the phone, and this guy would come out with mouthfuls of obscenities. If he phoned in the hours when I was up my mother would come in and tidy, and she would go round doing things, saying, 'Dirty phone call! Dirty phone call!' It really upset her, and I suppose years later I wanted to stand that thing on its head and to make fun of it, so that was one of the bases of the story.

The other story I don't think I would want to be terribly associated with is 'Between Two Shores' [*published in Secrets, 1977*], and the beginnings of that story. That story is about an Irishman who, because of his financial circumstances, has to spend a lot of time working in London. He forms a relationship with a woman and contracts venereal disease, and is coming home to his wife, realising that what he has to do on his first night home with his wife is make love to her.

That story began just out of a horrific journey that I had coming from Liverpool, sailing from Liverpool to Belfast, which is I think about eight hours. It was the most uncomfortable journey you've ever spent in your life. They seemed to have their architects to design the boats so that you can't put your feet up – you know, the chairs opposite you are just six inches too far away. And people constantly seem to get drunk and puke up; and the boat at first is too cold, and then it's too hot. And you go outside and you get frozen and the wind blows you. It was just a nightmare of a journey. And at one point I sat down and said, what could be worse than this? And then a thought occurred to me. (L) And then this story came to me in a flash! In a diseased flash!

But that story is the one that I think in the whole collection gives me most satisfaction. I think I spent two years writing that story. I wrote it, then I put it away, and took it out again, and put it away, and I finally finished it. I was talking to you about some things that keep you going as a writer, keep you moving from one word to the next. There's wee devices that you use yourself and you wouldn't ever worry about whether anybody ever saw them or not. I suppose I wanted that story to be a kind of life-journey. He starts off in a foetal position, and then he takes a couple of shaky steps because of the boat; and then he says something, he begins to talk (L). Then he has a cigarette and he begins to talk to girls: and at the end you know he's coming up to death between the arms of the Loch. Those wee, tiny devices are not tricks in any way, but they make the pattern of the work interesting for you when you're writing it.

IM   You put that story away a couple of times. Is that something you frequently do?

BM   No, that would be rare. By and large I would I think finish a story.

BT   You spoke about a couple of stories from the life which you just set down: did you mean that literally?

BM   No. What I mean about those stories – I don't know how many times I've rewritten – but I've certainly worked it over and over again.

IM   And it's not necessarily written in the week it all happened.

BM   No, no.

IM   I was thinking about *Lamb* and *Cal* and what made them different in character to the stories. I was wondering whether there was anything deliberate in the element of the thriller, the suspense, the hunt in both of them, in the same kind of way in which Graham Greene nearly always built his books. A basic hunt situation, so that you've got Michael and Owen being essentially on-the-run in *Lamb*; there's one kind of suspense about how Michael is going to cope with Owen, and another about whether the police are going to catch them. In the same way in *Cal* you've got triple kinds of suspense going on: will he tell her? Will he be caught? Will the IRA catch him? These are very powerful elements in a story.

BM That's probably why I used them. (L)

IM But were you conscious that when a story gets longer suspense seems to be more important, a more central element?

BM I just love that, when I read, that you can hardly wait to turn the page thing. You're really dying to see what's going to happen. It's pretty essential in *Lamb* and *Cal*, and in 'My Dear Palestrina' I think that element also works. Is this boy going to become very good? You would plant things early on to create interest: you want these points resolved in some way, therefore you read on. The same with 'Between Two Shores', and 'End of Season' [*published in Firebird 3, ed. Robin Robertson, 1984*]. It's a fairly long story, and the two spinsters and the man who comes in and makes them flutter a wee bit at the times when they shouldn't, or shouldn't want to flutter, and you want to find out what's going to happen. What's he going to do? And I find that is very interesting to work with. To have a plot.

Bernard MacLaverty's main publications to 1984, the date of the interview

Secrets and other stories, 1977
Lamb, 1980
A Time to Dance and Other Stories, 1982
Cal, 1983: Penguin 1984

The interview will also be of particular interest to readers of MacLaverty's 2001 novel, *The Anatomy School*, which is clearly partly autobiographical.

NAOMI MITCHISON

Naomi Mary Margaret Haldane came from Scottish stock. She was born in Edinburgh in 1897, and raised in Oxford, where her father, John Scott Haldane, distinguished physiologist, was a Fellow of New College. Her beloved elder brother Jack became J B S Haldane, the geneticist, and Naomi was interested in science from the first. Educated until puberty at the Dragon (Boys') School, Naomi was later a home student at St Anne's. She became a VAD, and married her brother's friend Dick Mitchison in 1916, travelling to France that year to nurse him through a serious wound. They had eight children, the eldest of whom, Geoff, died of meningitis at nine. She lost her last baby, a day-old daughter, in 1940. This was an open marriage, apparently on the whole very happy. Privileged Socialist and Feminist, Mitchison wrote constantly, and supported her husband's bids for Parliament in the 1930s. Her first novel, *The Conquered* (1923), marked the start of a long phase of historical novels, gradually followed by other developing genres, with emphasis on Scottish and later African subject matter, and latterly science fiction. Dick Mitchison became a Labour MP in 1945, and was made a life peer with a government post in 1964. He died in 1970. The family had moved to Carradale in Kintyre in 1937, and Mitchison served for many years as County Councillor and member of the Highland Panel. Although she travelled widely, Mitchison was based in Carradale until her death in 1999 at the age of 101.

IN SUMMER 1984, in the very early days of our interviewing project, Naomi Mitchison was 86. It seemed like a good idea to do our interview with such an old lady sooner rather than later. But one major problem with the undertaking was the range and extent of her work. It was a principle I started with, that I should read and reflect on all a subject's books, the whole writing career to date, before importuning her with a microphone. But when the subject has written some eighty books, including not only the famous historical novels of the ancient world and an epic of Scotland after the 'Forty-Five, but poems and plays, biography and philosophy, novels, stories and fairy tales, science fiction, a whole library of books for children, several volumes of memoirs and war diaries, pamphlets on oil for the Highlands and chapters on rural reconstruction after the war, the interviewer may have to be satisfied with falling short. I had read more than thirty volumes, some of them very hard to come by, and my husband, co-interviewer and sound technician Bob Tait, with specialist work of his own on hand, had read about six, when we travelled to Carradale to meet our subject, of whom I was considerably in awe.

We stayed at the Mains Farm on the estate, and spent a couple of days interviewing Mitchison at fairly long intervals – it's always a tiring business for the subject, and Mitchison was already having a little trouble finding words. Her brain was needle-sharp still, but she would stop, screw up her extraordinarily wrinkled face and grimace until the precise *mot juste* came to her.

We got on well. What had seemed to me a drawback – only having read about thirty books – turned out to be rather a treat for her, I began to realise. It was a long time since anyone had read so much, or asked about so many books with knowledgeable interest. She was widely celebrated, but much less widely read. I slowly realised she was enjoying herself, even when I asked about books she had almost forgotten herself, or had not re-read for a very long time. Her sense of mischief showed when, gently chastised for failing to pronounce 'Dione' in classical fashion, I fell back on her other name, Isobel. Mitchison twinkled that that was of course a witch name (p. 85). Again (p 98), she vouchsafed that people – even writers – could be quite complex. She was friendly, but awesome!

For any number of reasons, this interview was harder to conduct, to tape, to transcribe and to edit than any of the others, and may also be harder to read. The *oeuvre* is enormous, and the discussion often oblique or very rapid. There are more notes here than elsewhere, but the reader is still liable to be confused or puzzled, or feel inadequate. There is little point in a precise note if the general context is foreign to the reader, and with many of these books, some long out of print, this can often be the case. The reader is advised to consult Mitchison's *Saltire Self-Portrait* (1986), and Jenni Calder's fine biography, *The Nine Lives of Naomi Mitchison* (1998). Subjects such as the Highland Panel are fleshed out in both.

In interview, it took a bit of time to get used to her pauses, to questions that she seemed not to hear, and then too late I would realise she was still busy with the last question, considering it carefully and pursuing it regardless. Then she would surprise me by going on to the next topic I'd raised, when I had discarded it as not of much interest to her. Examples of this are on pages 72 and 81, and I have not edited them out completely smoothly, because what she had to say was so interesting. On page 72 she clearly thought I was asking something about her own attitudes to women, when I was intent on the male-dominated world of the early novels, before she developed her astonishing, strong female characters. On page 73 I asked two questions too close together, about the occurrence of the non-rational, and about the loyalties theme in *The Conquered*. She answered the second question first, at length, but she gets round to magic and nightmares and the non-rational by pages 81–2. We did not have time to get to know each other before starting taping, but soon there was less of a problem.

The tyro interviewer also knew few other people had read the books at that time (and this unfortunately remains true at the time of writing), and for the sake of future auditors of the tape or readers of the interview, found herself trying to summarise a plot or story to the patient author. There was also a tendency for Naomi and Bob to wander away from the subject, to engage in animated general discussion of Scottish politics or history until brought back to the tape.

The interview led to a long and rewarding correspondence. It further led to my attempt to solve a difficult problem for undergraduate students, whom I wanted to introduce to her work. Extended and complex novels such as *The Corn King and the Spring Queen* cannot easily fit into university reading lists, and even the leisurely Scottish masterpiece *The Bull Calves* with its extensive pages of authorial notes and commentary presents the same problem. So I asked and received Mitchison's permission to produce an anthology of her selected shorter fiction, which we could use to introduce students to the range of her subject matter, themes and narrative inventiveness. *Beyond this Limit: Selected Shorter Fiction of Naomi Mitchison* was published in 1986, and ranges from early cave painters and ancient world slavery through Scottish and African stories to a bleak account of a Scotland devastated by a 'small' nuclear device. The title story is the extraordinary collaborative effort of Mitchison and Wyndham Lewis discussed on pp 93–4.

Encouraged by publisher Richard Drew, Mitchison and I later collaborated on a selection of her stories and poems, published in 1990 as *A Girl Must Live*. Her memory by that time was more sporadic, and in many cases she could not remember whether individual items had been published before, or where, or when. It is still a vital record of much scattered material which might otherwise have been lost for decades.

I retain great affection for her second 'contemporary' novel, *Lobsters on the Agenda*, first published in 1952, and written out of Mitchison's experience of the Highlands, of Argyll County Council, and the Highland Panel. In 1997 I wrote an Introduction for a new edition, which was published by House of Lochar. The last time I met Naomi Mitchison was at the launch of Jenni Calder's biography at the Edinburgh Book Festival in 1998, when I contributed a piece on *Lobsters*, and everyone was thrilled at the appearance of a tiny frail figure in a wheelchair – and even more when she suddenly decided to speak, about her beloved Africa.

29 September 1984. Carradale, Kintyre, the home of Naomi Mitchison.
Present, Naomi Mitchison, Isobel Murray, Bob Tait.

IM Naomi Mitchison, one of the things everybody knows about you is that you write historical novels. But those of us who read some of your extraordinarily lively and entertaining memoirs keep coming across phrases like 'history bored me deeply', and 'the choking dullness of any history people tried to turn me on to'. So how does it happen that you started off in particular as a historical novelist?

NM I was very badly taught, I think. The school in some ways was very good [*The Dragon School at Oxford, which Mitchison attended until puberty as its only girl pupil*]; but at that period history was badly taught, and it wasn't until after I was married. My husband was a Double First in Greats, and was terribly keen that I should wander about the same world as his. And first of all he wanted me to learn Greek, and gave me a charming book called *Eulalie: ou le grec sans larmes*, but I didn't get far with that! Then I was always writing these imaginary things. Plays, usually, at that time. I just put my people anywhere. The first play I did, I put them in a remote part of the Andes, so remote that anything could happen. This was just fairy tales. And then I wrote one of these plays and he read it, and I said, 'Well, when could that have been?' And he said, 'I would think about the fifth century AD'. And I said, 'Oh, what's happening then?' And he said, 'Would you like to just read a bit about it?' So he gave me the appropriate volume of Gibbon [*Edward Gibbon, 1737–94, author of the monumental and multi-volume History of the*

Decline and Fall of the Roman Empire]. Then I thought, this is rather interesting; I wonder what happened before that. So then I read the volume before, and I gradually read backwards through Gibbon (L), and then bravely I read Mommsen [*Theodore Mommsen, 1817–1903, author of a three-volume History of Rome*]. And then by that time I was hooked.

IM   So the first novel that you published, which was *The Conquered* in 1923, is about Caesar's Gallic Wars?

NM   Yes indeed, a fairly simple period, and there's a lot that's badly wrong with it historically. I think I've got the Celtic civilisation quite a bit wrong on every kind of detail, but on the other hand, it gives *some* kind of picture. And by that time I'd read a lot of Yeats, and of course I'd got rather hooked on that: 'hard to remember, sick with tears, the swift innumerable spears' [*Approximation to two lines of The Wanderings of Oisin, 1889, 'sad to remember, sick with years/The swift innumerable spears'*]. An interesting thing you can do with Yeats is to substitute 'bottle' for 'battle' (L) in his many poems.

IM   I think that's a very subversive piece of advice! (L)

BT   Advice to students.

NM   Yes, that's for students. But then there was Lady Gregory, whom I read avidly. Then I also got hooked on the whole Irish Nationalist movement, and the first 'Demo' I was on was a Peace with Ireland procession which – I remember quite well – started the wrong way! (L) But then when I had written a book, when I went over to Dublin, everybody was very, very welcoming, and AE [*poet and painter George William Russell, who used this pen-name*] and people like that.

IM   Did they see that your book, apparently about Caesar's Gallic Wars, was in many ways about Ireland?

NM   Oh certainly. They saw everything at once; I think most people did, and my mother, who was a confirmed Unionist, a follower of Carson, was slightly shocked by it.

IM   It's a paradox: history at school was dull; you had to discover it elsewhere. Then you wrote about the Gallic Wars, although in a sense you were writing about Ireland, and in one of my copies of *The Conquered* it tells me there was a school edition in 1926!

NM   Yes.

IM   . . . And I find that very puzzling.

NM   People at school had been totally bored by the Classics when someone thought of this. I had a lot of letters from people, even a poem someone wrote, about how his school master had said, 'Well, one book that might interest you . . .' And he opened it, and there were all these beatings and so on. And it was a real bedside book. (L)

IM It still seems surprising in a way, that they didn't find that this book is deeply subversive, as so many people have found so many other of your books. Your message about Ireland in 1923 was not quite the Establishment line.

NM I don't think people were so fussy about subversion in those days. It was the pre-Thatcher world. Even civil servants might have read it.

IM (L) In the actual world of Gaul in the novel, for people who know of you as a feminist and socialist, it may seem strange that almost all the main characters are men. And the only female character who might be you slightly in disguise chooses death before dishonour early on . . .

NM I don't think I really felt myself very much interested in women, and I've always been pretty heterosexual (L), so that I never had a crush on a school mistress or anything like that.

IM But still, in your later books there are –

NM Oh yes.

IM Women have a much greater part, and are very often central characters.

NM I was much more into the problems.

IM So essentially it seems to me, and do correct me, that *The Conquered* is about loyalties.

NM Yes.

IM And about how people get very confused and conflicting loyalties. Your hero Meromic, who is a Northern Gaul, is eventually a slave to a Roman, and he is put into all sorts of intolerable situations because he begins to feel some personal loyalty to the Roman, and at the same time the Romans are attacking Gaul: and I'll put a marker down here, because I think this is something that also happens later. Meromic during the course of the book seems to get, to accept a series of wider loyalties.

NM Yes.

IM At first he despises other Gallic tribes, and says well, they're not our tribe. But by the end, when he has experienced what happened with Vercingetorix, he seems to be saying, this is Gaul, this is my country, so he has come out to a bigger idea.

NM This is what happens to people. I had a letter from Morgan Forster [*the novelist E M Forster*]. I was so thrilled by it, and he said in the letter that there are many Meromics in India, and he had picked up exactly all that about loyalties. [*See You May Well Ask, p 101.*]

IM I think that's something that goes on happening in different ways in many of your other books.

NM And in many a country.

IM Indeed. You said there are lots of historical details wrong in the book. Do you think that matters?

NM Yes. It worries me now. But I've said to myself, will I rewrite this book, and then I just couldn't, and I couldn't muck up a book by somebody else, and really at that time I *was* somebody else.

IM That seems eminently fair.

NM Then the stories that I wrote afterwards, some are very much by the other person, and sort of childish in a way, and others are beginning to be me.

IM Something that seems to be you right the way through and starts here, is that there is a vein in the book of non-rational belief of some kind or another. Meromic belongs to the tribe of the Wolf, and has a special relationship with wolves, and indeed he disappears *as* a wolf at the very end of the book. Is this an element that you feel is important in life generally, the non-rational?

NM I'm sure that one of the most interesting things that happen to anyone, is this business of loyalties and how to reconcile them. One's got a loyalty presumably to one's family to begin with, and then it widens out to one's village, one's town, one's country. Perhaps to being a European, and finally, I suppose, to being a human being. But one feels that *that* loyalty is the one that's got to be cultivated, because at the moment we are all threatened, whatever our colour or race or anything. And I always find it very interesting that when I'm here I feel myself basically a Scot, but in London during the Blitz, I felt tremendously a Londoner. Not English, but London. We set our will against yours, the will of London. We won't be bombed out.

IM Before we leave *The Conquered*, you wanted to call it 'Headlong Westering'.

NM 'We are young and setting, headlong westering, there is no recapture.' A quote from a very early poem by Aldous Huxley.

IM Do you think, though, it would have been as good a title, 'Headlong Westering'?

NM No. No, I think they were right.

IM You said in a memoir that you had to fight even for *The Corn King and the Spring Queen*, which I think is a wonderful title.

NM Oh yes, then I knew that was the right title.

BT That's terrific.

IM During the course of reading *The Conquered* with great interest, at one point I almost wanted to suggest an alternative title of *Meromic the Vacillator*, because he was always coming across these conflicts and having great problems trying to find out what he most believed in.

NM Oh he was. Then the title ought to have been *Who am I?*

IM Indeed I think a lot of your titles can apply across your books from one to another. When you call a book *Who Am I?*, or *When We Become Men*, or *You May Well Ask*, or *All Change Here*. They are all very striking titles, they are all very colloquial and immediate, and quite often they reflect themes that come up again. *When We Become Men* . . . it could be a title for *The Conquered*, couldn't it?

NM Yes.

IM The next novel that I read at any length was one which I think might puzzle a contemporary audience, or anyone since Greek and Latin came out of schools. This is *Cloud Cuckoo Land*, a title which has a very specific reference if you know your Aristophanes and the parliament of the birds. I didn't know what to expect it to be about, really.

NM Yes, yes, it was a reference like that. That again is a book for people who are interested in that period, and has been used a good deal in universities.

IM I would like to see it reissued. I think it is very fine. It hasn't got some of the rather rough early writing that you find in *The Conquered*. I think it's a very −

NM I haven't re-read it for years.

IM You must! (L) And again it's about choices in loyalties, and they are never easy. The hero comes from a small Greek island, in the time when Athens and Sparta are very much vying for power, and he has to decide what side to be on, and there isn't a right side; because even Athens is a bully at this stage. But Sparta is worse, and I think that in a lot of your books Sparta equals 'the baddie'. Is that true?

NM Well, you see, Sparta was a little bit like Germany, and at that time we were beginning to be aware of what was happening, and although

I don't think I thought of it directly, that was affecting us. We weren't going to have anything to do with the Hitler Jugend.

IM The whole discipline of Sparta immediately makes one fear a totalitarian kind of —

NM Yes.

IM Yes.

BT But the Sparta of Kleomenes is not the same.

NM No. Though to start with it was an aristocracy, it was rather less democratic than it was a couple of centuries earlier, more of an oligarchy, more top people.

IM But Bob's right; when we come to *The Corn King*, for example, Sparta is going through a good phase.

NM Yes.

IM In some ways we see the best of that phase.

NM Yes it is: it was an internal revolution.

IM So that Sparta there is intelligent, rational and modern, and it is being compared with the more intuitive virtues or (L) qualities of Marob.

NM But then that Sparta was squashed again.

IM So we can't just say that for Mitchison Sparta equals such and such, at all.

NM No. No.

BT Can I just pursue that point about the Sparta of Kleomenes, which comes about by an internal revolution led by an aristocracy, in a root sense of the word; some of the best, in every sense the best.

NM Yes: and the intelligentsia.

BT The intelligentsia: a part of that best in that context. And for a short time there is great popular hope.

NM Yes.

BT And it all occurs within a community which has a basis of tradition and custom and a sense of history.

NM Yes.

BT A very, very strong sense of history. And even so, the whole thing tumbles down, partly because of internal and largely because of external pressures, but for whatever reason, it all tumbles down. Do I detect in that an expression both of your hope and of your pessimism?

NM Indeed yes. But that's what actually happened, and no doubt in a sense I chose it, or it chose me.

BT It seems, looking back with the benefit of hindsight, almost the perfect model for you of the way that things tend to go, and I'm wondering how much of it in hindsight you view in a pessimistic light, since after all the whole thing crumbled. Or am I pushing it too far: is it a model or is it not a model? You were saying it sort of chose you: that suggested it.

NM Yes, I suppose it is. At the time one was feeling that there might be a very important social change happening in the UK, but it was endangered; and you see that scenario is repeated in my modern novel.

IM In *We Have Been Warned* [*1935: published only after long wrangling about censorship*].

NM There was a real sort of social change, and then there was a counter-revolution; and of course that keeps on happening. 'Es war oft schön in rote Wien' [*It was often beautiful in Red Vienna*]. And then comes Dolfüss and the counter-revolution, and a new and usually rather more brutal good time is born out of the blood. [*See Vienna Diary, 1934.*]

BT But that doesn't stop us all having to try to go with the tide in a positive kind of way, which is the message that you often carry?

NM Oh indeed yes. 'There's nothing but our own red blood/Would make a right Rose Tree' [*Yeats, 'The Rose Tree', in Michael Robartes and the Dancer, 1921*].

IM Yeats again! Do you sympathise at all, though, say with the character of Thucydides in *Cloud Cuckoo Land*, who after Athens has been defeated and is lost, says it was worth it because of what it meant?

NM Yes, I'm sure. It's always worth it. And a generation later the people who've been shot have a beautiful monument put up to them.

IM (L) Does that help a lot?
    Well, let's move to *The Corn King and the Spring Queen*, which is, I think, more than just a historical novel, although it's that. Why do you think, as you said recently on television, that this is the one book by which you are likely to be remembered?

NM It's the first book when I think I was really writing as myself. I don't reread it and think, 'Oh goodness, that's awful'. There are one or two bits I think I would perhaps like to re-write where it's got a bit sort of sentimental, a bit muzzy, but on the whole I think it is pretty good.

IM So far you have criticised things for whether they are historically accurate. Now you have brought in another criterion, sentimentality, so you are judging your novels not simply by their historical accuracy.

NM But also by the writing.

IM Yes. Right.

NM I mean by romanticising, or sentimentalising, going soft. I re-write enormously; I can re-write over and over again.

IM Do you re-write things after you have published them?

NM Well, I don't know: the two Virago have done, there was very little re-writing.

IM That's *The Corn King* and –?

NM And *Travel Light*, which is a fairy tale. But if anybody does *The Bull Calves*, about four or five places that I've got marked in my own copy where there have got to be alterations. Two of them are historical as far as I can remember, and the others are things that I think went soft in my writing.

IM (L) Yes. In the Virago Introduction – no, Afterword, to *Corn King*, you say that –

NM That I was in a hurry to end it. I was just feeling so tired.

IM Well, it's an enormous book, isn't it?

NM And it took a long time, but I feel that there should have been a bit more explanation before the last bit.

IM Should we have seen more of Tarrik and Erif?

NM Yes, I think so. But on the other hand that would inevitably have been a bit of a let down, in a way.

IM I don't know. You manage something of a similar situation in *The Bull Calves*, when Kirstie and William come. It starts together with them both having been through all they have been through, doesn't it?

BT Another relationship which I was fascinated by and wanted to hear more about was between Tarrik and Hyperides. That to me as a philosopher is an extremely interesting relationship. The extent to which Tarrik began to influence Hyperides' notion of the psyche, or a kind of ecology of mind and the natural world, which allowed for Tarrik's tribe's beliefs to have a function, to have a meaning.

NM At that time that was the thing that was interesting me enormously, and that interest has obviously increased as I write more about Scotland.

IM As is signalled perhaps in the title of *The Corn King and the Spring*

Queen: it's an enormously ambitious novel, because it's almost like the Fall, or the Birth – I'm not quite sure which – of man happening. The people of Marob, particularly represented by Tarrik and Erif, belong to a much older culture, which is full of unconscious or certainly unself-conscious things.

NM Yes.

IM And we don't see civilisations moving from Marob to Sparta, but answers coming from some attempt to learn from each other, so that you can have some kind of wholeness of person. Would you say that was so?

NM Yes, I think there was quite a bit of that.

IM You said in the Virago Afterword, and tantalisingly quite quickly, that you are *now* consciously aware of the great myths underlying the story. Would you like to specify a wee bit?

NM I think I am about the only person alive who has read through the whole of *The Golden Bough*, though it was much earlier and I read it almost as fairy tales. My grandmother, of all people, my Trotter grandmother, had the whole big edition, which I now have, and I just read it all through, and some of it stuck.

IM Obviously.

NM It's like when one reads the Bible, some of it sticks.

IM So there were obvious things about it that you weren't conscious of? The king dying for the people . . .

NM I think I was conscious of the king dying for the people all right, though in a sense that was very near the surface anyway.

IM Yes. But it even happened with the Spartans, didn't it?

NM Oh yes, and it happens everywhere, and this is what happens to political leaders. Jolly lucky if they do manage to die for the people and not long afterwards. I think that was so impressive about Lenin's tomb. There is obviously somebody who died for the people. His curious waxen figure . . .

IN One thing that is interesting is the very length of *Corn King*. Even in its time surely quite exceptionally long.

NM Oh, very long. Though of course, a generation before you'd have written two- or three-volumed novels.

IM But in the twentieth century, was it because you believed people would read it if it was good enough, or didn't you care?

NM I didn't care. (L)

IM Did you care about reviews?

NM A bit. *The Conquered* was set off by one review. I was discovered!
    And this was Raymond Mortimer, and he wrote a long review saying
    that I was the best if not the only historical novelist now writing, and
    – ooh er! – that started everybody else reading it. So then I had a
    crop of good reviews. I don't think it would ever happen now, but at
    that time good reviews were important. I'd never bother now.

IM What about the money that you got from books? Did that matter?

NM It mattered less then than it does now (L).

BT What a shame.

IM But again you weren't cramped or anything, you didn't think you
    had to write to sell, because you needed the money for anything in
    particular.

NM No, I usually spent the money on getting sort of frilly frocks (L) for
    the children.

IM You've already mentioned Morgan Forster liking *The Conquered*,
    and that meaning a great deal. The opinions of other writers were
    more important?

NM Oh yes. That was always important. Still is.

IM We know from your memoirs that you were friendly with a wide
    range; the Huxleys, Forster, Auden, Olaf Stapledon. Were there any
    Scots in your acquaintance as writers before you came to Scotland?

NM Not as such, I don't think.

IM And when did you encounter people like Hugh MacDiarmid?

NM I certainly didn't meet him till long afterwards. I probably read some
    of the early poems quite accidentally. Of course I'd been brought up
    on Scott and Stevenson. I found most Scott deeply boring, but when
    my father read it aloud, when I had scarlet fever, and I wasn't really
    allowed to read, he read me things like *The Heart of Midlothian*, with
    a lot of dialogue, which he read very well. And then Stevenson I've
    always liked.

BT The fact that there you were writing in the 1920s and you say you
    came across MacDiarmid's poetry rather by accident: that suggests it
    must have taken some time at least before MacDiarmid's claims for
    what he was doing impinged on you in any serious way.

NM Yes.

BT To what extent *did* you take MacDiarmid's claims to reconstitute a
    specifically Scottish culture seriously, in the end?

NM Not much. (L)

BT That's my impression. (L)

IM It interests me that you weren't really *with* any of the Scottish writers
    at this time, and yet, looking back, it is possible to discern an almost
    archaeological interest going through. Neil Gunn goes through this;
    you do; Grassic Gibbon does with *Spartacus*, and all the rest of it. All
    going back into history: even Eric Linklater does a Viking book.

NM Yes. Oh indeed yes, and his children's stories.

IM One wonders whether there is some common need being felt and
    understood.

NM Well, I think in a sense we were making something to stand on. A
    rock.

IM But there is nothing that I know of in your writing before *We Have
    Been Warned* in 1935 that is self-consciously Scottish.

NM No, I don't think so.

IM It's Dione in that one who is repeatedly and self-consciously
    Scottish.

NM I wrote some quite bad verse about Scotland earlier on, but really
    when I was half grown-up, during World War One.

IM So in a sense, Scotland could have been at the back of your mind as
    well as Ireland . . .

NM Yes.

IM . . . for *The Conquered*, it's just that Scotland wasn't in such a crucial
    situation as Ireland was.

NM Exactly, yes. And of course, every year we were going up to Cloan
    [*the Haldane family mansion adjacent to Gleneagles where Mitchison's
    Haldane grandmother used to gather the extended family*], but I have a
    pretty ambivalent feeling about it.

IM Yes, you have mentioned a few times in your memoirs how
    frightening it was, and how grim. Do you think it was in some
    sense Calvinist?

NM No, I don't really think so. I think it was just a house built that way.
    Two or three years ago my cousin Graeme who was just my age – he
    died last year – we were very fond of each other in a cousinly way: I
    asked him how frightened he'd been, and he said, 'Yes, I *was*
    frightened, but I managed not to show it'. And I said, 'Were you
    frightened of the Gorgonzola?' He said, 'Yes, yes'. So I said, 'Well,
    let us go up and see whether it's still there'. And he said, 'All right'.
    We crept up this winding stair until we got to this door. You see, the
    staircase goes up the middle, and one is shut in, and you open a door
    and you are in this Gorgonzola room, and the Gorgonzola might be

at the other side. We went to the opposite side so that we could really
see. He didn't appear to be there, but we weren't at all convinced.
(L)

IM It's a very striking thing, these childhood fears, and not only
childhood of course but recurrent nightmares as well: but you have
said several times that they do in some way nourish and make
possible your work.

NM Yes. Oh yes, you've got to have a look. Remember, 'Dauntless the
slug-horn to his lips he set, / And blew: Childe Roland to the Dark
Tower came'.

IM Browning. Terrific!

NM And you were to do all that.

IM Yes.

NM And make it up if it isn't real.

IM So almost before you write, you have a kind of subconscious
fearfulness. In your writings that very often comes out as magic
or whatever: there's a good and a bad kind.

NM Yes.

IM As for example in *The Big House* [*a children's novel set in Carradale,
1950*], which I read last night, where there's magic on both sides.

NM Yes. Oh yes!

BT Is storytelling a kind of magic too?

NM Yes.

BT You put the question to yourself, why write, in *You May Well Ask*.
And you leave the question open at the end. But it occurred to me
that the theme of magic and the healing power of magic is such a
recurrent theme that storytelling itself has got some of this healing
power?

NM Yes. Goodness knows what these powers are. Dowsing, when I have
the things in my hand, I'm never *sure* if I'm going to be able to find
water or not, or if what I feel is going to be water. I had one very
curious experience when I was doing this in somebody's garden –
they wanted to find some water – and I had a very strong feeling for
it, and when we dug down, no water, but a collection of Roman
pottery, all rather broken. (L)

BT Good God. That was a bit uncanny.

NM Well, I think there is just so much; and it's terribly difficult to say
what it is, and it doesn't respond to ordinary tests. And all one can
say is, well, this is how it's been for me. Perhaps it's all coincidence

and nonsense, but I just don't know. And I think writing is a bit like that too. You may strike water or gold or diamonds or whatever.

IM   Are you conscious yourself of where you struck diamonds and gold, and where you only found muddy water?

NM   Pretty much.

IM   Would you want to leave some of your books? Is there one that if somebody said, 'We'd love to republish this', would you say no to any of them?

NM   I'd certainly say – 'Well, I must think about it'.

IM   Perhaps why don't you do such and such instead? Because of course among seventy or eighty books, there are a great many out of print, and crying out, I think . . .

NM   And quite a lot which are of no interest.

IM   Why?

NM   They were just written perhaps for a series, or something like that.

IM   A topical interest?

NM   Yes.

IM   There is quite a lot of political writing, isn't there?

NM   And it dates rather.

IM   Yes. Mind you, I was reading a thing about rural reconstruction that you wrote in the middle of the war, which reads *very* sensibly still.

NM   Yes, but less and less likely to happen. And the way they're mucking up the Forestry Commission and everything. Oh dear.

IM   And you were telling me that one American student only knew of you –

NM   Through a pamphlet called *Oil for the Highlands*. [1974]. (L)

IM   (L) This year you were at a seminar for young American students, and this was the one place (L) where you struck oil?

NM   Yes. Well, I felt, swimming in this great sea, here's a little plank I can hang on to. (L)

IM   And is there any book you would rather see reprinted than *The Bull Calves*?

NM   No, I'd like *The Bull Calves*. [*The novel was reprinted in 1985 by Richard Drew, Glasgow; in 1997 by Virago*]
The book I can't see why people haven't, didn't read, really – it hardly sold at all – was my last historical one, *Cleopatra's People*.

IM   I haven't been able to get that one yet.

NM   It just sort of fell into limbo: nobody wanted to read it. Yet I think the history is very good in that.

IM It's about the time of Cleopatra?

NM It's done in two bits of history. One is straight of the time, and the other is twenty years after, with a girl who is the daughter of one of Cleopatra's ladies.

BT When was that published? Roughly.

NM Roughly I think it must have been the early seventies [1972].

BT I think at that time there was a fairly widespread lack of regard for historical novels. I wonder if something as simple as that, in terms of literary fashion – it was not the time for historical novels?

NM And yet the funny thing was, all Mary Renault's things were selling very well. And you know, she wrote to Virago, saying that it was *The Corn King* which had started her off.

BT Did she? That's very interesting to know.

IM In fact you haven't been writing so many historical novels. Science fiction, for example, has taken over –

NM But on the other hand, the thing that I am writing *now* is further back in history than I've ever been [*Early in Orcadia*, 1987].

IM We'll look forward to hearing a little more about that.

Tape Number two. 29 September 1984. Naomi Mitchison, Isobel Murray and Bob Tait at Carradale.

IM We have been talking about history and the accidents by which you choose to write in one historical time or another.

NM And I was thinking how attractive it was to do the historical digging out that one has to do. And sometimes in the actual book it is a couple of sentences, but one's had all the pleasure of finding out what it is. And I remember in the children's book *The Big House*, when they do a bit of time-travelling, I had to find out what a possible country radical could have been reading at the beginning of last century, and that was great fun. I remember Douglas Cole telling me a lot about what was going on. Then I had to consider what might have got as far as the West Coast of Scotland. That sort of thing, it all ends up in a sentence, but it gets things right.

IM And also it's marvellous that you get such pleasure from it. It indicates to me that you could have been very happily a historian, or an archaeologist, or an academic of any sort.

NM Yes.

IM These days, do you come up with an idea first – a story, as you told us you did early on, and then look for a period to set it in, or does it ever work the other way?

NM I think it works the other way as well. This book that I've been writing – really a set of stories – was very much started off. It really started off years and years ago, when I was on the Highland Panel. We were up on that coast, talking to estate owners about sheep and so on, and going along that road one was always seeing these white, shining cliffs of Orkney across ten miles of sea. And that stayed with me and stayed with me, and I did nothing with it. And then I started going to Orkney a bit, and to Isbister, where there is this very curious tomb, and it all started coming together, and now I'm at the point of worrying archaeologists. [*Early in Orcadia was published by Richard Drew in Glasgow in 1987.*] I think the people who are doing the really important, technical work, the discovering and so on, the historians and archaeologists, are quite pleased to see something being done with it. I knew Professor Adcock at Cambridge, long dead, how he enjoyed reading the manuscript of *Cloud Cuckoo Land*. We were talking about the Persian Satrap's court, and he said, perhaps there were peacocks there, and I said, 'Right, I'll put them in'. And there are Adcock's peacocks! (L)

IM (L) And we've been mentioning this book you are currently writing about Orkney. Has it a working title?

NM No. I'd like to call it *The Shining*, but somebody else has got that title. So I can't think what else to call it because it is still that in my mind.

BT It's set very early in history, or pre-history?

NM Yes, pre-history. About the fourth millenium BC, about which little is known.

BT (L) Yes, in a sense you're on safe ground there! You said that people who are doing the important technical things are in general quite pleased when someone comes along and makes use of what's happened. Are they always so keen, or are they anxious about your historical accuracy?

NM I've never found that. I've always found them interested. I'm sure there *are* some who haven't liked it, but then they didn't let me know.

IM Well, getting back to the writing career. In 1935, after all these historical stories and novels, you suddenly came out with a hyper-contemporary novel called *We Have Been Warned*. A novel with which you were setting out to corrupt the young, so they said – to corrupt everybody! First of all, you had a lot of trouble getting it published, didn't you?

NM Yes, and it was very badly cut. Luckily I have the bits which were
. cut, and if it ever gets reprinted, they'll be in. Now, there's nothing to it, of course, but at that time they were just so *fussy*. Anything to do with contraception, and by that time you see I'd been working on the committee of the North Kensington Family Planning Clinic, and I was deeply into all that sort of thing.

IM Do you think they would have made so much fuss if you hadn't been a woman writer?

NM I think that certain things could not have been said, by anybody.

IM But you had had some fairly hectic scenes in the historical novels, but obviously without the rubber goods. That seemed to get past all right.

NM That was all right, yes. Well, in those days at least there was no contraception. (L)

IM (L) But in *We Have Been Warned* there is a virtual rape scene . . .

NM Yes.

IM Which you have to reconstruct backwards afterwards because it's so –

NM I've had now to reconstruct it. I've now rewritten it as I think I would have written it then.

IM It's now a historical novel, in other words. (L)

NM Yes. I think probably Virago's going to do that next. [*There has been no reprint of the novel to date.*] On the other hand, there's a lot of rather turgid writing in it, which I must really leave because it's of its period. I sort of ran away with myself over the descriptions. Adjectives: I used too many adjectives.

IM And clearly, not only the main female character but also I think her sister are both in some senses you, are parts of you – both Dione and Phoebe.

NM Yes. She's Dione [*three syllables*]. Don't you remember the *Pervigilium*? 'Cras Dione iura dicit'. [*Pervigilium Veneris: an anonymous poem from the second century BC: II 1.4: 'tomorrow Dione declares her laws, high enthroned aloft'*].

IM I'll just call her Isobel – that's her name too! (L)

NM Isobel, of course, is a witch name, as you probably know.

BT Ah! That explains a good deal.

NM (L) Well I think it's important to have a witch name. You see, my suppressed name is Margaret, which is another witch name.

IM Dione is 'the' central character, 'the' central consciousness.

NM Yes.

IM And I wonder how she is going to go down in the 1980s.

NM Because she's very wuzzy. She doesn't make up her mind.

IM There's no harm in *that*, I think. And she's a feminist, and that's fine, and she's a socialist of a very personal kind, working out very personal dilemmas about what she thinks about it. I wonder, though, about her magic side?

NM Phoebe?

IM Well, no, not Phoebe so much here – or Phoebe as well, the magic bits, the Campbell women, the Kelpies.

NM The Kelpies, yes.

IM Do you think that necessarily entirely works?

NM I don't know that it would, you see. It would be very difficult to take it out.

IM Oh yes, it would be impossible. I mean, it's a period piece, and I wouldn't want to take it out, but when you were writing in, I think, *You May Well Ask* about Stella Benson, you said that she was less fashionable now because of an element of fantasy which you said very occasionally verges on whimsy [*p 129*]. And I wondered whether . . .

NM Yes. I think this is probably so. But whether one can take it out.

IM No, no, I'm sure not. You wouldn't write it that way now, but she's there, and . . . It's interesting that all the baddies in her head are Scottish, although in many other ways she is fairly British. (L)

Dione goes to the Soviet Union, as you fairly controversially did.

NM Yes.

IM Do you think she or you were deceived or over-impressed or anything?

NM Of course it was so lovely in the south, and I think I've probably put too much of that in, the kurgans and so on, down there. [*See Mucking Around: Five Continents over Fifty Years, 1981, pp. 63–67.*] But oh dear, they were such nice people. In a way perhaps I found myself among friendly people because I was friendly.

IM So many people say that people in the twenties and the thirties found in Russia what they went to find.

NM Well, I expect one did. And I so remember, I had just finished writing *Corn King*, and I wanted very much to see some of the things. I went to the Hermitage, and I told Orbelli about my book, and about what I'd been reading, and I remember his opening a case and saying, 'You will have seen pictures of this; caress him now', and put this beautiful little bronze beast into my hands. [*See You May Well Ask, 1979, p. 188.*] And you know, I felt that was a very Russian thing: it certainly wouldn't have happened in Germany.

IM Have you been back to Russia recently?

NM Oh, several times, but not for about six years, and again I found people very, very friendly. Last time I was just only in Moscow. It's a rather grizzly place. I felt very doubtful, and I felt some of the people I saw were really very unhappy with the situation but couldn't do anything about it. I'm sure it's all going to work out, but so long as people can't express themselves . . . There's a book I really want to write, but no publisher is interested. It is about the Authors' World Peace Appeal, and how we all went to Russia.

IM When was that?

NM That was in 1950, at the time when there really *was* the possibility of a Cold War, and when the Americans had the Bomb and the Russians hadn't, and we were all very, very worried and anxious about all this, and we went as a delegation to the Soviet Union. And a lot of this book if I wrote it, and I'd write it partly with Doris Lessing, would be on how we reacted to this.

IM Why do you think people wouldn't want to publish such a book?

NM They are not interested in that kind of book.

IM Would it be a novel?

NM No. A straight book.

IM And Doris Lessing was there as well?

NM Yes, Doris and I shared a room, and we argued like mad. We used to argue till about two in the morning, then we'd get up about four so as to walk around before our guide came. (L) It was a very exhausting time.

IM Well, back with *We Have Been Warned*, the first really contemporary book. It is very clear and very important apparently to Dione that she is Scottish. This Scottishness of hers is frowned on, particularly by other socialists, who seem to think that socialism and Scottishness are incompatible.

NM Yes. At that time Scottish Nationalism tended to be a rather sort of romantic thing, and the people who were talking Nationalism tended to go back rather than forward. I think there is a lot that I have got wrong in that book.

IM I think that both Dione's wishes to be Scottish and only Scottish, and also the other socialists' suspicion of Nationalism – these are still both the case, aren't they?

NM Yes.

IM I mean, that particular split lasted right up almost I suppose to the devolution debacle.

NM Well I think it's still there.

BT Absolutely still there. We've suffered from it a great deal. As soon as someone detects that we might be described as Nationalistic at all, the immediate suspicion is that you have got really rather quaint and romantic and sentimental notions. Perhaps there is a reason, a perfectly good reason, for this perception, in that it has proved very, very difficult to construct any notion of a unifying culture belonging to Scotland.

NM Yes.

BT And the attempts which have been made have been based on bogus materials and bogus presentations very often, is that not so?

NM I think so.

BT Anyway, the thing is that in historical novels you seem to be saying that you have to go back in history in order to go forward, or go back and forward at the same time. In that there must be traditions to build on. Is it simply that it's harder to do that in the Scottish context, to find life-giving traditions?

NM Yes, I think it is; it probably is harder because they've been so mucked up, and the more people are conscious of them, the more they get changed. And so it's much harder to get at anything real. One might have thought a place like Carradale would have real traditions, and I think possibly it did have, but they've all disappeared now. There would only have been perhaps the people I first met here, and some of the older people had this quality which was important.

IM Both *The Bull Calves* and *The Big House* take a careful look at the Highland/Lowland division, a curious kind of schism that divides Scotland very deeply.

NM Indeed, yes. And what's very curious is that there's Campbeltown dialect, and there are bits of Gaelic in it, and a lot of very odd words. There are two or three songs. I remember once the Young Farmers did a play which was all in this dialect, and I went with several people, and I was the only one who understood it at all. But I don't think anybody uses them now. And a lot of them are about agricultural and fishing things, which are now in the past. But I would use a certain amount of them. Currently I would say 'graip' rather than 'fork'. I would say the 'sock' of a plough rather than a 'ploughshare', and so on. And in building materials; but it's all going.

IM   Do you think it's necessarily bad that it should go, if the traditions of the different parts of Scotland are so divisive?

NM   Well, I think the difficulty is that it's a vulgarising all over, and it is only the tones of voice that remain in some parts. In Edinburgh and Glasgow the common man still speaks quite differently, but it's not the use of words. The East coast again – when I was a child the farm servants at Cloan [*the family home near Gleneagles*] were mostly from the Mearns, and had a splendid vocabulary, and one picked things up a bit, but for all I know they are all now American.

IM   I think the Mearns and Buchan are parts of Scotland where the old language ways have stayed clearest. After twenty years in Aberdeen I can still have to ask for repetitions from someone from Buchan: it's extraordinary.

BT   But in the way that people *order* their lives there's not much left which is distinctive, is there?

NM   I don't think so.

BT   Not in the living sense that one finds in a tribal society.

NM   Not a bit, though even those are changing and breaking up.

BT   You seem to be suggesting that it's not just a shame for the sake of human variety that they are breaking up, but that something very important in people's sense of reality disappears when this happens.

NM   Well, they made a framework, something people could hold on to.

BT   Are they necessary for the Kataleptike Phantasia? [*See The Corn King and the Spring Queen, 1931, especially Part One.*]

NM   I don't know. I think that can be done in other ways, but I'm sure there's a lot of strength.

IM   Well, certainly in your more recent books which have approached the science fiction sort of thing, there seems to be quite a considerable undercurrent of horror at people becoming blander and blander and more alike, possibly even clones, and differentiation and individuality disappearing with the loss of the past and the standardisation of the present.

NM Yes. And people have got to have a certain amount of things to hold on to, and if they don't have the traditions and what have you, they'll go in for fancy religions and what not . . . And I think some of it is not very good for people. With architecture, you've really got to know your materials, and this is the same thing, that you've got to know strengths. I think you can get a good deal of this in science, but in ordinary life a great deal has gone. Of course your host Dougie is from Iona, and he has got a lot of background. [*At Carradale we were enjoying the hospitality of Mr and Mrs MacCormick of the Mains Farm.*]

IM I think it is important to know where you are from. Can I come back briefly to *We Have Been Warned*, which is, I think, in many ways an imperfect novel, but it's so full of life that it is also a very impressive one. You have a note at the beginning disclaiming any relationship to any living people and any political situations, and I think it is a bit of flannel, isn't it?

NM (L) Well yes, I have the people to whom it's dedicated for . . .

IM And they are strangely similar to the people in the book!

NM Exactly.

IM (L) So it was hardly a real pretence that there isn't an awful lot of Naomi Mitchison in the book. And indeed not so much of your life's *plot*, but your life's situation as you have described it elsewhere.

NM Yes, and the sort of people who were one's friends.

IM The very list of places. The chapters tend to be named by their setting, and there's the Scottish place, there's London, there's Oxford where they actually live, and there's Tom's constituency of Sallington; and that again is very similar to the kind of pattern your life was in.

NM Yes.

IM And other similarities are for example the fact that Dione, the main character, although she is happy with her husband and children, wants to be open to other sexual experiences, and Tom also. Dione even seems to have a kind of romantic notion that sex is the only real way to get rid of class barriers.

NM Yes. Of course that was also what various other novelists thought, and of course Lawrence, although I can't read him now – I'm sure he was quite an influence on all my generation.

IM Did you have a real involvement with the Hunger Marchers?

NM Oh yes, but what I did was more cheerful than Grassic Gibbon; I collected the Scots in the South and asked them all back, and we had this great party.

BT   Good for you. (L) An excellent thing to do after a hunger march. (L)

NM   (L) Well exactly. They took to it like mad, and we danced and danced.

BT   Splendid. That's one of the best stories about hunger marches that I've heard.

IM   But Dione's own personal politics are a bit individual. They are not just ordinary Labour Party. She tries to come to a very personal notion of value, a different notion of value. She puts on one side all the things that are to do with money and 'deserving', and she puts Christianity and a lot of other things there as well. She is looking for 'an idea opposed to all the bargaining of the East and the Mediterranean basin, opposed to the idea of the scales of justice . . . an idea opposed to the Jealous God of Scotland, the Family Grocer visiting with his wrath those who questioned the price of his sandy sugar or attempted to evade an extortionate bill'. [*We Have Been Warned*, 1935, p 443.] And what she puts against that is an idea of good will.

NM   Yes. And sharing.

IM   Is this wild sentimentality, or is it more than that?

NM   No. It must. That why one was so – America, nice as it is, is so shocking. You have just got to get away from it.

IM   How does one get away from it?

NM   Only in little bits.

IM   It's almost as revolutionary and yet not revolutionary as the Christian ethic itself, or the way in which Victorian people said you have got to change inside before you can change all the institutions.

NM   Yes.

IM   Does it come down to that?

NM   I think it probably does.

IM   And is it possible for everybody? Dione thinks about 'Good will, that curious product of consciousness, of leisure and energy to spare and share' [*Ibid, p 482*]. Can we expect good will of people without these things?

NM   Very difficult. The difficulty is, that in a society which is living – I mean after all we are living in this country, however much we grumble, at an enormously comfortable level compared with Africa and India and wherever, and all we do is to envy people in America who are living still better. Though of course there is a pretty nasty layer at the bottom. We don't notice that.

IM But do the most deprived people of the Third World have any opportunity to develop or understand this idea of good will?

NM Well, except in so far as they've had to develop it in order to survive. And the bushmen can still do all this extraordinary healing, which is a group thing, and they are pretty well down at the bottom.

IM And for example the tribe in Africa to whom you are Mother: you talked about them on television as being in a very bad state of drought. Do these problems bring them together? Do they really react as a group to that?

NM Yes. On the whole. At any rate the people who are still in the tribal areas. They really do share their last crust.

IM That's very impressive. But perhaps again in the same breath depressing, because the tribal areas, presumably, are not where people are going to go *more* . . .

NM No. They'll go more to the towns. But then I don't know, I think that all this may crack up. What is going to happen in China, and what is going to happen when you have one couple having to look after up to eight elderly relations? [*Given a policy of limiting family size to one child*] I think even when you've started off like that, you've got the most terrible problems coming. And India is very difficult, because you've got all these groups, and people may behave very well within their groups and not so well otherwise.

IM Do you think it's true, really, that in order to have a group you have to have at least a consciousness of a non-group, and your group gets stronger if the other group's the enemy in some sense?

NM Well, I'm afraid so.

IM (L) Very depressing, isn't it?

NM It is, it is, I mean I can't say I'm totally cheerful about how we're going to develop.

IM But that is something you are still at. As I said, you were doing this with Meromic discovering the idea of all-Gaul: in much the same way, in *When We Become Men*, your characters have to come to terms with what tribalism means, when they come to understand it better, and then they can understand better what Africa creates.

NM Yes. I think this is so, but you've got to be fairly intelligent and conscious of what you are doing and being, and that's not very easy.

IM I'm sure too few of the African would-be freedom-fighters learn as those two do, from being in the tribe. Most of them will learn from being at the other end of guns.

NM Yes.

IM And that's a different kind of nationalism, isn't it?
So when *We Have Been Warned* gets republished, you'll feel it's mostly by you. (L)

NM (L) Yes.

IM I can see entirely that you wouldn't rewrite it the way it is now, but on the other hand I think you find yourself very sympathetic to Dione. Now I said that Phoebe is also a bit of you, or seems to me to be a bit of you. She doesn't have a *very* big part to play in *We Have Been Warned*. But she comes up again, doesn't she, in *Beyond This Limit*?

NM Yes of course, so she does. Yes.

IM And this book was published on beautiful paper and I imagine in a small edition: it's a different sort of book looking for a different kind of public. Wouldn't you like to see that reprinted?

NM Oh, that would be lovely. And it should be, of course, now, with all the interest in old Wyndham Lewis. [*IM edited a volume entitled Beyond This Limit: Selected Shorter Fiction of Naomi Mitchison in 1986. The novella 'Beyond This Limit' was included, along with the Wyndham Lewis illustrations.*]

IM And these days black and white illustrations could easily be reproduced.

NM I'd love to have it republished, but . . .

IM It's very different in tone and mode and everything . . .

NM Well you see, it's a fairy tale, and we did – and I was *telling* it, and what we did was that one or other of us would get ahead, and then . . .

IM Wyndham Lewis was doing the pictures.

NM He would do a picture and I would say, what's that of, and perhaps what was going to happen, and then I'd rush ahead and it's happened, and then gone on, and so on.

BT A pretty unique way of composing anything, really.

NM Well it was great fun, we got on madly well. And then at the end he wanted it to end in the hotel room, and I said, 'No, no, you can't leave Phoebe there, I won't have it'. And that was when he was acting as the guide of souls, and with this great black hat he always wore, and I was wearing this headscarf that I always wore, and the guide of souls relents slightly, and they all get into a lift and go down to meet the powers of darkness, but no doubt it will be all right. [*See the Wyndham Lewis illustrations, which make it clear that the artist is the porter and the guide of souls, and the writer is Phoebe Bathurst, the central character.*]

IM I think the writing in that book is not only different, it's a bit special. For one thing, it is not just a fairy tale; it's not a bit like your other fairy tales. It's more surreal. And it has a little bit of Alice in it, doesn't it?

NM Yes I think so. And in a sense it's a London book. And it's picking on, jumping on various London things.

IM The Gorilla Arts Theatre.

NM Yes.

IM And the British Museum.

NM But it was a bouncy book, and I think the way we both enjoyed doing it is reflected.

IM Yes, I think so. And did you co-operate in the same way for example with Eric Kennington in 'The Powers of Light', or did he just . . .

NM No. I wrote it, and then he liked it very much and he did the pictures, more or less at the same time as he was doing the pictures for T E Lawrence's book. The *Seven Pillars* one.

IM You wouldn't think I was daft if I said that *Beyond This Limit* should be republished, and that in a sense it's a category completely of its own in your work? I don't think there is anything else at all like it. You've done other fairy tales, but this is not like that.

NM No, it isn't a bit.

IM It is very grown up and special, and although it makes use of all sorts of old myths and stories, it really makes its own, doesn't it?

NM Yes. And it's got things of its own date in it.

IM Yes. I hate to think of the day when it will be published with footnotes. (L)

NM Oh dear.

IM OK, let's break off there and stop punishing the lady for a wee while.

NM Well.

Tape number three. 30 September 1984
Present: Naomi Mitchison, Isobel Murray and Bob Tait, at
Carradale.

IM We are going to start off by asking Naomi to say a little about her
    Scottish book *The Bull Calves*, and possibly also the children's book
    The Big House, which is very Scottish, and a contemporary comedy,
    Lobsters on the Agenda. [*We failed to get to Lobsters on the Agenda,
    1952, but IM got it reissued, with an Introduction, by House of Lochar
    in 1997.*]

    I would like to suggest, Naomi, that much as I admire *The Corn
    King*, I think *The Bull Calves* is your best book.

NM I think you may be right. It is much shorter, which is one good thing,
    because almost a third of it is notes.

IM Ah, but the notes are essential. [*NM had said this firmly, off-tape.*]

NM The notes, I think, are essential.

IM You took a long time writing it. It was during the war, and you were
    immensely busy. But the long time meant that the structure of it is
    more interesting and complex than anything else you have done.

NM It's *very* complex, and one of the things that happened was that I was
    building up Black William at the beginning, and then I suddenly
    realised that he'd been telling lies all the time to me, his creator, and
    I mean I felt like God (L), but it was very curious because I thought,
    this doesn't fit; this isn't quite right. What is happening? There it is:
    he just came alive.

IM He hadn't told you he had an Indian wife?

NM All that, yes.

IM So in a sense you were discovering it in this extraordinary narrative
    form . . .

NM Yes.

IM . . . which I think makes the book so special. It almost obeys the
    Aristotelian Unities, doesn't it: it's two or three days, just, in 1746,
    but it goes back one way or another through all of Kirstie's life in her
    first marriage, and all of William's, and a lot more.

NM And then of course that was great fun, doing the characters who were
    actually my ancestors, and one's sort of interested in the genes.

IM Yes, being you (L), you always would be.

NM And Patrick in a sense is partly based on my brother, so that it was all
    very close to the heart.

IM   And Patrick is a fairly ambivalent figure: one doesn't exactly trust him all the time, but he turns up trumps in the end. And he's the one that goes to Kirstie's wedding and so on. And do you see it as a political novel?

NM   Yes. But not directly, but again going back to the intelligentsia I think, and to the people who should be giving a lead.

IM   So in a sense it was addressed to at least the Scottish contingent of the people that *We Have Been Warned* is addressed to. You should be leading; you should be doing better than this –

NM   Yes, indeed, indeed.

IM   Because certainly one of the features of the family in the book is their enormous sense of responsibility, isn't it?

NM   And this is what I have inherited.

IM   What Lew Gardner was accusing you of? [*In a television programme earlier that year.*]

NM   (L) Yes. I am quite aware of my family, and of course I think in some ways they were pretty awful. And there are these two, Robert and James, who went round preaching to the Highlands, who were apparently needing conversion almost as much as the heathen Indians or whatever – building little churches for them. But then you see they had this fun thing that they would be preaching on the hillside, and the local laird would send out the police to get rid of them, and then it turned out that they were gentry, so it was made awkward. And one of the pleasures of life is making things awkward for the top people.

BT   And this is a pleasure which you evidently take, but from another perspective it might seem as if, since you are a member of a family which has always been among the top people, why should *you* take this particular pleasure, which is more associated with the rest of us who aren't?

NM   Well . . . (L)

BT   A streak of straight mischief?

NM   Maybe, maybe.

IM   You said on television at some point that it was rather fun to kick the police.

NM   Yes.

IM   Anyway, back with *The Bull Calves*. One of the reasons I asked you if it was a political novel is that it seems in some ways very adult. Scots, even placid Scots, tend to get emotional about the '45, but your novel does not simply take a side, does it?

NM No, no, it very much doesn't take sides, and the thing is best forgotten, only bits of it remain. And there's no nonsense about the Prince.

IM No, there's not a lot about the Prince at all, in fact, as I recall.

NM The only bits that were like that at all was a story about the Lanrick girl, now I've forgotten her name.

IM I'll put it in a footnote. (L) [*Isobel Haldane of Lanrick: see The Bull Calves, especially pages 5–8 and note.*]

NM But they were all real people. And there you are.

IM And certainly there isn't anything of the Prince Among the Heather thing; it's much more a country facing up, a stratum in a society facing up, to the fact that some appalling things just happened in recent history, and they have to learn how to live with each other again without too much considering it.

NM Yes. And whether I'm right in having Forbes in as the *deus ex machina* I can never quite make up my mind, but it seemed at the time quite a possible thing. Do you know that statue of him in Edinburgh? [*Duncan Forbes of Culloden (1685–1747), Lord Advocate and Lord President of the Court of Session. The statue, by Roubiliac, can still be seen in the 'Hall of Lost Footsteps', in the Parliament Hall in Edinburgh, a surviving part of the Parliament House erected between 1632 and 1640. It used to accommodate the Scots Parliament, and continues to accommodate the Supreme Courts of Scotland.*]

IM No.

NM It's in the Hall of Lost Footsteps in the – oh dear, I can't remember what it's called, but it's where the lawyers go to and fro, and one that I always felt should have been used for the Scots Parliament instead of the old school; but still you couldn't turn the lawyers out.

BT (L) They wouldn't have allowed –

IM They would have been sitting in the Scots Parliament.

BT I suppose so, yes. But can I ask for a little clarification about the sense in which it is a political novel? Do you see it as drawing parallels between the political situation of 1746 and the political situation of the culmination of a disastrous world war, and people being called upon to clear up the mess?

NM Well yes, that's really it. And that they are now in a position where they have just *got* to work together. The thing that I find is rather good politically, is the beginning of a book which I'm sure you haven't read, called *Behold Your King* [1957], where Caiaphas and the others are arguing about politics, and what you do if the Messiah . . .

BT   Mm. Yes, awkward, yes.

NM   Which is quite an interesting thought.

IM   (L) Indeed. Religion is something which is quite interestingly dealt with in *The Bull Calves*, between Kirstie's first husband –

NM   Yes, yes, yes, yes, who's such hell, yes.

IM   And his sister, who's a witch . . .

NM   And *she'd* been really religious in a way. [*Kirstie*]

IM   And towards the end, the religions of Kirstie and William and the way they co-exist with the rest of the family, is somewhat like the theme you are trying to give in the whole book, about how they accept differences. Is it William who's Episcopalian? And Kirstie marries into it, but they don't go on being factious; they come to some kind of toleration. But religion isn't generally a subject that you usually treat with a great deal of favour, is it?

NM   No, no.

IM   You think it's a bad thing?

NM   Dangerous. (L) I mean, I think that really of course all preaching is dangerous, even if it's politics. But when you invoke something it may well be a devil.

BT   Do you mean that you can conjure up this spirit in effect?

NM   Yes.

BT   Whether it exists or not?

NM   Whether it exists or not.

BT   Mm . . . and having let it loose, the consequences are unforeseeable, and could be disastrous?

NM   Yes, you can't then do much about it.

BT   Quite. So to that extent the spirit is real, in the sense that it has an effect, whether it has a reality of a supernatural order.

NM   Yes. (L) I mean after all one is, people are quite complex.

BT   (L) They certainly are!

NM   Even writers. You can't say we are always like . . .

IM   (L) Yes. But you don't do a great deal of preaching yourself. The things that you do preach you don't do preachily, and they are not usually religion. For example, there is *The Big House*, the other Scottish book, which is supposed to be for children. Having read it last night, I think it will do for everybody, (L) thank you very much.

It's not really religion there, is it, but there are good magic and bad magic.

NM Well yes, and it's also again about loyalties and –

IM Tell Bob, because he hasn't read it.

NM Well, it's the girl in the 'Big House' but who is at a local school, and is having quite a bad time. This of course being based on one of my children. And they change places in the past and so on, and she becomes involved with the other side, and they have to be very loyal to each other in what appear to be very dangerous circumstances.

IM She's very good friends with a village boy, *one* village boy, who comes from a very different background. So they go back both sides to that.

NM And he out of loyalty to her has to give up being a chief in the past.

IM Because she can't get back to the present unless he comes too; and in the past he was doing nicely, thank you. That's very much a question of personal loyalty over-ruling everything else, which in a way again is a fairly predictable Mitchison thing.

NM Well, yes, that goes right back to *The Conquered*.

IM Yes. Although in *The Conquered* certainly Meromic never knows whether he is right.

NM No.

IM And in fact you half suggest he is wrong, don't you?

NM Well, quite.

IM (L) Because authors are never as simple as all that!

In 1955, to leap quite a bit, you published a book which very much fascinates me. It's called *To The Chapel Perilous*, and it's about the Grail story. The story of King Arthur and his Knights, only told through the medium of two very twentieth-century newspaper reporters and the rather nasty newspaper empires that they represent. What do you think is the thing you are most interested in doing in that book? [*Note: what a ridiculous question to ask out of the blue in 1984! IM.*]

NM (L) One of the things, but I don't know if it was the most important, was dealing with language, because the occasions in the book where I've really got the screw tightly on I'm actually quoting verbatim from Malory, and I've got to make the book so that it's as good as Malory, and I suppose that's one of my aims, what I was trying to do. (L) But of course it's also about newspapers, and it's quite genuinely about the limits of what should be said.

IM And the way things get warped in the saying.

NM Oh indeed, yes.

IM And the totally accidental nature of the truth that sometimes gets told, or the part of the truth that gets told. For example, at the beginning the two reporters see several knights one at a time coming out of the Chapel Perilous bearing grails. They don't know what to do about it, so they choose one as *the* Grail.

NM Yes.

IM I began to feel in a way that the book was making some of the points Orwell made in *1984*, about how the person who can control history, or the telling of history, is able to control the present and the future. If Lord Horny and Merlin and all the rest of them could actually decide what the real version of the Grail story was going to be, then there was only this terribly faint hope that the hermit might be reporting to God, and that's the only possible truth there was.

NM Yes, I think there is all that.

IM And it's very funny in places; you get a stray knight coming in, wanting to make up a four for jousting.

NM (L) And of course some of it is portraits, and there are bits of the various people on the *Guardian* and so on, and I change them around.

IM So you don't want to go on record as saying that somebody is the basis for such and such a character?

NM No, no.

IM (L) The laws of libel after all, still . . .

NM But I mean there's a bit of Cameron.

IM/BT James Cameron?

NM Yes, who I am very fond of, and you know, various people.

IM Is he in Merlin?

NM Yes.

IM I think that is one of the books I would like to see reprinted.

NM Yes, so would I, and I wouldn't really want to alter much of that.

IM No, I don't think so. As you say, on the one hand, where the language is going for that, it's as pure and clear as Malory, and on the other it's very deliberately in other places made twentieth century, colloquial, slangy, to point up the –

NM Yes, exactly. I think as a matter of writer's art, it's probably my best book.

IM It's up there in the list anyway, it's very difficult to choose when it gets to that. I thought it was a most interesting book, and liable to make people more aware again of the Grail legend. Because, alas, people don't have the same reading childhoods as some of us had any more, and I imagine a lot of people now would meet the Grail story first through your book.

NM Of course they have also met it with T H White. And I think a lot of people have taken it. It is one of *the* stories.

IM Yes. That was one of the points that I was going to ask you about: how the satire is almost all at the top, but at the bottom there is a sense that the Grail story itself is something which enormously *means*. The whole Round Table and the Grail have a resonance and a meaning beyond anything that can be made funny.

NM Of course I read all the relevant books, and thought about all the possible grails.

IM That was lovely, when they came out, each one his own grail! (L) Luckily the hermit was full of wonderful Christian philosophising about how if there's one there can be many, and if it's been discovered once it must be discovered again, and so on, which helps the story enormously. And one thing that makes it very serious at the end, I think, is these two reporters, who start off being light and trivial and so on, waving their legs in the air —

NM Yes, they've grown up.

IM They've grown up, and they give up reporting, and they go on a quest themselves. Which goes to indicate that questing is really what it's all about, and reporting is either a highly dangerous or a trivialising activity.

NM Yes, it's dangerous, and yet it matters terribly if you can do it well, and you are probably *not* going to be most highly paid; and Lord Horny will clamp down on you much sooner than old Merlin and the *Guardian*.

IM Yes, but you've got rather inhuman subs on both sides.

NM Oh yes!

IM Even if you were totally true to your job as a reporter, it's a bit unlikely, one feels, in this book, that the story as you write it will ever appear in the paper.

NM In a way I owe quite a lot to my son-in-law Mark [*Arnold-Foster*], who in a way is the *Guardian* reporter, and he saw that his stuff went through. He was on the much better-paying *Observer*, which he left because they'd altered his piece.

IM I think it's really a very important book. And on the Orwellian point,

I think it's easier to understand in the particular fable version you give it than in this Minitruth thing of Orwell's, with Winston just rewriting little stories all the time. Throwaway remarks in the newspaper office like, 'Well it's easy to make Lancelot a villain; or any of them', make you suddenly do a treble-take. The Hermit seems important, and the way that the two reporters grow. One of them says: 'There were plenty of facts that could be used; one wouldn't even have to invent them. Things that hadn't seemed significant enough to put in, the way everything had been going before. If Mordred had won there would just have to be a new kind of test for significance. Simple. [*To The Chapel Perilous, 1955, page 138.*] Even in retrospect, the whole newspaper campaign can change the whole meaning, and make the baddies into goodies.

NM Oh, indeed.

IM One other thing. We have talked about magic a few times. I'm interested in Lienors, and the White Lady. It's not very spelt out, but Lienors, instead of simply going either to the Devil or the Churchman, goes to the White Lady.

NM No, the White Lady – you were talking about Graves before, and of course this is Graves's White Lady.

IM Yes, I wondered. The White Goddess, yes.

NM I caught Graves out, in a bad bit of botany. (L)

IM (L) I like it!

NM No, he should have known better. He put down the silver fern, the *abies*, as one of the White Lady's trees, and of course it's not even a European tree. (L)

BT Right: (L) footnote for Graves scholars. Yes.

NM That's the sort of mistake I wouldn't have made. Lots of mistakes I would, but I wouldn't make a botanical mistake.

BT That's right: I'm quite sure you wouldn't.

IM So basically, is it a pessimistic book? Is it a book that really suggests that anything we think of as truth simply can't be known?

NM Oh no, but you may have to dig round a bit, and you may have to do something to protect the honesty of the reporters.

IM In a way it's an elaboration of the old idea that history is always written by the winners. The idea that if Mordred wins they'd change the whole thing makes us aware of the media we tend to trust. So the nature of truth is something we don't think we'll go into.

When you are writing, do your books overlap?

NM Oh yes. When I was writing *The Corn King* I wrote several others. When I wrote *Powers of Light* I wrote a couple of the plays I wrote in Paris with Lewis [*Gielgud*]; and what else did I write? I wrote *The Home*, which isn't at all good [*The Home and a Changing Civilisation, 1934*], and probably wrote one or two children's books. You know I could break that off fairly easily and then it would go on cooking.

IM Yes. Is there anything cooking beyond the Orkney book at the moment?

NM Not really. I mean I want to write one or two things, but now it's the difficulty of finding publishers for anything which isn't very straightforward. I want to write about the Authors' World Peace Appeal, and that would be a quite solid book about the politics of 1950, and everybody's bored with that, but I think it's interesting because it was an attempt to make a bridge.

IM Yes, and a very necessary one at that.

Well now, one of the big things that happened, I suppose between *To The Chapel Perilous* [*1955*] and *When We Become Men* [1965], was your Botswana connection. Meeting an African chief, befriending him, eventually becoming a mother to the tribe. This is very clearly all subsumed into the experience of *When We Become Men*, not only because the young man arrives at the chief's coronation – I can't remember what it's called – at the end. Is that one of the books you're pleased with?

NM I haven't re-read it for a very long time. I don't know how it would read now. I think I'd probably feel that it was a bit romanticised, that it was in too bright colours. I think that probably the political thing is all right, but whether anyone would feel like that about the tribe I'm not sure. And it's curious that the two older people in the Bakgatla whom I knew very well were in a curious way – they had a sort of nobility that I don't see coming up among their successors. They were people who believed strongly in the ethos of the tribe, and who were deeply kind in a gentle way. They had, I suppose, all the things that one imagines the ideal Highlander should have, and I don't know whether the next generation is going to feel at all the same.

IM But in this novel *When We Become Men*, you didn't portray anybody at any length, who was that wise and kind, and so on.

NM No.

IM In fact, although the old chief who's dying is clearly a good fellow –

NM Yes, the old man –

IM And his son, who is eventually to succeed him after a few conflicts about where his interests really lie, is a good fellow too. But there is nobody special: there *is* a 'baddie' –

NM Yes.

IM Motswasele.

NM And the women, who are on the whole the competent and sensible ones.

BT Yes, that was a very striking aspect of that book to me. You said early on when you were writing your earlier books you weren't really very much interested in the women. All right? By the time you wrote *When We Become Men*, paradoxically, given the title, it's the women really who are most rounded, and most interesting and most intelligent.

NM Yes, and they run things, even if they run it from behind.

BT Quite. Seneo is a very wily politician, apart from anything else, and Tselane is even wiser, without having the formal or informal power in a political sense. Isaac for much of the time is plain dumb, stupid, until he gets a bit of insight. And the same with Letlotse; I mean he is a mixed-up kid and a young fool, isn't he, until there are certain realisations which are almost – well, which certainly require the women to pick up the pieces. So that's a whole shift, isn't it? Is that a shift in your perspective on male/female relations?

NM How do I know? (L) One isn't conscious of these things. After all I think I've had more women characters who were really running things, like Aud the Deep-Minded in the children's book about the people from Caithness going on to Iceland; and of course this is just taken from history. [*See The Land the Ravens Found, 1955. The postscript scrupulously indicates Mitchison's considerable debt to Icelandic literature.*] And I think at certain points of history, including this Norse period, the women were very important. And they come in, even in these stories which were largely written down by monks. You couldn't ignore these women. And the fact that the women weren't actually out fighting meant that they could stay at home and look after things, as indeed the people in *The Delicate Fire* do. [*The Delicate Fire: Short Stories and Poems, 1933, has the sequence of stories about ancient Mantinea which includes 'The Wife of Aglaos', reprinted in Beyond this Limit: Selected Shorter Fiction, 1986.*] When the Ionian men were off trading and so on, the women stayed at home and ran things, and incidentally wrote poetry.

IM   And as we come nearer the present time, there's a number of books which for want of a better word we can label as science fiction, although you are going to disagree with me about one of them. [*Off-tape, Mitchison had rightly refused to call Not By Bread Alone, 1983, science fiction: it is about possible disastrous consequences of genetically modified foods.*] In those, because you are able to make certain happy assumptions about the future as well as bad ones, men and women seem more at ease —

NM   Yes.

IM   And there is less differentiation. You don't have people making a terrible fuss, whether their boss is a man, or their boss is a woman, or anything like that.

NM   Well, exactly. Yes, and this is *perhaps* something that is happening. Something I think one can see the beginnings of. It is still more difficult for women to get up to the top without doing rather more treading on people's faces than a decent woman wants to do. I mean, we aren't quite as vicious. Even in academic circles. (L)

IM   Perhaps we don't value some of the things that people are fighting for as much. But if you think about *Solution Three*: that I would say could be fairly labelled science fiction.

NM   Yes, that is science fiction all right.

IM   What would you say was the main thrust of that, or the thing that at this distance first comes into your mind as being what it was about? (L)

NM   I have some very good jokes in that!

IM   Yes. (L)

NM   (L) I don't know. It's loyalty again, and loyalty being considerably stretched but still holding, and quite a bit of women with women.

IM   Yes, yes. Sexuality and homosexuality indeed is quite an important thing. Now you said in one of the books of memoirs in a splendidly ambivalent way that you had perforce to write sympathetically about homosexuality in your early books because the Greeks went in for it. [*You May Well Ask, 1979, p. 78*].

NM   Yes.

IM   And therefore you got some very sympathetic friends in the twenties (L) who thought this was a splendid thing. Homosexuality doesn't seem to have to be in these later books, so is it something you have become interested in writing about?

NM Well, it had to be in *Solution Three*. It was basic to that.

IM Yes. One should explain to the reader, or rather the non-reader, that in *Solution Three*, the only births that take place, with a few exceptions, are births of favourite clones, and that men and women have been conditioned to fancy their own gender as perhaps one of the simplest ways to birth control, isn't it? (L)

NM Yes: it is very much the simplest way of planning.

IM The question is whether you find yourself basically sympathetic or unsympathetic, or completely indifferent. You said you had always been strongly heterosexual yourself; I just wonder whether you have any . . .

NM I've always been a little scared of too much contact with other women.

IM Mmm . . . That's interesting.

And *Solution Three* in the last resort is asking – *one* of the questions I suppose it is asking – is it ever going to be possible to have a peaceful world community?

NM Yes. That's what one's really asking oneself, and at this moment, with everything being completely in the balance and so much depending on what an American actor who has stomach cancer, which is going to kill him within four years, is going to say and perhaps do. [*A faulty prognosis for Ronald Reagan*]

BT Mmm. The possibility of a peaceful world would suggest the possibility of a world where we managed to do without violence. It seems fairly clear throughout your books from *The Corn King* onwards that some forms of violence seem to be justifiable. Is violence on behalf of some loyalty which one commits oneself to?

NM Yes, but that's very dangerous.

BT But Erif Der does kill her father.

NM Oh yes, yes, and there are other people, yes.

BT And Tselane also kills that man who is about to betray –

NM Yes, and pretty nastily too.

BT And very nastily, that's right. But in certain contexts the morality of it seems to be more or less unquestioned as to right.

NM Of course these are people killing for – on their own. They are not being told to kill by somebody else, nor are they in the grip of some emotion which is being run by other people. Those people have made up their minds quite definitely what they should do.

BT And so they are aware of the evil that they do?

NM Yes.

BT And the good they do by it, and both?

NM Yes. I mean, one could lose one's temper, but that's very different from perhaps being told to press that knob which is . . .

IM Mmm. But I think one of the things you are saying in *Solution Three* is that you can't take a sane, real humanity, and make it perfect or perfectly peace-loving. It's not going to work. That we have violence in our emotions and so on, even if we don't – and so –

BT That can't be subdued, I take it.

NM No.

IM The idea of the clones which are being brought up in the society with foster mothers, as it were, the idea is that the world council will sooner or later give up all its authority to the clones, because the clones will be perfect and amicable and rational.

NM Yes.

IM And it becomes quite frightening, this business of the clones, except that I'm reassured when it goes wrong.

NM (L) Yes. I don't know: it's very difficult to know how this book strikes a reader.

IM I see particularly the similarity. There's the two things that call out to be looked at. One of them is this business of the clones, and the fact that I'm depressed by them, and delighted when one or two of them start behaving a little unpredictably. And on the other hand, your interest in genetics comes in the way they have purified the world cereal crops, and made them much more efficient. But because they have just thrown away a whole lot of genes and don't have a gene bank, the crops themselves begin to be attacked by new things, and can't survive.

NM Well you know, they've had a lot of this sort of thing happening, and actually in maize quite lately; so that what I was saying was something which *at that time* had not happened, but which is happening, I'm afraid, now.

IM Yes.

NM And the question is whether it can be stopped.

IM But it almost comes to a moral question. And it's a question that comes up again in *Not By Bread Alone*, which you say is not science fiction, where again the idea of feeding the world and then something going wrong with a marvellously cheap and plentiful food supply is crucial. Is it something you think really might happen, or is it more a metaphor for –?

NM Yes, I think it *is* something which might happen.

IM So that the individuality must in some ways be retained in the genes, in the person, in the plants, and all the rest of it.

NM You have got to keep something you can go back to. You've got to have the original genes kept. That's being done.

IM So it's almost the same again. It's a parallel in the cereals and among the people. The people also have to have something to go back to, to come from, in order to know where they are – clones don't come from anywhere.

NM I think it's all terribly difficult, because however much one wants to be a person of good will, one's running into contradictions the whole time. I mean one can only avoid contradictions by shutting one's eyes quite a bit. If you are a good Marxist you can probably avoid certain contradictions, but then other people are outside. There are always people who are outside, and even if America and Russia got on terms and hugged one another, there would still be people like the Ayatollah. And what do you do? I mean, you can't shut up a whole country in a loonie bin.

   I do think that the main religions of the Father God are very dangerous. I mean the original one, Judaism, and the two that sprang out from it, Christianity and Islam, dangerous.

BT Why these religions in particular?

NM Well, a great many other religions don't have a sort of God telling you to do this or that. Buddhism is a very reasonable religion. Of course, it can be distorted in various ways – I mean, religions are there to be distorted. And presumably what the Aboriginals in Australia have is a very curious feeling about the earth and so on, which enables them to do rather curious things, like communicating over long distances in some way which can't be measured. But I don't know: it's easy, it's these religions that tell you exactly what to do.

IM Is it important that it be a Father rather than a Mother? Is a Father more dangerous?

NM Well of course, the Mothers were pretty awful, in their time.

IM I wanted to give you a chance to admit that? (L) You were perhaps being sexist about the Father God?

NM (L) Yes.

BT There's the authoritarian aspect of it. Mothers can be vicious, though.

NM And they can turn themselves into wild boars. 'I fear their bodies in pieces torn'.

Mitchison Books mentioned in the interview

The Conquered, 1923
Cloud Cuckoo Land, 1925
The Corn King and the Spring Queen, 1931
The Powers of Light, 1932
The Delicate Fire: Short Stories and Poems, 1933
Naomi Mitchison's Vienna Diary, 1934
The Home and a Changing Civilisation, 1934
We Have Been Warned, 1935
Beyond This Limit, 1935
The Bull Calves, 1947
The Big House, 1950
Lobsters on the Agenda, 1952
Travel Light, 1952
To the Chapel Perilous, 1955
The Land the Ravens Found, 1955
Behold Your King, 1957
When We Become Men, 1965
Cleopatra's People, 1972
Solution Three, 1973
Oil for the Highlands, 1974
All Change Here: Girlhood and Marriage, 1975
You May Well Ask: A Memoir 1920–1940, 1979
Mucking Around: Five Continents over Fifty Years, 1981
Not By Bread Alone, 1983
Beyond This Limit: Selected Shorter Fiction of Naomi Mitchison, ed. I Murray, 1986
Early in Orcadia, 1987

IAIN CRICHTON SMITH

Iain Crichton Smith (Mac a'Ghobhainn) was born in Glasgow in 1928, and was taken to live on the island of Lewis at two years of age. Gaelic was his first language and English his second, and he went on to write widely in both. He first left the island aged seventeen to travel to Aberdeen University, where he did an honours degree in English (1945–1949). This was followed by two years' National Service, when he served in the army, loosely involved in education (1950–1952). He taught English in Clyde-bank (1952–1955) before moving to Oban, where he taught until he became a full-time writer (1955–77). He looked after his widowed mother until she died in 1969. He married Donalda Logan in 1977, and they lived in Taynuilt, Argyll from 1982 until his death in 1998.

WE RECORDED OUR interviews with Iain Crichton Smith early in 1986, when he was Writer in Residence at Aberdeen University. An old friend, Iain regularly came for an evening meal on Sundays when he was in Aberdeen. [*He dropped in on another Sunday evening a few weeks earlier, and joined in one of our interview sessions with Norman MacCaig: see Scottish Writers Talking*, 1996.] We recorded two tapes on February 9 and one on March 22, both at 14 Devanha Terrace, Aberdeen, then the home of Isobel Murray and Bob Tait. We finished the taping at Iain's home at Taynuilt on 29 and 30 March, when Iain and his wife Donalda had invited us for a weekend. There was little difficulty with continuity, because of the constant quality of Iain's interests at the time.

We were all old friends. Isobel Murray first met Iain Crichton Smith at an Aberdeen University Student Teach-In in 1971. She had previously reviewed some of his books, and has reason to remember a party she hosted then, when she requested him to sign a couple of the novels. It was late in the evening, and, declaring he wanted to give a name he respected, he signed *Consider the Lilies* 'Robert Lowell'. Alasdair Gray beside him joined in: 'this signature is authentic. Alex Tolstoy'. *The Last Summer* was triple signed: 'Hugh MacDiarmid: Hugh Bariet Stowe: Sidney

Goodsir Austin', and Gray further embellished it: 'these signatures are authentic: signed Wolfgang McGillicuddy'.

Bob Tait, in his capacity as Editor of *Scottish International*, had known Iain longer. While his mother was still alive and he was still teaching, Iain would periodically escape from Oban in party mood, and undergo the equivalent of what Dylan Thomas used to describe as 'Capital Punishment' in Edinburgh, often at Festival time. Bob might encounter him at such times, and *Scottish International* was the first place of publication for many of Iain's poems, including the fine sequence 'The White Air of March' [*see below, p 148*]. As he indicates in the interview, Iain was very prolific, and he often tended to rely somewhat on other people to sift wheat from chaff. On one occasion he sent Bob a boxful of work, saying that if none of it was any good, he should just dispose of it. Needless to say, that did not happen!

Crichton Smith's coming to Aberdeen was thus a splendid opportunity for all concerned to get reacquainted, and better acquainted. Old acquaintance meant we could at times press him for answers slightly further than initial politeness might suggest. He was a fine Writer in Residence, generous with help and encouragement to young writers, and supplying Introductions to their work or contributions to their anthologies.

Iain Crichton Smith enjoyed thinking, and engaged in it compulsively. He also welcomed the discussion of serious ideas, as these pages demonstrate. Unselfconscious, he found it easy to ignore the tape-recorder, but for the marvellous moment [p 131] when he caught himself being a little over-serious, and declared, with a wonderful giggle, 'This is too difficult for your readers'. The interviews generally followed the directions that interested him at the time, and a surprising amount of the discussion centred on his fiction, or ideas about ideology, and the meaning and conduct of life that underlay both fiction and poetry.

Tape number one.
Aberdeen, February 9 1986

IM   What I'm going to ask Iain to do is just tell us as much as he feels
        inclined to tell us about his background, his family, his parents, his
        childhood in Lewis.
ICS Well, I was born in Glasgow; and I spent one year in Glasgow, and
        then I was taken up to Lewis by my parents. My father was a sailor;

he was married twice and my mother was the second wife. She was married rather late in life, I think, and she used to go away from Lewis quite a lot to be one of the herring girls, down to Yarmouth or Lowestoft or places like that. My father died when I was about one or two of tuberculosis, and consequently our upbringing was very poor. I think all our mother had for the three of us – there were three boys – was a widow's pension, which was something like eighteen shillings a week in those days. And because my father had died of tuberculosis, my mother was very worried about me, because I had bronchial tendencies, and I was off school a lot when I was young.

My mother was a very strongly religious person. She also had moved into a village, Bayble, which wasn't her own original village, and in that sense she had to be accepted by the villagers, which was a bit of a problem. I think in the islands unless you belong to a particular village for a long, long period of time, you have to work your passage in a sense. This is probably true of a lot of rural areas. It was also tricky for her because it was my father's village.

IM   Bayble was your father's village.

ICS   Yes. And she was always going on about Glasgow. When she was young she had been in Glasgow, and she loved Glasgow, and she was never really happy in this village, and so consequently we were never really happy in the village either.

IM   You were born in Glasgow. Had your parents been living in Glasgow then?

ICS   Yes.

IM   And your other brothers were born there?

ICS   My older brother I think was born in Glasgow; my younger brother was born in Lewis.

IM   And so your mother had always looked back to that time in Glasgow?

ICS   Yes. In fact I tried to find the place – Blochairn it was. When I left Aberdeen when I was a student here and went down to the job in Dumbarton, I tried to find where Blochairn was, but I don't think it any longer exists, or it doesn't exist under that name. [*It does, not only physically, but also featured in Alasdair Gray's Lanark, pp 175–6, notoriously concerned to put Glasgow on the literary map, where it is precisely placed: 'On the far bank of the canal stood the vast sheds of the Blochairn ironworks. Dull bangs and clangs came from these, an orange glare flickered on the sky above them, the canal water bubbled blackly and wisps of steam waltzed on the surface and flew in a cloud over the*

towpath. A high railing divided the path from the Alexandra park'.]
They were living in a kind of tenement, and I think she found a kind
of closeness in this tenement that she never found actually in the
village. And she was always saying the Glasgow people were very
nice, very kind and all the rest, but when we went to Dumbarton
many years afterwards she never wanted to visit on holiday. Never
wanted to go back.

IM How much older was your elder brother?

ICS He's about six or seven years older than me.

IM Six or seven; and then there's another one.

ICS He's about two years younger than me.

IM So he was born almost at the same time that your father died?

ICS That's right, yes.

IM So this leaves these three boys, very poor, with a widowed mother
who has a strong religious sense and a domineering personality.

ICS Yes, very domineering.

IM So you didn't perhaps have a very happy childhood?

ICS No. Mainly I think because of her, because she wouldn't adapt to the
village, because she was a very strong-willed, unchangeable sort of
person. Not very malleable. And as far as I myself am concerned I
was cosseted to such an extent that I felt almost half strangled.

BT Whenever you had a cold you spent long times in your bed – literally
in bed.

ICS Yes, sometimes seven weeks at a time. Probably I was bronchial, and
probably I had a weak chest, but I think it was over-done. There was
a kind of possessiveness there which probably has something to do
with the fact that her husband was dead. This showed not only with
regard to me. Much later on my elder brother was going out with this
particular girl, and she smoked, and this was considered enough for
him not to have anything more to do with her. This is the way they
looked upon things like that in those days, or she did certainly.

IM I was just going to say, was there a difference between 'they' and
'she'? Was she perhaps even harsher in some of her ideas about social
behaviour than the Free Church view of the village?

ICS No, I think she would have been just the same, but I think it was
made worse because she was a widow in a very tricky situation. But
she also must have been fairly ambitious, because she was willing to
postpone us earning money by sending us to university.

IM Was she determined to send you to university?

ICS I think she was ambivalent about it. I think she felt it was a good
thing, especially if we turned out to be ministers or something (L),
but at the same time she would say to you, 'after all I've done for you
. . . you aren't doing anything for me in return'.

IM She was domineering. Was she affectionate?

ICS No, not at all.

IM Totally undemonstrative; for all she cosseted you, she wouldn't
cuddle you?

ICS No, she was not at all affectionate in that sense. In fact I think this
was a thing that I had to learn for myself, to show affection to people,
because she showed no affection whatever. I don't mean to imply
that she didn't have any, but she never showed it. I suppose she must
have felt something that she should have looked after me all that
time.

IM Did she apparently care for any one of you more than the others?

ICS Probably me, more than the others.

IM Because you were ill, bronchial and weak? I'm sensing a certain
element of fear in this little boy's relationship with his mother, which
would perhaps stop him communicating with her very much?

ICS Yes, I think I was afraid of her.

BT You were also deeply affected by love for your mother, weren't you?

ICS Yes. Now this is an extraordinary thing. I was teaching in Oban, and
I felt free at first, when I went to Aberdeen, and then when I went to
Oban. At the same time I felt a sense or responsibility that she was
totally on her own, and I was staying in this flat in Oban.

IM Hold on, can I interrupt a minute? She was staying in a different
place from you?

ICS Oh yes. This was in about the 1950s. First I was teaching in
Clydebank High School and I was staying with my mother in
Dumbarton, commuting from Dumbarton to Clydebank. Then I
left Clydebank to go to Oban High School, and she stayed in
Dumbarton. But I used to go down every weekend from Oban to
see her, mainly because I felt a sense – I don't think it's as simple as
responsibility. I did feel that she was on her own, but much more
than that, she was becoming a bit difficult in relation to the
neighbours in Dumbarton, and eventually I felt compelled to take
her up to Oban.

The difficulty showed itself in various ways. She told me that
someone from next door had come to borrow a ladder. And she told

him that she didn't have one, although she did have one (L). Maybe it was because she was completely on her own, but she turned against all the neighbours and they found any communication very difficult.

One weekend I went down to Dumbarton, and I took her on the bus to Luss. She was saying to me all the while that there were people in the bus talking about her. The way she said she knew that the people were talking about her, they were waving their arms. And a lot of people do wave their arms when they talk. Eventually this became even stronger because there was a place directly below the window in the flat we were in in Oban; there was a roundabout, and a traffic policeman. He was always waving his arms about, (L) and she considered this man was talking about us. I'd never experienced this, before, which was really a kind of madness, and I thought it was the loneliness that was causing it, which it probably was to a certain extent. So I felt responsible, and of course by this time there was no one else. My older brother was in Africa, as I was telling you, and my younger brother was in New Zealand –

IM Would it be a cruel thing to suggest that they'd both got as far away as they comfortably could?

ICS My older brother certainly didn't care much for her, because she was the kind of person who can damage marriages, extremely possessive. I think there is a certain element of truth in that, yes.

BT You were afraid of your mother when you were a child, but when other members of the family went off, you took care of her.

ICS This is a thing I don't understand: I've thought about it a lot. Donalda has said to me, and I think this is very true, that I used my mother as a shield [*Iain married Donalda Logan in 1977, eight years after his mother's death*]. I took her up there that would mean that if someone wanted me to do something I wouldn't be able to do it because I had to look after her. So in a strange way beneath this guise I was able to get on with my writing. I could assuage my own feelings of whatever guilt I had. I don't know why I felt this guilt, but I did have this guilt feeling. I don't know whether exactly it was love as such: the mind is very complicated, and I often wonder about this business of sacrifice. There is a poem that I wrote, 'Statement by a Responsible Spinster' [1959.] I think sacrifice is always more complicated than it appears, and when you are thinking of sacrificing yourself for somebody else, you're actually doing it for yourself.

IM And possibly to yourself?

ICS And something to yourself. Which may be irreparable, yes.

IM   That poor spinster didn't leave herself much time to have a life, did she?

ICS And she ended up, of course having nothing in the end. But she must for some reason have deeply wanted to do it. This is why my attitude to Lear has changed considerably over the years: I'm moving away from the Cordelia complex towards a Goneril one. And I've often written about that kind of thing.

BT   You've written amazingly about women.

ICS Old women especially.

BT   In a very understanding way, and a critical way. These are major figures.

ICS Yes they are. They are almost like painteresque themes, like Braque with his white bird in all his paintings. I suppose it does deeply come from her, and it must come from my ambivalent relationship to her. On the other hand you get a lot of Celtic poetry, and especially Irish poetry, in which the old woman is a very dominant figure. In Celtic countries whether they like it or not the woman is actually the matriarch, the dominant figure. Though it appears as if the man is dominant, behind the man is the woman. I really do deeply think that women are stronger than men, are more enduring. I think of men as being more boys, really, on an extended scale. (L) I think that men are extended adolescents in a way that women are not just extended girls. There is a kind of maturity among them. And of course my formative years were the war years really, 1940–46, which meant that the village was composed mostly of old people and very young people, because the able-bodied were away in the war. So there was a kind of artificial society because a lot of them went to the navy. I was happier I think being with old people than I was with people of my own age. I was quite happy to be sitting listening to their stories.

And I was reading an enormous amount. We also had a loft in the house, and I remember this. I must have been about thirteen, fourteen maybe at the time. My older brother had this book, and he had hidden it up in the loft, and I climbed up and found this book and I started reading it, *No Orchids for Miss Blandish*. And D H Lawrence. I used to climb up into this loft and I was quite happy sitting up there and reading. I read a lot and probably my first writing was book-based, and I suppose this must be true really of most writers. When I started first, I think I was imitating a lot of other writers – like Shelley. I remember I used to like Kipling a lot.

IM The poetry or the prose?

ICS It was the sound. When I was reading poetry first, I never could understand a poem unless I read it aloud. It was many years before I could actually read a poem without first reading it aloud, and the thing I liked about Kipling was the swing. I wasn't interested in what the poem was about, at that age, I was only interested in the sound of it. I liked poems which had a very sonorous quality.

IM The mind boggles a little at the thought of your Lewis voice getting round Cockney. (L)

BT What strikes me about this is simply that you are talking about English writers, strikingly in the case of Kipling, imperialist writers: not Gaels.

ICS Yes. One of the most interesting memories I had was reading a book about a boy in an English public school. And he was dying in this bed in this English public school because something was wrong with him, and he was listening to people playing cricket. I can't remember the name of the book, but the extraordinary thing was I was crying over this boy in this English public school dying. [*IM guesses this was The Fifth Form at St Dominic's by Talbot Baines Reid, 1887: she wept over it too, at an early age.*] The stuff that I read would have been more or less the kind of stuff that would have been read by someone not brought up in the Highlands at all. When I was growing up there were no books in Gaelic for my age group. It is only in the past few years that books have been written –

BT By you.

ICS Yes, some of them by myself, for pupils in schools where there was nothing at all for the age group.

IM At home and until you went to school you were only a Gaelic speaker.

ICS Right. Until I went to primary school.

IM Until then you spoke nothing but Gaelic. Then you had to learn English, and you had to learn all your other subjects in English.

ICS Now this was common to everybody.

IM But it was a very strong thing to push you toward English and away from the Gaelic.

ICS Yes it was. I was reading an Irish writer who said that if you are an English boy everything that you do or read from the moment that you are aware reinforces your Englishness. If you are an Irish boy who is brought up on Irish – and similarly if you transpose it to the Highlands you start off learning Gaelic – after that everything that you do is inimical to your culture.

In fact I can't even remember how I learned English, I can't remember the period. It seemed to be something that just happened. At the time you don't realise. There is a poem by Derick Thomson called 'Coffins' ['*Cisteachan-Laighe*', *1967*]. When you are very young, before you realise, the coffin is being prepared for you with the Lowland or English writing on the lid. At the time you don't realise this is happening to you. It is only when you look back that you realise exactly what has happened. That you have been conditioned in this way. I've talked to a lot of people older than me who have said that when they were growing up, in schools speaking Gaelic was a punishable offence. I don't think it was a punishable offence in my day, but you spoke Gaelic in the playground. There were a lot of teachers in the school spoke Gaelic but would never speak it to you in the school. When I was growing up, Gaelic was spoken in the playground, not spoken in the schools. Now Gaelic is spoken in the school but not in the playground, This is the paradox. Now they have made a cult of Gaelic and they teach it in the school, but the kids are not speaking it.

IM Do you remember whether as a child you spoke Gaelic to your mother, how much English she spoke? In what language did you speak to her?

ICS Oh, always Gaelic. When I was growing up you would never dream of speaking to your mother in anything but Gaelic.

BT Why would your mother speak Gaelic in Glasgow?

ICS We went down and stayed with my brother. My mother was going to be on her own, because I was going to be away, and my younger brother was doing his National Service at the time, so she wanted to leave Lewis. So we went and stayed with my older brother, who at that time was teaching in Dumbarton before he went to Rhodesia. He was married by that time to a girl from Helensburgh. My mother wanted to leave Lewis, so we went down and stayed with him. Well, she didn't get on. She caused bits of problems, and so eventually we had to move out of that flat and get another one in Dumbarton. So myself and my mother were staying in Dumbarton, and my brother by this time had escaped to Rhodesia with his wife.

IM And your mother by this time was obviously a fluent English speaker?

ICS Oh yes.

IM She never chose to speak English to you?

ICS If you go back to Lewis, and you go back to the village, you'd never speak English to someone in the village you grew up with. It's just one of those things, you just don't. If you speak English it becomes a kind of class thing. You just don't, if it's someone you know well. To do that is almost like saying, I'm superior to you.

IM So basically you would normally speak Gaelic to a relative, but supposing somebody came in to visit you you'd both immediately go into English.

ICS Yes, if the person spoke English exclusively.

IM Before we move away too far from Lewis, let's talk about the Free Church and all that that entailed. What it meant in your young day in Lewis, and how much you seem to hate it now.

ICS I hate it really because it was very constricting. If you were walking about on a Sunday you could actually be reported! I was up only about a year ago seeing my cousin, and I went to the church with him; and when we came out of the church I lit up a cigarette. You mustn't do that, because the minister came up and talked to someone who did exactly that about two weeks ago, for lighting up a cigarette after they had come out of the church.

I don't understand why in Lewis especially the Free Church is so strong. It is stronger in Lewis than for instance in Islay – well, it's not very strong in Islay at all. Maybe more in Skye, but it seems to be much stronger in Lewis than anywhere else, and I feel it's a sort of dictatorship. There have been ministers in Stornoway who have a kind of almost absolute power, and I hate anything to do with any ideology controlling you. I hate anyone trying to control my mind, and I think this is what they were doing. And the reaction of course is a lot of drunkenness: you get a lot of drunkenness in Lewis, which is in part reaction against the Free Church.

IM Do you remember whether even as a little boy you believed in God?

ICS No. I can't say that I ever had any great belief in God at any time.

IM Do you think your brothers did?

ICS No, I don't think so.

IM Do you think your mother did?

ICS Oh, yes.

IM It wasn't just that she accepted the ideology, she actually believed.

ICS I resented the authority. You could still love someone and resent
their authority, and I resented the authority that my mother exerted
over me, and I'm not being vain. I'm sure you would be in the same
situation and probably you are in the same situation. I'm not being
vain when I say that I thought I was brighter than her, and I'm sure
that the kind of God she was concerned with I couldn't believe in.

I had a very ambivalent attitude to people up there, because a lot
of the people who were Free Church people I could admire as
people, but I couldn't believe in the things they believed in. In
Dumbarton a lot of Lewis people would become policemen, and I
think this must be because they were trying to hunt down sin. (L) It
wasn't just crime they were hunting down. They were hunting down
sin.

BT Why were you so free of sin, your good self? You obviously felt free
of sin.

ICS I've never actually felt guilt. I've never actually felt that I was
sinning.

BT But how come you managed to escape sin, as a problem?

ICS I don't know. Sin is something which is theologically orientated, and
therefore if you don't believe in God you can't believe in sin. I've
done wrong: I think most people have done wrong in all sorts of
different ways, but I've never actually thought of them as sins.

BT I'm interested in your absentee brothers. I don't know what your
attitude to them is.

ICS First of all they were different from me in the sense that they weren't
interested in writing. My older brother is very bright. My younger
brother could have been bright, but he didn't particularly care for
school, and he was always in trouble there. They were not interested
in the kinds of things that I was interested in. And the main reason
they weren't was because they were very healthy, outgoing boys who
mixed freely with the other boys, but because I was sickly I didn't.
They strongly reacted against my mother in the same extent as I did.
But the problems weren't so obvious for them, because I had more
time to think. (L) If I was lying in my bed for several weeks I
thought about the things that were happening to me in a way that
they wouldn't really.

I was very close to them when I was young, but I turned against
them. I turned against my brother in a way. I don't think it was his

fault, but when someone sacrifices himself – and again with all the reservations I made earlier – someone always has to carry the can. (L) And I felt my brother didn't carry enough of the can. I carried two-thirds of the can. (L) Although I disliked my mother, I still had enough of whatever it takes to put myself in the position of someone else – this is probably the problem with me – and I could put myself in the position of my mother in this village, strange, a widow and all the rest of it. I don't know whether my older brother was more honest or took the better part. Maybe because of his wife, he cut himself off almost completely, and I was at the stage where I didn't want any more to do with him because I couldn't see any reason why he couldn't see there was something to be said on her side. People don't become as difficult as my mother was without a reason.

It doesn't matter how much these kind of people wreck your life, in a way you have to do something about them. One should look after the old simply because they are old, without any regard at all to what they are like.

BT I don't know, Iain. I have noticed, like everybody else, that you married late. Why didn't you marry earlier?

ICS That's a point. Probably I could never have married when my mother was alive, because I knew distinctly that if I married in my mother's lifetime she would do exactly what she has done to my brother, she would have deliberately set out in some way to wreck it.

BT Why should you carry your responsibility for your mother so far? It was excessive.

ICS Yes, it was excessive. I think I was probably immature, for my age.

IM And perhaps that could have been her fault as well?

ICS I think intellectually I wasn't immature, but emotionally I was till very, very late. I was very, very immature emotionally, and I hated revealing myself, for many, many years, until in fact my madness. [*ICS suffered a breakdown in 1982. His fictionalised account of it is in his novel In the Middle of the Wood, 1987.*] I hated to reveal anything about myself to people, and certainly not my emotions if possible. Maybe in writing, but not in reality.

BT You've been a very prolific and a very philosophical writer. What kept that going?

ICS It's hard to know the sources of these things. I'll tell you maybe a clue to all this tortured thing. (L) Talking about Kierkegaard: why did I become so interested in Kierkegaard?

BT   Indeed why?

ICS Unless I saw something on a lesser scale. Something in myself that I
     saw in Kierkegaard, and it was Kierkegaard's inability to relate to
     people. Especially to relate to this girl, Regina. Also the fact that he
     was a very peculiar person in that he had both an aesthetic and a
     religious dimension. So I was attracted to him, and the fact that his
     intellect was in advance of his emotional commitment. I had a very,
     very strong commitment to Kierkegaard's writing at a certain stage
     in my life, and he influenced me tremendously. It would have been
     in the '60s, I think. The thing that Kierkegaard taught me, among
     many others, was that one should try to be an individual – however
     painful it is – at the expense of an ideology, and this gave me the way
     of escape from the Free Church. Here was a man who was very
     interested in religion, but at the same time was an artist or a poet.

IM   Kierkegaard opens up a whole spiritual realm for people who are
     unbelievers.

ICS One of the things he does is that he makes it appear as if the most
     important thing in the world is the choices you are confronted with.
     It's an anti-ideological thing – you are yourself in the end. He says
     that you have to make these kind of creative leaps, in his case towards
     God. I didn't actually make the creative leap towards God, but at the
     same time he taught me that you don't need ideologies. Ideologies
     are hateful, and also it was all mixed up with his attitude towards a
     kind of dedication towards something or other, in my case art but in
     his case religion, such that it would go beyond human feelings.

BT   Comprehension and reason.

ICS Yes. I wrote a short story in Gaelic called 'Abraham and Isaac' which
     is based on Kierkegaard ['*Abraham is Isaac*', *1963*]. Kierkegaard had
     analysed the Abraham and Isaac story, and he said that the inter-
     esting thing about the story was that all the way to the sacrifice
     Abraham never spoke to Isaac at all, simply because there was
     nothing he could say to him. This fitted in with my ideas about
     language: being bilingual and all the rest of it I was very interested in
     language. I also wrote another story about a chap who believed he
     was the new Kierkegaard, and that he had the right to say to this girl,
     'I abolish my engagement with you because I am Kierkegaard'.
     Kafka and Kierkegaard, these kind of people I found more inter-
     esting because they were people who were dedicated. Kafka was
     dedicated towards art and Kierkegaard was dedicated towards

religion, but in their lifestyles they seem to me to be so alike that it
didn't really matter whether it was God or art. There was something
about the two of them I really did identify with at that stage.

IM And did it have something to do with being humanly lonely?

ICS Probably yes, and also it had something to do with this feeling that
one had to break out of the system. I had partly done this too in that
long short story 'The Black and the Red'. [*See The Black and the Red
and other stories, 1973*]. About the chap who comes to Aberdeen
University, and writes home, and finds that he is breaking away
systematically from the kind of environment in which he has been
brought up. And to him this was a huge undertaking, to make
himself an individual at the expense of the environment in which he
had been brought up. This chap actually got involved with this girl
at the university, got involved with CND and all the rest of it, and
this to him was an extraordinary thing to do: it was a tremendous
thing to do.

IM And it was a way in which he made himself free of his mother, and
therefore for the first time able to sign himself 'your loving son'.

ICS Yes, because before that he had been signing himself 'your dutiful
son'. Then suddenly he broke free, and he was on the same level as
her; he could talk to her because he had made himself free.

But you see it not just in me. Maybe in Sorley MacLean and his
brother. I mean Sorley broke away. He broke away from a Pres-
byterian strongly Seceder background to become a Communist, and
then his brother Calum broke away from the Seceder background to
become a Catholic; and these were huge decisions. They are really
massive decisions. I didn't become a Catholic or a Communist
because I don't believe in either. I don't believe in any ideologies
at all, because I was taught by Kierkegaard to be an individual.

When I was writing the wee thing I did about MacDiarmid, *The
Golden Lyric* [1967], I said that this was my interpretation of what
happened to MacDiarmid. There was one point MacDiarmid was
writing sort of hallucinatory lyrics, and then there was a point where
he felt that he had to gain some kind of security, and he became a
Communist, simply because if he hadn't he would have disinte-
grated.

IM Needing a framework?

ICS Yes. Eliot also moved into the framework, and I think these people in
a sense have had bad faith. I hope not to opt out in that sense: I hope

to keep going as an individual who can make absolute decisions all along the line.

IM   You said in your University lecture that churches and ideologies and even the bizarre schematisms of Yeats, while all of them were understandable as ways of trying to make some sense of life . . .

ICS I think they are a cop-out in a sense, against loneliness, against the hallucinatory.

BT   I'm fascinated by the repetition of the word hallucinatory.

ICS I was thinking about it in terms of MacDiarmid. I think that when you read *A Drunk Man*, when you read the lyrics, I think the only alternative for MacDiarmid apart from joining a group would have been insanity. Because I think that his insights were so extraordinary, and so many and multifarious, that he would have had to surrender himself to some form which would make sense of what was happening to him, or he would have simply gone mad. I think the level of the hallucinatory in MacDiarmid was very high.

BT   The poetry you most admire in MacDiarmid apparently is hallucinatory?

ICS Yes, the early lyrics and the *Drunk Man*. Well, after his conversion to Communism his poetry is still good, but it's not on the same level, because I think that in the first instance he was accepting things as they were as a sleepwalker does, and then he schematised them. And whenever one schematises things one becomes frightened. I think nearly always schematisation arises from some sort of fear.

BT   That is doubtless right. I am very struck by the repeated use of the word hallucinatory to describe his *best* poetry. Are you serious?

ICS Yes, and the schematisation arises from fear almost of some kind of insanity.

BT   We presumably don't mean the same by hallucinatory? Hallucinatory is to have illusions, and surely his best poetry is very clear.

[Tape number two].

ICS Well, the way I use hallucinatory is as pushing perception to the furthest limits. This is the feeling I have with the lyrics and with the *Drunk Man*, that MacDiarmid had pushed perception to the furthest possible limits while still remaining sane, and if he had continued without a scheme which could assimilate these perceptions he would have gone insane.

This is a continual feeling I have, and that there is a safety factor, and I think it's possible that the same thing arises with Eliot. The kind of perceptions he had in 'The Waste Land' were hallucinatory, and therefore he had to schematise things, and so he jumped into the safety of the Church of England, in exactly the same way as MacDiarmid jumped into Communism.

IM I wonder if we could look at the difficulties, the shortcomings, for a poet who refuses all these frameworks. Who can only use his own life experience and his own imagination. I wonder how far you feel your own work, poetry and novel, has been fairly directly autobiographical.

ICS Let me put it another way. Let me go back to Lowell. Now Lowell was a person who had extraordinary insights and didn't in the end choose to accept a scheme. In fact the reason why I liked Lowell myself was because I sensed something akin to myself in Lowell. That he had broken out of a religious, strict situation towards eventually a free verse. Which was exactly the plot that my own poetry has taken, and in fact he –

IM He put into the odd spiritual harbour that you weren't willing to put up with, didn't he?

ICS Not latterly, no.

IM Did he not shed his New England Calvinism and become a Roman Catholic? And only after many years leave that?

ICS Yes, I know, but what he did took almost the same time as I – well, pretty much the same paths as I have taken. His last book was *Day by Day* [*1977*], in which he is breaking away out of the system: he notes the things that are going on, the ordinary things that are going on day by day. Now the danger, as you very rightly say, is that you are back onto the autobiographical, and you don't choose to have any masks at all. And Lowell chose not to have masks. I think really that my ideal of the poet would be someone like D H Lawrence; him I always keep coming back to, someone who reacts to the moment. This is what I want to do eventually, to react to the moment, to make every moment a privileged moment. If you consider the book *Consider the Lilies* [*1968*], which is in many ways a very flawed book –

IM Oh, nonsense, Iain. (L)

ICS In the sense that it's full of anachronisms, but the whole point of the book was this. What I was trying to do, I was taking this woman who had been involved in an ideology, which was the ideology of the Church, and I was trying to make her human. I was trying to say to her, destroy the ideology of the Church, and can you come out and live as a human being needing no ideology at all, and can you survive? Can you survive into the kind of person who is continually open to experience, wary, but still open to all experiences all round about him? When you accept an ideology you're automatically cutting off whole areas to the left and right of the ideology. No ideology can incorporate life.

IM But don't you find that there are other things than ideologies which have to shut off parts of experience, relationships with one person shut off the possibilities of relationships with other people?

ICS Well, that's true.

IM Loyalties to individuals. I think that what you were just describing as an ideal is in fact a very unfinished picture, a life of somebody who has not made any choices. I think whenever you choose you do shut off some possibilities to concentrate on others.

ICS Oh, I think you do, yes.

IM But you don't mind that on the human level; it's only on the ideological level?

ICS On the ideological level, yes. Let me put it like this. If I were to make a criticism of Norman [*MacCaig*], I put the human at the centre of everything I do, while Norman sometimes puts animals at the centre of what he does. I am not really interested in animals, because I don't think that we can really make much contact with animals in that sense, and therefore the most important being is human. The thing that I think I can do best is analysing people's minds, and this is because I have been used to analysing my own mind. Maybe, of course, I'm wrong: possibly I impose on other people the way I analyse my own mind, which may be wrong.

BT Norman doesn't put animals in the centre in the sense that he excludes human beings, does he?

ICS Well, let's take that back. Just say that as far as I'm concerned the human is the centre of everything I do.

IM Norman describes himself as looking at a landscape, which includes landscape, people and animals, but for you people come very much at the centre.

ICS Yes, basically I'm not interested in landscapes. And this is extra-ordinary because by all the history of my development I shouldn't be interested in people at all. It may be that it is through my writing that I communicate with people though I couldn't in real life.

IM Well, what was it like coming to the mainland for the first time, to Aberdeen University?

ICS I left school at seventeen. I left in fifth year because in those days there was nothing much for me in sixth year. There was no Sixth Year Studies or anything. So I did the Aberdeen Bursary Competition in fifth year.

IM Did you get a bursary?

ICS Yes, I got about £60.

IM Where were you placed, do you remember?

ICS I can't remember. It wasn't that high, but the point was that normally this was sat in sixth year and we were given extra tuition. I wasn't given any tuition at all: I sat it immediately after the Highers.

IM So to be placed was quite significant.

ICS Well, I took English which I was doing at Higher. You couldn't sit a Higher in History in those days, so I was doing a Lower in History. I took this bursary competition with a Lower in History, and I think I took Celtic.

IM It's interesting that you took Celtic somewhere.

ICS Anyway, I left Lewis at the age of seventeen. I arrived at Kyle of Lochalsh, and I saw my first train for the first time, and then I went to Aberdeen. And I think I told you already about this beggar, the ambivalence I felt about it, the first time I'd seen anybody begging.

IM Not the first time you had seen anybody who was indigent. What happened to indigent people in Lewis?

ICS Well, if you had an indigent person in a village, everybody would look after him.

[Tape number three. Aberdeen, March 22 1986]

ICS I think probably I started writing poems in English first, and then there was a period when I wrote poems in Gaelic and short stories in Gaelic, and then I started writing short stories in English, novels in English – and somewhere in the middle of writing novels in English I wrote a novel in Gaelic, *An t-Aonaran* [*The Hermit*, 1976].

IM Does the Gaelic play fit in there?

ICS The Gaelic plays would have been written maybe in the early 1960s.

What happened was that when I was teaching in Oban there was a drama group, and they were short of material. It was very, very hard to get hold of Gaelic plays, and they asked me if I would write some Gaelic plays for them, which were really one-acters. The first Gaelic play I wrote for them was called *A' Chuirt* [*The Trial, 1966*]. This is the courtroom, or the court, or the trial. And this play was based on Sartre's *Huis-clos* [*1944*], and as you know it's about people in Hell and so on. I'd actually been doing this with my Sixth Year in an English translation. I put Patrick Sellar in this court in Hell, and he was being tried for what he had done. I also wrote a Gaelic short story on the same theme, and then after that I wrote *Consider the Lilies*. It was written very quickly because I'd found roughly what I wanted to say with the other two things. But generally speaking I would say that English would have come first, but there were periods when I got especially interested in the Gaelic short story. The plays were written mainly because people asked me to write them, not because I particularly wanted to write them.

IM   Did they ask for the subject matter, or did you choose that?

ICS I chose that: they didn't specify.

IM   Do you remember why that particular theme?

ICS It's very hard for me to remember. Certain books came before other books: I have a feeling that *From Bourgeois Land* came before *Consider the Lilies* and also probably before *A'Chuirt* [*in order of actual publication, A'Chuirt, 1966; Consider the Lilies, 1968; From Bourgeois Land, 1969*]. As far as I remember, what happened when I was doing *From Bourgeois Land* is that I was creating this idea that it was possible for Nazism to appear in Scotland. This was the theme of the poetry book. And then it suddenly occurred to me, was there any particular point in Scottish history when you could say that a certain kind of Nazism had appeared, and like Hitler's treatment of the Jews. It struck me that the Clearances was the period when this had happened, and so in a sense it was a continuation of what I had been doing. It was a continuation, the idea that things like that had happened in Scotland, and people had been treated in that way.

IM   When you wrote on this most emotive of Scottish themes, were you aware of what had already been done, MacColla's *And the Cock Crew* and Gunn's *Butcher's Broom*?

ICS What I was most aware of was the Prebble and the Grimble [*John Prebble, The Highland Clearances, 1963; Ian Grimble, The Trial of*

Patrick Sellar, 1962]. What I actually read was more historical and documentary stuff, rather than novels. I hadn't actually read Gunn when I wrote it, and I hadn't actually read the MacColla – in fact I don't think I've read them since! What I really wanted was to have some idea of the backgrounds and the facts, and not make too many errors, though I *did* make a lot of drastic errors. There are a lot of anachronisms in the book, but what I was really looking for was dates and historical background.

IM   I'm interested in why a novel in English. Were you looking for a broader public than you could get by writing anything in Gaelic or poetry in English?

ICS I've been asked why I didn't write it in Gaelic. It might have been better for me to have written it in Gaelic from the point of view of the language. I don't think I've ever thought about a public for anything I've written.

BT   What do you mean, from the point of view of the language?

ICS Well, she would have spoken Gaelic. On the other hand it would have been rather complicated because Patrick Sellar would have spoken English, and this was the perpetual problem, whether to make him speak in a different kind of Gaelic. It was really ridiculous. These contradictions in Gaelic limit what you can do. I avoided this kind of complicated problem by giving her a kind of simpler English than for instance Sellar might have used.

IM   Yes, your Preface shows that you were totally aware of all the problems of language.

 I was wondering whether you had by this time found how little money there was in writing poetry, and whether even when you started writing novels you were hoping to be able to give up teaching and write full time?

ICS I wrote this when I was still teaching.

IM   I know.

ICS These kinds of questions have never really occurred to me. I have never thought of an audience for anything I've written. I've never written anything specifically geared to any particular audience. Anything I've ever written, like *The Search* [*1983*], has usually been partly out of my own experience, partly out of things I've become interested in at the time.

IM   You've never felt that you have a message for either public, your Gaelic or your English public?

ICS Well I had a message in *Consider the Lilies*. In one sense what I was
trying to do, I was trying to work out of my system the idea of
someone brought up inside an ecclesiastical carapace, a religious
shell, and I was conscious of what I was doing here. I wanted this
woman to be broken out of her religious ideology in order to become
naked, bare, and see how she could cope as a human being. Again, all
the things that I do are very intertwined with each other. This is also
intertwined with the essay I wrote on Hugh MacDiarmid, *The
Golden Lyric* [*1967*]. I said that MacDiarmid at a certain early stage
in his development was operating at a very high degree of nakedness
to the universe, and I maintain that in order to survive as a human
being he had to put this carapace of an ideology around him. He
happened to choose Communism, but it need not have been Communism: it could have been anything. When you're a poet of that
kind of talent, the whole world impinges on you and you have to
make yourself a clearing somewhere along the line. Therefore his
later work is inferior, because he is not as naked to the universe as he
was. It was a self-protective thing. If he hadn't adopted some kind of
ideology he would have destroyed himself because things, images
were coming at him from many directions, and he was so open to the
universe that unless he had some kind of covering from this hail-
storm of things he would have destroyed himself. This is too difficult
for your readers (L: *wild giggle*).

   I'm getting back to *Consider the Lilies*. Mrs Scott had the Church,
and MacDiarmid had Communism, and I don't believe in ideologies, and I think that MacDiarmid made a mistake in trying to
escape, which on a human level I think he did, and therefore the two
things were quite intertwined with each other. The idea of ideology
as a shelter and the idea of what happens when the shelter is taken
away. Mrs Scott was unsheltered at the end, but she managed to
cope with it, and the ending is on the whole optimistic, which is not
so true of my other novels. But that one is optimistic.

   Her mother had visions of Hell, which obviously came from her
own religious background, and these were transmitted. This religious background obviously made her rigid in her attitudes, and it
was these religious attitudes that lost her both her husband and her
son. This is what I intended: the mother's visions of Hell were
transmitted to her, her whole way of life was to do with the Church. I
actually made this anachronism: I made her church the Free Church

and the kind of people that I knew in my childhood. [*The Disruption in the Church of Scotland which produced the Free Church did not take place until 1843.*] Her whole nature had become rigid and a lot of it was to do with the Church.

IM   There's a crucial point in the middle where Donald Macleod is listening to the story of her life, and she has never, ever been able to tell anybody.

ICS   She isn't able to tell anyone a story. Not only can't she tell the story of her life but she can't tell a story to the children. Because telling a story would be a kind of vanity. The only story really is the Bible story. This idea of lack of love, I base her on the kind of rigid churchgoers I knew in Lewis. Again everything comes together so much: they were unable to hear what you might call 'the unpredicted voices of our kind'. [*See 'Two Girls Singing', 1965*].

One has to look at her in a clear-eyed manner, and the fact is, she is not a likeable person. My job in the book was to try to understand what made her unlikeable, and maybe make her likeable at the end. I didn't want to sentimentalise her: it's easy to sentimentalise a single person, or one of two or three against a whole structure. I wanted to present her as really unlikeable.

Again I keep coming back to the intertwined nature of what I do. I wrote a poem, 'She Teaches *Lear*' [*1968*]. I was very interested in old age for personal reasons at the time. With Lear, you start off with someone who is extremely unlikeable (L), and by the end of the play you have made him into somebody understandable. I'm not sure how Shakespeare does it, but our feeling changes as far as Lear is concerned, from beginning to end. He is a cantankerous old bugger really, and she was an unlikeable old woman. I have always been interested in whether there is a duty on you to help people who are essentially unlikeable (L): she is helped by someone whom she would not normally have spoken to, that is an atheist. He has a certain compassion for her. He sees what is happening with regard to the Clearances and the traditional. The historical Donald Macleod did see this, and was exiled because of it. The whole point is that you can help old people even though you don't like them, and this is one of the problems we have to face. Old people can be very devious, very difficult, but nevertheless there may be a human compulsion on us to help them in spite of that.

BT   I wonder what process you went through in order to establish where you are with regard to human compulsion. You obviously have confidence in a set of values which you see as quite different from the carapace of the old persons, or an ideology adopted by writers.

ICS What I'm talking about are felt compulsions. I'm talking about the Pharisaic external Law and the felt compulsions from within yourself. A Pharisee for instance might do certain things, or demand certain things without actually feeling them deeply. I think this is the basic problem, do you feel it is a value that whatever old people are like you have to look after them? I feel it. I can't justify it, but it is a personal thing to me. It's not a law that has been imposed on me from outside, like the Free Church, but I just feel it myself that you do it.

BT I'm interested in what set of values you think you acquired to give you the strength and integrity to hold together as a human being. How did this happen?

ICS It goes back to Kierkegaard. One of the things that he taught me is that you must try to be an individual. No matter what the other people around you are like, you have certain sets of values that you believe in, and you go ahead. And as an individual you do the kind of things that you feel are necessary, even though they bring you up against problems from the society outside you.

IM Do you feel that this individual can be created quite as much by books you read as by religion?

ICS By experience.

IM Personalities of other human beings who can deal with life with a kind of clarity and charity that we all recognise and admire and follow?

ICS Yes.

IM Would I be right to suggest that, if one was to add up all the felt compulsions of your life, they would be not unadjacent to a lot of the felt compulsions in the life of a good Free Church person? But you feel you've arrived at these by some experience of your own which internalises them.

ICS That's right. As I say, I went back to Kierkegaard. You are confronted by certain choices, and strictly speaking I tend to evaluate these choices as far as possible for myself without allowing an ideology to dictate to me, at least consciously, how I should evaluate the choices. In other words, I try to be as much as is possible a free person. It is very difficult, but I have always tried to be that.

BT   What's interesting surely is that quite a lot of your impulses to the
     good and to responsibility are impulses which an outsider from, say,
     Aberdeen or Mars, might well say are the sort of impulses which a
     Christian person might have. A Christian person of a somewhat
     puritanical disposition of the type you might find in the Free
     Church.

ICS A Kierkegaardian might have, perhaps. (L)

BT   There's a funny grafting on of values which are Greek, humanist,
     intellectually adventurous and so on, onto something else which is
     very culturally distinct to the Highlands and Islands.

ICS I feel a lot of kinship with somebody like Hawthorne. I think he is an
     individualist in the sense that he does his own thinking, and this is all
     I am trying to say. I try as much as possible not to go along with the
     system if I feel the system is wrong.

BT   That wasn't a disguised critical question. It was just to try to bring
     out how the person from Mars might place you. A free thinker
     within a tradition.

ICS Yes, yes.

IM   There's another way to look at how the values of a Free Church
     young man who rejects the Free Church begin to evolve. The second
     novel, *The Last Summer*, very deliberately and a long time afterwards
     [1969] goes back to the last summer that the fairly autobiographical
     hero spends at home before going to university.

ICS That's right, yes.

IM   Did you feel any need to differentiate yourself from that hero?

ICS Not basically, I don't think. In fact even when he chose Mathematics
     at the end. I was actually swithering myself between doing Mathe-
     matics and English. I suppose Mathematics could be considered an
     escape from the complexities and intertwining roots of things, the
     messiness of life. This is probably why I liked it so much.

     I could do a Geometry problem, and it had nothing to do with
     particular pains or guilts. I was very attracted to it, and nearly did it,
     but I changed my mind later on. But I don't think that there's
     anything much, if I remember correctly, in that book that I would
     disassociate myself from.

     There was one thing which actually was important to me when I
     was growing up. I don't know whether it comes into the book, maybe
     it does. I was brought up in this village of Bayble and then I went to
     school till about the age of eleven. Then I went to the Nicolson

Institute, which is in Stornoway, about seven miles away, till I was about seventeen. There was a problem about the football teams, because I was asked to play for the village and I was also asked to play for the Nicolson Institute, and at the age I was then this was a vast problem to me, which I should choose to do. In fact I did play for the village team, but these kinds of decisions, I certainly felt them as very important to me. The other thing I felt was very important: when I went to the Nicolson Institute I was an individual leaving the community where the other boys were, and maybe they wouldn't speak to me because I was considered to be someone who was different. The idea of the individual, which again comes back to Kierkegaard. Individual as against the community, how far the individual can disassociate himself from the community, how far he feeds off the community. These are questions which I've thought about a lot, and I think they were there in *The Last Summer* as well, at least in embryo.

[Tape number four, Crichton Smith's home in Taynuilt, March 29 1986.]

IM Iain, you said earlier today that you thought perhaps *Consider the Lilies* was one of your best books because it wasn't directly about your own experience.

ICS Yes, yes.

IM I would have thought it might be that you had so much experienced your mother that you were able to do that old woman.

ICS But what I meant was that there was nothing of myself in it apart from the actual writing. Some of the other things I do are sort of disguises for myself in a way, like *The Last Summer* and 'The Black and the Red' and one or two things like that.

IM The one that comes after *The Last Summer* is *My Last Duchess* [*1971*]. Is that one in which you feel in some kind of sympathy with the main character, Mark Simmons?

ICS Yes, in the academic kind of background, I suppose I put myself in his position. A lot of these things I do are really about academics who are brought face to face with some kind of reality, even *The Search* and one or two others. Poets and academics who are brought to face some kind of reality and sometimes find it very difficult to survive it, and similarly in *My Last Duchess* too.

IM I find it quite constant. It can come to a bad end, as it does, relatively, in *My Last Duchess*, or a much better one, as in *Goodbye, Mr Dixon* [1974], but again and again you come back to this theme, which must, if I'm guessing right, have been some temptation in your own life. To escape from certain ordinary human concerns into a world of books. These heroes tend to be lonely people, in a self-inflicted loneliness, and whether the book is happy or sad, the question is whether they can achieve some kind of movement towards other people.

ICS Yes, I think that has been a lot of my temptation really, escaping into the world of books: because I do read a lot, and I think probably it's the only real hobby I have. I read books from when I was ill a lot when I was young. It meant I read more books than was common for someone of my age group. I think that is a temptation for me, and therefore a lot of them are about academics who get their learning from books confronted with something in the real world, or maybe surviving or not surviving in the real world.

IM Obviously it's not so simple as to say you are always writing the same book. There seems to be a cluster of problems: there is the positive thing towards books, and a certain withdrawal from people, and communication – whether or not communication is possible.

ICS Yes, I remember the first book of poems that I ever published, which was *The Long River*, and this was the first review I had ever read of anything I had ever published, and it was in *Lines Review*. And it was actually published by Macdonald, so this was the magazine which came from Macdonald. [*M Macdonald, Loanhead, published Lines Review, and also The Long River, 1955. Laurence Graham reviewed the book in Lines, 10, 1955, p 35. His review, which clearly made a big impact on the poet, is reprinted by permission at the end of this interview, pp 154–5.*] The writer praised the technical virtuosity, but he did say that there was a lack of a kind of common humanity in the poems, and that when I learned humanity my poems and my work would improve. (L)

G K Chesterton said you ascend toward common humanity. What I've been trying to do is to write something which is an attempt to communicate with common humanity, and this is partly why I like *Consider the Lilies*. In some sense, there was more of common humanity there. Academics and so on are really not what you would call a common class of people, in whatever use of the word common here. (L) Probably a lot of them are outside the range of the ordinary reader. Whereas Mrs Scott isn't. Somehow in that book I think I succeeded in establishing a small society of common humanity, if you like.

I think that to a certain extent I possibly succeeded with *A Field Full of Folk* [1982], where again I was trying to write about common humanity. I think the thing that is wrong with *The Tenement* [*1985*] was probably that there are too many people outside the range of common humanity. They are the extremes, they are either eccentric or they are twisted in some way: there was a strange gallery of lonely people without enough compensation from common ordinary humanity.

IM   Do you think that beginning to write novels, prose fiction at all, was perhaps an effort to reach a common humanity, an audience of ordinary people who didn't perhaps read poetry?

ICS Well, in spite of what that man said [*Laurence Graham: see pp 154–5*], I think you can get away in poetry with studying yourself to a greater extent than you can in the novel. Actually I'm not really a novelist at all, but the reason I started writing fiction was to fill in the spaces between poetry. I recognised that it's very easy to over-write in poetry, and I was a very prolific writer anyway. Partly I just wanted to fill in the spaces between the poems.

IM   I'm sure there was more to it than that.

ICS Maybe there was a more specific impulse than that.

IM   When you quoted that early review it seemed to me that it might be quite easy to argue that for at least a short time twentieth-century poetry in English *is* a bit unhuman.

ICS I would agree with that.

IM   It's not just Crichton Smith. Pound, and Eliot and Yeats. MacDiarmid.

ICS Yes, I think this is very true. Maybe I didn't realise at the time that there is some kind of compulsion on the artist somehow to give his readers hope, and that simply to write a passive reflection of the despair one finds around is not enough.

I sometimes feel like that about Beckett. I quite liked his novels, where there was quite a lot of humour, but I find some of the later things very despairing. I feel there should be some kind of attempt to establish some kind of hope without at the same time being untrue to your experience.

IM   In general that would seem to me entirely right, but it wouldn't be a good reason for not from time to time expressing the gloom or despair. It seems to me that *My Last Duchess* is a very gloomy book. Mark Simmons is a very honest and searching portrait of somebody who appeals, doesn't he, on two occasions in the book, to writers as if they were God or something. This character Frith at the beginning – I think you told me once off-tape that in a very loose way he might be based on MacDiarmid – and then there is Hunter, the character who works in Easterhouse, who is fairly clearly based on Archie Hind. I'm sure Archie is proud of that. Mark has hidden away from life in books, and then he gets married, and the marriage doesn't work at all. I think we are supposed to see it is because of him: it's not because of Lorna.

ICS It's because of him, yes.

IM   So, is there anything positive in it? Can we feel that just by living through this experience he has become more human at all?

ICS The only possible sign of hope at the end of the book is that he has reached a point where he can go no further, and I suppose what I'm saying is that self-knowledge in itself – and the deeper it is – is maybe a sign of hope.

IM   This book doesn't have an ending really; it just breaks off, and you're very conscious of that. You have Mark saying to himself, 'I must have willed it to be like this because this is the way it is', which has an appalling logic, though I don't believe it's true about life in general.

ICS At the end I think he's come to some kind of self-knowledge, in the same sense possibly as Mrs Scott. This may be a wrong belief – it's almost like the Freudian thing that you are partially healed if you can understand your own motives deeply enough. Freud is someone I've always been deeply interested in, but whether this happens I'm not sure *now*, whether it is true that if something is uncovered and brought to the surface it does help.

IM   This book is the first where several things come up. Lorna is not just an ordinary human being, she is an artist, and she and Mark are contrasted, because we see her and her friend going into good works and starting to try to help the first of many hermits that abound in your fiction. Can you remember about that hermit in *My Last Duchess*? Is he based on a real person?

ICS I think all these hermits started off from one man. I used to see him. He lived in a kind of tin hut. I think it was on the road to Crianlarich.

And he just lived by himself in this hut, and it's the kind of thing that I've often wondered about. How a hermit can actually live, how he can live without any communication at all with other people, and this is one of the central things that I do. A lot of the things that I do are really dealing with people who are on the edge of things, or who are in pain, or who are extremely vulnerable. I suppose that is a limiting factor in what I do. On the other hand I think that if one thinks at all one has to come to these kind of positions. In something like *King Lear* the healing is actually created partly by the language, and I think it's much harder now for the writer to get away with that (L) – to get away with healing a painful problem by means of metaphor or by means of language. People see through it more quickly now. And because we are living in a post-Freudian age people understand more about themselves and again the easy solution is very, very hard to get. People are not deceived so easily by the easy solution. I think a lot of things I do are almost like internal soliloquies of people questioning their own motives, and that there isn't all that much narrative in a sense. There's enough, I think, to carry the thing through, but I'm not deeply interested in narrative.

IM So you very often juxtapose things, rather than tell a story. One of the points of these hermits is that they fairly place your hero who is apparently on the edge. He actually turns out to be in the middle compared with the hermit, and he half envies him and is half appalled at him, because the hermit doesn't disappear into books or something academic; he disappears into self-sufficiency, some appalling, almost threatening state to everybody else.

ICS That's right. The threat of this. I'm really interested in what happens to people, starting off with Mrs Scott, when all forms of protection are removed from them. What I'm trying to find is, does a human being need this kind of protection in order to survive, and could you survive from day to day without self-deception? I don't know whether it's possible: it's very hard to know.

BT The implication of this fascination of yours is that you think that a great many people actually do live on the basis of self-delusion and self-deception, ideologies being one form of them.

ICS I've found it more and more interesting since I came out to Taynuilt [1982]. Art is one way. A strong belief in something is one way, and it could be a strong belief in art, where this gives a future to your existence. If you live in a small village, you're looking for news. Most people in a small village are looking for news, which helps them to survive from day to day, because they talk about this piece of news. It sounds bad if I say ordinary people – I don't mean that I am any more extraordinary than they are. If you are a practitioner of art, that gives you a specific way of dealing with the world. If you don't have a specific obsession, then the world must become more diurnal. It's a kind of day-to-day existence, and that is the mystery I'm trying to get at. Towards the strength people can have for doing that. In that sense I'm ascending, or trying to ascend, towards where you set aside all questions of protection and ascend towards the diurnal.

BT   Would this mean that the artist gave up his obsession with art as unnecessary?

ICS It implies that I think they are stronger than the artist, those people who don't need protection. I think that 'ordinary people' respond to influences which come from outside them, very often in an un-coordinated way. And the artist forces his own interpretation on the impulses which come in from outside. A lot of people think the artist is heroic, but the more I look at reality the more I think that there are lots of people more heroic than the artist. I tend to find heroism more in the events in ordinary people's lives, which are unnamed and unmemorialised.

IM   Mark Simmons is not an artist. And with the next hero, Tom Spence in *Goodbye, Mr Dixon*, the whole plot is about how he has un-consciously retreated from life almost completely, seeing himself as an artist as a way of escaping from things that happened to him in his real life that he simply cannot face or cope with.

ICS That's right, yes. I used to think that Hamlet was an admirable person, but the more I actually look on Hamlet, the more I think of him as a child in a cradle, beating his fists against the cradle. There are so many people in the world to whom terrible things happen who don't do that. People who are unemployed, people of 49 or 50 who are going to find themselves being made redundant next week. I suppose this is really the kind of thing Brecht was saying, there's been a kind of con-game played on us, in the sense that these people like Hamlet and Lear have been made very important, simply because they happen to be kings or princes. I come down to the idea that there is at least as much heroism going on without being known about in the ordinary world.

IM   You always come back to the single quotation I most blatantly re-use when I'm reviewing, which is the Thoreau one about most men living lives of quiet desperation.

ICS Yes, I think this is very true, and how do they survive? I remember one of the things that I was quite ashamed of. When I was 17 or 18 at Aberdeen University, a friend of mine died of tuberculosis, and he was quite young. I was asked by his mother to write a piece about him for the *Stornoway Gazette*. I was very proud of this piece, especially after I quoted from Paul Valéry. Looking back on it now, I think this was a kind of cleverness that was really stupidity (L), as if to say, look at me – I know about Paul Valéry.

Maybe I'm trying to do what that man [*Laurence Graham: see pp 154–5*] advised me without my realising it. Or maybe because he advised me I was doing it. Trying to find my way towards some kind of common humanity.

IM On your way back. Interesting. With both Mark Simmons and Tom Spence, when they become aware that there's something very badly wrong, they both almost literally retrace their youth. Mark is on this terrible sort of pilgrimage to find somebody to help him, but he ends up going to the place where he was at university, which is oddly like Aberdeen.

ICS To find out what's gone wrong, yes.

IM Simply retrace your steps. I was here: what happened? In *Goodbye, Mr Dixon* [*1974*] in the most melodramatic way Tom Spence does go back to an actual point where he is suddenly allowed to remember a completely traumatising thing that he saw, that changed his life.

ICS That's right. And one of the images I have of Aberdeen is of meeting myself when I was seventeen, and this person who was seventeen meeting me now, and this person of seventeen walking past me because he doesn't like me. He doesn't recognise it was possible for the person I was at seventeen to have become what I am now.

IM It's a very simple affirmative thing at the end of *Goodbye, Mr Dixon*, that Tom has decided to face life again, and he has found one person with whom he can relate, and the hope that then he can relate to others. And after that novel we move on to *An End to Autumn* [*1978*], where you have a couple who could almost be those two a lot of years on. A pair of teachers married in this fairly similar situation. And interestingly there the old lady comes in again: she's very important.

ICS Again a problem of having to deal with age. You can use old people as a screen, as another defence mechanism. When I brought my mother up to Oban I cut myself off from going out much, and this went on for years and years. But was I in fact using her as a screen so that I would not be distracted from my writing? I could always use her as an alibi. It boils down to self-deception. How far can we go in self-deception? I keep coming back to the Cordelia/Goneril thing: which was the more honest of the two? Was Goneril actually more honest than Cordelia? Did she see more clearly than Cordelia? She was saying, I'm not going to sacrifice myself for Lear because it would be self-deception.

It comes back to my fascination with Freud, and how if you allow free range to your mind you might alienate something which is human in you. Alienate a quality of humanity in oneself. Unless there's a kind of balance between the mind and something else. And sometimes I feel that this man [*Laurence Graham: see pp 154–5*] was right in a sense, what he said about the poetry. That maybe in a sense you can't do it, move yourself towards humanity by an effort of will.

IM   The questions, I suppose, are more interesting than the answers. And the symbols, the images – that hermit who just crops up everywhere, or Robinson Crusoe [*'The Notebooks of Robinson Crusoe', first published in Lines Review 47, 1973, then as The Notebooks of Robinson Crusoe, and other poems, 1975*]. How human can somebody be in isolation? Even that kind of imposed isolation.

ICS   That humanity implies at least more than one person, and if there's only one person, can you call that person human?

IM   If only because they have a past, perhaps.

ICS   Only because they have a past, yes. I think 'Robinson Crusoe' brought together a number of things I was interested in. The idea of community. The idea of isolation, and the fact that he was on an island (L). The idea of language. A lot of things came together in that particular book of poems. I often wondered, would someone who was totally alone end up by losing his language. I don't know what happens in an extreme situation like that. Language obviously, like being human, would also be something which is a network, an intertexture of some kind. I don't realise it myself at the time, but when I look back everything seems to be somehow connected with two or three things, and they spring from there.

IM   You talk about using your mother to allow you to get on with your books. In all those years, were you ever consciously lonely?

ICS   In a funny sort of way, not when she was alive. Somehow the very fact that there was someone there was important. But after she died I became extremely lonely, and there was a period when I was slightly disorientated. Partly because I had been in the house for so long that I'd cut myself off from a lot of things – except that I was going to school. I think it was very important to me that I should have been teaching in the school at that time, and this was a kind of community inside which I existed, and which helped. Loneliness is actually like a kind of disease. It can actually warp your personality as a disease may warp you physically; and it can make you extremely un-nice.

IM   Teaching keeps you in communication with other people, but it is a very special kind of communication: it's not an equal communication.

ICS It's not an equal communication, no. There were a great number of reasons why I left teaching, but one of them was that I noticed that a lot of teachers become almost childlike, and if you're too long in the world of adolescence there's some kind of maturity that you're missing. I saw it in other teachers quite a lot, but I don't think they saw it in themselves.

IM   There's also the possibility of a kind of arrogance and superiority – again figures that you draw who are or have been teachers or ministers. Who have always been in a superior position, and become very strange.

ICS Yes. The other thing I've always been wary of is having any form of power over anyone. This is another thing about teaching that I didn't realise at the time, that I did have a sense of power; and I don't like that. The kind of people I like are people who are actually vulnerable but not so vulnerable as to make them unable to function. They have to have a certain sense or air of vulnerability about them, and I think that comes from the fact that they are willing to examine themselves; they try to uncover as many layers of self-deception as they can. The people I don't like are very often the people in power, who have a lot of self-deception, and that is why they remain in power. I'm absolutely sure that the more self-deception you have, the more fit you are to hold on to power.

30 March 1986, Taynuilt.

IM   We were talking on the last tape about how the figure of the hermit seemed to be quite important in your writing. And we've talked a little off-tape about the novella-length story you eventually wrote, 'The Hermit', and the fact that you can't remember what language you first wrote the story in, or at what length even [*The Hermit and other stories, 1977*]. Could you tell me a wee bit about it?

ICS It's set in the village in Lewis where I grew up, but the characters in it are not necessarily ones I met in this village. During the war there were some airmen stationed there, and they left these huts. And there was one at the corner of the road of our village, which was a bit away from the houses. I don't know how it came into my head, I'll maybe put someone into this hut who is actually, physically, on the edge of the village. And I thought of this figure of the hermit, and he'll not interfere with anybody in the village. He wouldn't be a nuisance or anything, but he'd just be there, and this will in some way disturb the community of the village. And as far as I know this was all that happened in my mind, though I had actually used the idea of the hermit already. I suppose the hermit would be the kind of person who was going to the ultimate experience of living very vulnerably and apparently not needing anybody. It's all to do with the idea of loneliness and everything else I was exploring. I made him self-sufficient and almost happy, and this was the thing that the people in the village couldn't understand. The man could live like that and be happy! Then it began to affect them, because some of them wanted to do what the hermit was doing, and leave behind their wives and so on. It kind of disturbed the pattern of the village, and eventually he had to be driven away from the village before he could do any more harm. But in actual fact he hadn't tried to harm anybody.

IM But people found him very threatening. They were investing him in their own minds with their own obsessions.

ICS Yes, that's right.

IM The women thought he was dying for love, and the religiously anxious person thought that he had some sort of mystical wholeness, and so on.

ICS As if they were putting pictures on a screen, their own pictures were being put on the hermit.

IM You wrote that story in English twice. Is it a story you would write again?

ICS I don't know that I would do it again now, because I extended it even more in 'The Notebooks of Robinson Crusoe'. Where someone is completely unprotected and is totally alone; and that was the furthest one could take the idea. It brought together a number of my obsessions, the idea of loneliness, the idea of community, and also the idea of language, since the hermit didn't actually speak to anyone. Even when he was getting his messages he wrote them down on a piece of paper and got the shopkeeper to give him the messages. In a sense it's like a mathematical construct. I didn't actually know any hermits. I've never actually spoken to any hermits, but I'd seen one, as I said, on the road to Crianlarich. And he lived in this kind of hut with a chimney sticking out of the top, and he had lived there for years and years and years. But this one wasn't strictly speaking a complete hermit, because when the tourist buses were passing he used to come out; and this is actually how I saw him the first time. He used to play a fiddle or something when the buses stopped, and would board the bus and play to the passengers, and the passengers would give him money. So he wasn't strictly speaking a complete hermit, but I started off from him.

IM   I was interested when you inferred there that the whole thing got carried to its ultimate conclusion in the Robinson Crusoe poems. I suspect that you think your poems, when they work, are rather more important than your fiction.

ICS   I suppose so. I suppose I really am more naturally a poet than a novelist. I think the short story is different, because I'm a reasonably natural short story writer, but I don't think I'm a natural novelist. I have to work much harder at my novels than I do at my stories and my poems, because they seem to come more naturally.

IM   You also have an interest in the novella length. The hermit story and the Murdo story are both non-commercial lengths, but they're both exactly the right length for what you wanted to do. [*The original 'Murdo' was published in Murdo, and other stories, 1981, but see also Thoughts of Murdo, 1993 and Murdo: The Life and Works, ed Stewart Coun, 2001.*]

ICS   Yes, I'm very interested in novella length, because they seem to me a kind of extended short story. And I think my problem with the conventional novel is that I find it very hard to imagine people, and I sometimes find it very hard to give them the kind of language that they would naturally speak. Mainly because of lack of experience of a variety of languages. So I find it very hard to write a novel, for instance, and the other thing is that writing novels in the Highlands, and for that matter writing plays in the Highlands, is very, very difficult, because the range of people of interest is narrower. The range of people of interest is narrower, I think that is important.

IM   It's important that the novella comes most naturally to you, and you said to me yesterday off tape that another reason why you go back with pleasure to *Consider the Lilies* rather than other things is that it is, actually it is a novella too, isn't it?

ICS I was just going to say that. Actually it's a very short book. It is almost like a poem, because there are certain images, and it works in images I think, a lot of it. As in a poem certain images are taken up, the images of the dead sheep and so on. They are taken up and repeated in different ways, and this is the way I quite like to write, when I'm successful.

Another thing I find about novels is a kind of artificiality. I have great problems in creating names for people. (L) Somehow with really great novelists you get the sense that the name of the person seems to be exactly right. The names Dickens gives seem to be exactly right, but I find that the names I give seem to be arbitrary. Another thing I discovered about novels is this business of he said, she said, he repeated, you know, this kind of drudgery, a bit monotonous.

IM   I would like to say that you've sometimes taken risks, precisely that, leaving out the things that are boring. In 'Murdo' you go on to the next bit that interests you: you don't bother about the conventions of ordinary fiction.

ICS Yes, I think this is true. I'd like to be able to do a novel which would be really totally unconventional, and yet it's so difficult. Trying to read on the train short novels by a chap called Ronald Firbank, I found I was stupefyingly bored by them, and yet they were beautifully written and all the rest. I think I really want some sort of a plot. I would actually like to write a novel which would be like a poem, and at the same time I think people would find it very boring.

I don't know whether it works or not, but I've got about three sort of long poems which are actually like novels. Quite long. One of them is a report on my visit to my uncle. It's called 'My Canadian Uncle', and it's mostly soliloquies from what he was saying. [*This was eventually published in 2000, with 'A Country for Old Men'.*] Also one called 'The Divorce', which is based on a divorce. The poems themselves now are beginning to become like novels. I don't know whether I can do that. I don't even know whether they work or not, because I haven't shown them to anyone yet. They're just lying about there.

IM   That's very interesting, because you haven't very often up till now written many long poems, despite the fact that so much has been said in praise of 'Deer on the High Hills' [*1962*], for example. You seem to accept that that's your best poem, and I don't know whether you really think that or whether it's what we've all so often told you. (L)

ICS No, I always thought that that was my best poem, mainly because I don't understand it. (L) This is true. I've always thought this was an unusual poem for me to have written, like MacLean with *Hallaig*, and I think it really is my best ever. Certainly on a long scale I think it is.

IM   There is also 'The White Air of March' [*1969*].

ICS I like that one as well.

IM   In 'The White Air of March' it's almost a question of building, as Eliot did, out of shorter things. There's something very finished and chiselled about 'Deer on the High Hills'. 'The White Air of March' is more a collection –

ICS Yes, it's less unitary in a poetic way.

IM   And it has this wonderful comic quality. In some ways it appals me to think that somebody will be reading or listening to this maybe in a hundred years' time, and think they know you because they have read *Consider the Lilies* and 'Deer on the High Hills'. Because to me if you just read these you wouldn't encompass Crichton Smith: you also have to read something funny.

ICS I find it very hard to write funny things. It's much, much harder than writing serious things. I've certainly done it, and it's a part of my personality. A lot of people before they meet me think I am going to be very serious, and I think they're quite surprised to find I'm not all that serious. Though I'm fundamentally serious about certain things, I can still make fun of them. Even of poetry.

IM   And of yourself. There's a sense in which all the way through 'Murdo' you are making fun of yourself, because he's closely related to you, and he comes out with the same kind of anarchic humour as you come out with yourself.

ICS I wrote it just because it appeared in my mind, but at the same time, thinking about it afterwards, and the kind of person he is, and the kind of environment he came from. If you try to convert people from the kind of religious environment I came from, you can't make

anything of it. So you have to try and do it by making them funny.
The best way of dealing with people like Paisley would be to make
them figures of fun, rather than rebutting their arguments step by
step. I think that something like that was at the back of my mind
when I was doing 'Murdo'.

IM Because again, 'this is the land God gave to Andy Stewart' . . . It's so
funny.

ICS Yes, yes.

IM What did you feel about it, Bob, when you first had it to read? Did it
immediately strike you as being something special?

BT Yes, this question arises because Iain sent the poem to *Scottish
International* while I was editing it, and I was just absolutely
delighted to get it, and certainly humour was one of the things that
first struck me about it. Then the underlying seriousness of purpose
and tone. The humour was a humour of indignation and exasperation, and that quickly came across to me, and I think also came across
in the same way to Eddie Morgan and Robert Garioch [*the other
literary editors of the magazine*]. Robert Garioch in particular
thought it very funny, and also very painful. This was a poet
who was saying, God, this bloody country really is impossible
any which way you look at it, and he thought it was one of the
best achievements of exasperation and indignation in poetry that he
had come across, and I certainly agreed with that. [*'The White Air of
March' was first published in Scottish International 7, September 1969,
pp 28–34.*]

ICS This was at the back of it. When I was at school in Stornoway I used
to go down to the library reading-room every dinnertime, and this
reading-room had these things like *The Illustrated London News* and
The Tatler – they used to be covered in leather. I used to read these,
and I used to see pictures of skeleton-faced aristocrats like Alec
Douglas-Home, standing together, and it said 'a shared joke'. I
thought this was hilarious, because I couldn't imagine any of them
coming out with what would even appear to be a joke. They looked
half-dead, and the contrast between their half-deadness or their
almost-deadness and the idea that they were joking seemed to me
absolutely hilarious. And this came back to me when I was writing,
because things do come back to you from long periods, things you
think you had forgotten about. I thought years afterwards, how
utterly ridiculous it was that I, a small peasant boy of 11 from this

wee village of Bayble, should be sitting in that library reading things from *The Tatler*. I mean people carrying bundles of pheasants and foxes' skins. It was such a ridiculous notion. (L)

BT   If your writing was all about that sense of the absurd and the ridiculous, there would be quite a lot of it, wouldn't there?

But yesterday you seemed to be implying that in recent years you've become more and more concerned with ordinary people without the recourse to art to deal with things. And that you want almost to dispense with art. Which leaves us wondering, well, what does the artist contribute which is of any great value? If the point of the exercise is to do away with it at the end of the day, what was the exercise about? (L)

ICS Art itself is a compulsion for the artist. He cannot do other than do what he is doing, but I think also that it's limited. I place art along with the other things that people believe in as a method of controlling randomness. I remember when I was over in Yugoslavia just before I became ill. I didn't realise at the time what was happening to me in Yugoslavia, but I was definitely on my way towards this illness. I remember I didn't have any books or newspapers or anything. What happened was I did have various magazines when we arrived, and it was the time of the Falklands crisis, and people were saying, could we have a look at these to find out what's going on at home, so I just gave them all away. I was a fortnight in Yugoslavia, in a country whose language I did not know, without any books. And it suddenly struck me – and I think maybe it was part of my breakdown – the actual meagreness of the world, and this was the word that I kept coming back to. I remember this woman, the psychiatrist at the hospital, asking me various questions, and I kept saying to her, but don't you realise that the world is really meagre? I don't think she understood what I was saying, but it was as if without these things to hide under in a way the world was meagre. That's why I keep coming back to the idea of the unprotected and the ordinary. The greatest thing of all would be to operate in the meagreness of the world without protection. (L)

BT   To be reconciled to it?

ICS Yes.

BT   The artist transfigures?

ICS Yes, without actually making an order. I haven't actually thought it through, but what I mean is that you don't have to order it in an artistic way, and yet you still survive in person-to-person relationships without having to be driven to the desk to create new persons, ideal persons, and ideal things, which is what the artist is really doing. In effect he is saying, this world is not enough for me, so I have to create another world to take its place. And yet ordinary people appear to live in this world without having to create alternative worlds. This is a mystery that puzzles me: I find it a mystery, anyway. (L)

BT   The artist, then, by your definition, is someone who is unusually aware of human vulnerability and disappointment, his art a way of both acknowledging vulnerability and coping with it.

ICS   It both copes with it and in the process reconciles it, and also tries to take the randomness out of it. Because you couldn't have a random art; it would be a contradiction in terms. But you could presumably have a random universe. So he creates a plot; this is the important thing. He creates this plot which takes the randomness out of things, and also puts into the plot people who are either more intense than the people one normally meets, or he sees them as more intense, or better or worse, at least more intense. This is the experience he creates, actually more intense than the experience that we often live through in the real world. Therefore he gives the world a kind of meaning. If he is a great artist this meaning will become more and more important for a greater number of people. If he is a minor artist it will only be important for a certain number of people.

BT   In your work, if anything, you become more and more interested in the fragility of the protection which anyone can make, artist or non-artist. Would that be fair?

ICS   Yes, that's fair enough, and this is why the image that keeps coming up throughout my work is this image of the vase, which is the fragile thing. It's vulnerable: it can be broken. It's a beautiful thing but it's also very fragile, like the beautiful wrist watch in one of my poems about Dante. The image of this very fragile wrist watch which is very easily broken: the more complex something is, the more easily broken it is ['*What's Your Success?*', *in From Bourgeois Land, 1965*].

BT   Can we now talk about a word which has cropped up quite a lot, the term self-deception. You've been exploring, could people possibly live without any kind of self-deception at all, and somehow get the satisfactions in relationship with each other, but without the self-deception. This has driven you to explore the self-sufficient person, the hermit. And of course the paradox here is that the very thing which the self-sufficient non-artist person has to have is some kind of solitariness which cuts them off from what you would like to think is possible for ordinary people. *They* have normal relationships, and they get on with things and do things.

ICS The paradox is that the novelist who is trying to express truths about humanity is by his very craft being cut off from humanity. A basic example of that is Proust, who sits in a cork-lined room designed to shut out any noise at all of the world which he is describing. (L)

But this business about self-deception. When I was in the hospital, one of the things that I thought was that I was living in a kind of theatre. I thought I was living in a theatre and everybody was acting a part. They were all trying to deceive me about their real motives. How did I react to this? To keep this system consistent, my mind would obviously have to look for theatrical images or somebody talking about the theatre. Now people in hospital talk about a hospital theatre, an operating theatre. Also, there was this chap who came in when I was in this bed. They pulled the curtains round, and when he was going out, when he was pushing the curtain aside to get out, he said, this reminds me of the time I used to act in amateur plays. And a sister said to a nurse, I could make a scene if I wanted to.

Now the point I'm trying to make is that there is something in the human mind that if it has got an obsession, even an artistic obsession, it will look for things which will confirm the obsession, no matter how stupid or unreal or absolutely ridiculous the obsession may be. When my mind was at its craziest it was also at its most rigid. Madness is not, as some people believe, a destruction of logic: it's a strengthening of an absurd logic. When you look at a really mad person he walks like a machine. Some of these mad people walked as if they were just wound-up machines. A lot of ideologies that you create are probably of that kind in the way they are created. Their content may be more sustainable but the way they are created is that you look for things. The universe is immense, so no single ideology could possibly explain it. Every ideology is therefore only a small clearing in the darkness, and I suppose what everybody is trying to do is to find in the world around them things that will confirm. I was trying to find a shelter in my madness in order to prove that what was happening around me was what I thought was happening around me.

BT And don't you think that most people do indeed require some kind of shelter, and that they will fight very hard if somebody tries to disturb that shelter?

ICS The difference with the artist is that he tries to make that structure more coherent and more conscious, and ordinary people live by fragments of half-beliefs that they've inherited. But they don't actually set out to make a coherent strategy, and this is what the artist does. It may be that what happens with writers when they become less good than they used to be is that they start echoing themselves in a second-hand way, and they are cutting themselves off from the mercilessness and the randomness of life.

BT Which ordinary people by implication suffer more of. But another paradox: if the artist is any good, he's aware of the fragility of the shelters and the likelihood of self-deception. Isn't he also going to be sceptical, more vulnerable to knowing how far short of protection this is? He might be aware of the ultimate paradox of the hermit or the solipsist, that here was somebody who doesn't want any truck with nonsense and fripperies, including the fripperies of art. He might divest himself of ordinary commerce with other human beings, things like religion, beliefs, families, all the sort of things that people get bound up in. He winds up in a very self-conscious state of trying to protect himself artificially.

ICS The more I see self-deception in myself and in others, the more I think how complicated the mind is and how easy it is for us to see others. You get lots of artists who have been poor in their youth, and anarchic in their youth; and they become rich, and somehow they justify to themselves a conservative view of the world. And a lot of them maybe don't realise they are deceiving themselves. Maybe they think that the arguments they are putting forward for a conservative view of the world are quite reasonable, and more reasonable than the ones they had in their youth, when they were much younger and less experienced. It may in actual fact be the case that without these self-deceptions the human being couldn't actually survive: that he has to have them, and that a confrontation with what you would call naked truth would be so annihilating that it would simply destroy him as if in a flash of lightning. Anyone who could confront himself and see himself as he really is would probably be annihilated by it, if he could see it truly.

BT This connects to my mind with another point that you have mentioned, and that is the business of people who have power and can exercise power. A curious ambivalence in a number of things you said about some people, characterised quite often by Fortinbras. He comes on to the stage and is obviously very bewildered at the very notion of a man like Hamlet, who had everything on a plate and yet creates such disaster around him. Stands astonished: what the hell was he mucking about at?

The ambivalence is that on the one hand Fortinbras would seem to personify the kind of political animal who you think is always a self-deceiver, and is uncritical of himself. On the other hand, Fortinbras is the guy who comes in and clears up the mess. So how far do you go, in two directions? In one direction, where do you want people to stop simply being vulnerable to themselves so that they are shattered by the sense of the meagreness of the world, its absurdity, its lack of meaning? It wouldn't appear to me from your work that you want people to go that far. And in the other direction, to what extent are you prepared to allow people to invent meanings and invest things with meanings and cling to this, simply because the alternative is a mess or a disaster?

ICS Yes, this is a real problem for me. This is why I have been so obsessed with Hamlet throughout everything I have ever done. If Hamlet had carried out a command that he had been given according to an orthodoxy which he had inherited, the lives of six or seven people would have been saved. And his kingdom would have been saved. People of his kind are not made for power, and the artist is not made for power. Maybe there have been one or two exceptions. I suppose the thing that I find incomprehensible about Goethe is that he could have exercised power in the way he did. And this is why, although I don't know German, I find it hard to believe that in some sense he's a major artist. I don't think he was vulnerable enough. There was some kind of self-satisfaction about him, somewhere.

To get back to Hamlet. I think though Horatio said what a great king Hamlet would have been, in actual fact he wouldn't have been. It was impossible. In the end it must mean that the artist cannot exercise power because he tends to be like Hamlet, someone who examines his own motives.

Laurence Graham's review of Iain Crichton Smith's first volume of poetry, *The Long River*, reprinted from *Lines Review* 10, 1955, p 35:

Away back in 1947, I remember reading a poem in the now defunct *Scots Review* – a poem which has stayed in my memory ever since. It was called 'Elegy'* and its author was Iain Smith** – a name then unknown to me. What struck me most about the poem was the ease and mastery of its style and the quiet passion which underlined the whole thing. I was astonished to find out later that the author was still an undergraduate.

Reading his first published collection of poetry, *The Long River*, I am still astonished at this young poet's maturity. It is a difficult poetry to assess, not because it is obscure, though there are moments of obscurity, but because he is tackling themes in his verse which almost defy the net of words, and which can only be caught momentarily as it were, in the language of myth and parable. A tremendous task for any poet; for, to use his own words, what can he be but

> A blind man hunting a key
> On a night of terror and storm?
> ['*Calling the Roll*']

His poems are really meditations, milestones marking a pilgrimage of the spirit. He seems to possess what he so admirably describes in his poem addressed to Hugh MacDiarmid, 'That masterful persistence of the spirit/ that wears like a long river through the stone'. That he chose the title of his book from this same passage shows that he senses his kinship with MacDiarmid in this particular respect. ['*Meditation Addressed to Hugh MacDiarmid*']

Iain Crichton Smith is a Lewisman, and it is only natural that his native background should colour much of his writing. Perhaps 'colour' is hardly the right word to use when we recollect the stark, bare, almost bleak landscapes much of his imagery evokes for us. Take these typical examples:

About us the horizon bends/its orphan images, and winds/ howl from the vacant north . . . ['*Dedicated Spirits*']

'. . . the toothed rocks rising/sharp and grey out of the
ancient sea . . .' ['*Some Days were Running Legs*']
'. . . the sea heaves/in visionless anger over the cramped
graves.' ['*Poem of Lewis*']

There are many others.

One feels, behind all this, a vague resentment against the defeated
blackness of the life he had sprung from – a hatred almost of his
heritage. He laments in 'Poem of Lewis' that 'Here they have no time
for the fine graces of poetry'. It is only in a *Tir-nan-og* of his
imagining that he finds a country akin to his Heart's Desire:

> It was a land made to be written on
> With words carved out of the shining sky.
> Everything new and clear and scrubbed by sun;
> The old had long ago rocked purely by
> Into oblivion. There was nothing to be done
> But let your shadow in the water lie.
>
> ['*It Was A Country*']

Perhaps he will some day discover the more positive virtues of
his islands and his people, and with that discovery will come the
one vital thing still lacking in his verse, warmth and humanity.
Meanwhile, we can only give thanks that here is a young Scottish
poet from the furthest reaches of Gaeldom completely master of his
medium, writing in English and doing it supremely well.

---

* 'Elegy'. This poem is now very hard to access, and the poet chose not to
reproduce it in his mature collections. It is not included in Grant F
Wilson's excellent *Bibliography of Iain Crichton Smith* (1990), and it may be
of interest to peruse it here, with reference to Laurence Graham's
prophetic comments, and because it constitutes an early treatment of what
were to be basic themes. It was published in *The New Alliance and Scots
Review*, vol. 8, No. 3 (June, 1947) p. 41, part of a feature on 'New Poems':

ELEGY
I have come home to an unheroic people,
To the pasteboard mountains and artistic sunsets,
Tremulous horizons and the bewildered traces

Of a lost endeavour.
Faces shadowed with grief,
The stoic, the unheroic,
And the fatalistic duel with life,
(Though there have never been here the thrust and the parry
In a silver immaculate dawn,
And the pinch of snuff after the killing).
There is little meaning in it, O my people,
You who have hunted the deer in the usual recesses,
Tugged at your creels on the violent sea-shore,
Storing the bitter seaweed for your angry land,
Despairingly fought with the ancestral cutlass,
Thought never of counting your losses.
Sang of your darling's argosy of hair
In the old conventional lyric:
Moralised on the skull, the death and the funeral,
Carved never the monumental phrase,
The quick stab at the heart of the problem
But sang the sad songs in the mist of the twilight
And the smoke of your campfires.

Summer comes furtively here
Like a guest unsure of his welcome
(Not like a song from an opera
Or a flower trapped in a flame).
But securing the requisite footholds
On the drab, ungenerous land,
And the rock where the seagull is harried,
Cautiously, uncertainly,
Summer comes never assertively
To this land of corn and of fishermen,
Dedicated to the sea
And the subtle goddess of the sail.
Heart of my heart, thou daffodil
That grows swiftly in my breast,
Locked in no chaste garden,
Unhardened by the frost.
Blossom of my repose,
Blow the gospel to my people,

Show them in the innocent ripple
Of the white swan on the lake,
There is no grace in their living,
In the grieving dawn, awake.

The cock crows in the afternoon,
Dry and sexless winds arise,
The old fences are broken
And cut my delicate eyes.
Time your antiquated watches
On the white and skeleton beaches,
Sing a sonnet to the sea,
Catch a facet of the riddle,
Caress it on your dripping saddle,
Bondman drooping on your steed,
Fling your bonnet and applaud
Your voluntary slavery,
But I shall mourn you in the morning,
Your linen body and your head
That whispers in the wind.
I shall weep for you, my people,
I shall lament your arid land.

                                    Iain Smith**

**Iain Smith. The poet signed himself Iain Crichton Smith from
January 1948. Donalda Crichton Smith notes that 'Crichton' was the
middle name of Iain's younger brother Kenneth. On his mother's side
of the family the name Crichton goes back to 1838, when John
Campbell married Margaret Crichton in Knock and settled in Garra-
bost.

[I sent Laurence Graham the interview to read, and to comment on if he
wished. The following is an extract from his letter of reply, in December
2000.]

One event which did cheer me up immeasurably was the arrival of
your letter and manuscript regarding Iain Crichton Smith. It did
more for my rather battered ego than all the antibiotics and
dubious drugs doled out to me over my long-delayed recovery.

Your typed interview with Iain was fascinating to read – the most revealing of any interview I've come across so far.

Looking back now over the original review, I think I was a bit hard on Iain. Unlike me, coming from the more or less pagan environment of Shetland, he came from an island community where a remorselessly bleak repressive religion ruled. It must have been torture to a sensitive young lad, a torture only made worse by the daily guilt he must have felt for his widowed mother left alone and craving always for his love, care and affection. The bare windswept island, the angry seas, the people who 'have no time for the fine graces of poetry', and the harsh unforgiving creed which hung over all this – these are the recurring images which haunt his poetry. Even in his later work, in 'A Life' [*1986*] for example, the old image still recurs:

'The island is the anvil where was made the puritanical heart'

But he does celebrate too, 'warmth and humanity' in many of his poems, for example in 'The "Ordinary" People' [*1984*], and supremely in 'The Human Face' [*1997*], that eloquent, passionate tribute to the great humanity of Burns. I'm very happy that perhaps my few words away back in 1955 made some contribution towards the development of that more positive note, realised so magnificently in his later work.

Books and poems mentioned in the interviews

All the poems without volume titles are to be found in the *Collected Poems* published by Carcanet in 1992. Fuller details of work by ICS to 1990 are available in a meticulously researched volume edited by Grant F Wilson, *A Bibliography of Iain Crichton Smith*, 1990.

'Elegy', 1947, *The New Alliance and Scots Review*, June 1947
The Long River, 1955
'Statement by a Responsible Spinster', 1959
'Deer on the High Hills', 1962
'Abraham is Isaac', 1963, *An Dubh is an Gorm* [*The Black and the Blue*]
'Two Girls Singing', 1965
A' Chuirt [*The Trial*], 1966

The Golden Lyric: An Essay on the Poetry of Hugh MacDiarmid, 1967
Consider the Lilies, 1968
'She Teaches *Lear*', 1968
'The White Air of March', 1969
'What's Your Success?', 1969
From Bourgeois Land, 1969
The Last Summer, 1969
My Last Duchess, 1971
The Black and the Red and other stories, 1973
Goodbye, Mr Dixon, 1974
The Notebooks of Robinson Crusoe and other poems, 1975
An t-Aonaran [The Hermit], 1976
The Hermit and other stories, 1977
Murdo, and other stories, 1981
A Field Full of Folk, 1982
The Search, 1983
'The "Ordinary" People', 1984
The Tenement, 1985
A Life, 1986
In the Middle of the Wood, 1987
The Human Face, 1997
A Country for Old Men and My Canadian Uncle, 2000

[ICS also published a volume of essays, *Towards the Human* (1986), which is invaluable as a guide to his ideas and attitudes.]

ALAN SPENCE

THE INTERVIEW WITH Alan Spence was conducted in two widely separated sessions, when Alan and I managed to find time to prepare and record them. His Aberdeen University job is concentrated into intensive periods of work, when he teaches Creative Writing classes, sees individual clients, organises visiting writers, and co-ordinates the planning of the biennial Word Festival. Between times, he lives in Edinburgh, where he and his wife Janani run the Sri Chinmoy Meditation Centre, and both spend parts of the year preceding or accompanying Sri Chinmoy to concerts, talks and conferences in all parts of the world, particularly New York and Japan. My obstacles to clearing time when Alan is around are more mundane: it is always term time, when students, seminars, supervisions, preparation and marking tend to interfere with sustained research. Both were recorded in my room in the Old Brewery at King's College in the University of Aberdeen, where Alan has spent part of the year as Writer in Residence since 1995. He was made Professor in Creative Writing in 2001.

Alan was an excellent interviewee, unselfconscious, interested in the process, intent on truth or accuracy, whichever seemed in context more important, and always willing to mock himself or his choice of language.

The list of Alan's publications at the end of the interview indicates the range and variety of his work. As a Writer in Residence in many parts of Scotland, he has done much to assist and inspire younger writers. This is especially true in the University of Aberdeen, where he has also been Artistic Director of Word 1999 and Word 2001, and is engaged in planning Word 2003. His widespread popularity among other writers, in a small country where rivalries can sour relations between writers, has been a major factor in attracting galaxies of talent to these events.

The first session, then, was on 29 March 1999, with just the two of us present.

Part one. 29 March 1999. Present: Alan Spence and Isobel Murray

IM   I want to start by encouraging Alan to talk a bit about his childhood and perhaps today about his mother, because she hasn't tended to figure anything like as much as his father in what Alan has written. Is that true?

AS   Maybe less so than my father, because my mother died when I was fairly young, I was eleven. So she's there very much as an absence in the stories, I think. Liz Lochhead saw my play *Sailmaker* and said it was a very powerful feminist play although there wasn't a female character in it. It was strong because of that, and it showed the lives of these men turned in one themselves without the female influence, and that was what was seriously lacking in their lives. In my earliest memories of my mother, I remember her as a very gentle woman. She worked in the local bakery, Peacock's Bakery, near Ibrox, which was not far from where we lived. She was a packer and then a checker on the assembly line. But she had perks like bringing home pies and cakes for lunch and for the evening meals, which she regularly did. I can't remember at what stage she had to give up the work. She'd always been a bit weak: she'd had problems with her chest – asthma and bronchitis, which she traced back to having her tonsils out when she was quite young. Whatever that did to her immune system made her very susceptible to infections of one sort or another.

    So she was never healthy; she was never a strong woman. In my memory she was always wheezing and having to take a lot of rest.

IM   I think you told me earlier on that she'd also lost two babies before you, so she may have been a bit healthier to start with, before you ever met her.

AS   That's right. My father never talked about the circumstances: they weren't stillborn but they died very soon after birth, maybe a matter of weeks after being born, both of them. And I suppose they were very anxious to have family, so I was welcomed with open arms when I did arrive. I think partly because of that I was treasured and generally looked after well and doted over.

    I think my mother was quite talented in her own kind of way. She could draw very well – I remember her doing wee doodles for me. You know when you're a kid and you're trying to draw something you always go the parents and say, draw it for me, draw me a tree, Mammy, or a tractor, a Centurion tank, Mammy. (L) And she would do it, she would draw space guns for me and she had a talent for that which had never been developed. Like my father she had left school at fourteen and never had any further education beyond that.

IM Was there an extended family?

AS Not really. My father had a number of brothers. My mother was the seventh daughter in her family – in fact she was the seventh daughter of a seventh daughter – in occult terms supposed to be very significant. We would go and visit aunts and uncles on a fairly regular basis. We lived in this room and kitchen in Govan, so huge gatherings were out of the question. We'd occasionally get one or other of my mother's sisters dropping in. My father's side of the family didn't tend to socialise so much: there were probably ongoing family feuds dating back to before I was born. (L) Relations would pop round at New Year, birthdays, that kind of thing. But never much sense of a close extended family. All of my grandparents had died before I was born. They all died fairly young: longevity doesn't run in my family at all. (L) Apart from my mother's father, who lived into his eighties. He worked in the Dixon's Blazes and had worked on the railways before that – some kind of engineering. I always remember he was a cantankerous old character – my mother said he would regularly throw his dinner against the wall if things weren't to his liking. He ruled the house very much in the Victorian patriarchal tradition, but I remember him as quite a nice, quiet old man, sitting in the corner, smoking his pipe. (L) And I remember him being quite desolate when my mother died, that his youngest daughter had died before him – in fact I think one of his granddaughters died before him. He seemed to ponder deeply on these matters.

IM Was he a religious old man?

AS I don't think so, no; I didn't have any sense of that at all And neither of my parents were, particularly. My father as a young man had been involved in the Boys' Brigade. He'd been an officer in that, and continued well into his twenties. So that was a very strong Church of Scotland connection. But at some stage in his life he had drifted away from that. I don't know if he had a falling-out with the church or if the interest just waned. By the time I knew him he wasn't particularly interested in any of that. Nor was my mother. They were happy enough for me to go along to the wee local Mission Hall and go to the Life Boys and the Boys' Brigade.

IM Were you happy enough?

AS   I was indeed, except that by the time I got to the Boys' Brigade, which was when I was twelve, it all seemed a bit too serious for me, these attempts to instil decent Christian values into us – Christian manhood, that was the expression. (L) You have to swear an oath of allegiance when you enter the Boys' Brigade, and I'm sure there was a line about Christian manhood. And I stuck that about six weeks, I think, then faded out.

IM   That was the end of your first religious phase. (L)

AS   Indeed it was.

IM   What about politics? Were your parents at all involved in that?

AS   Not actively or in any obvious way. Certainly when I was younger, my father was that strange phenomenon, a working-class Tory. That was partly the Protestant background: we lived within spitting distance of Ibrox. And I think it was just assumed that all those values went together, Queen and Country, the church, Rangers, the Tory party, and it was only later in his life, after a couple of spells of unemployment, that he began to question that allegiance. He was regularly voting Labour towards the end of his life. My mother I never remember voicing any strong political opinions. She was very much against the whole Protestant ethos. My father was never heavily committed to things like the Orange Order, though he took me along to watch Rangers play, and had that kind of emotional involvement with the Protestant cause. He never went as far as actually joining anything, but two or three of his brothers did, and wanted me to join the juvenile Orange Lodge, and learn to march in a band, and all of that. I was quite keen, because this was exciting, this was vibrant, this was alive. Strutting my stuff along the streets of Govan would have been great fun, but my mother very firmly put her foot down against all that. I think I put the kind of words she said in the mouth of one of the characters in a story, that it was all nonsense and turning people against each other. 'I'm not having you go along to the likes of that'. [*See eg Brian's mother in the first chapter of The Magic Flute, pp 5–6.*]

IM   It's the sectarian aspect of it: she wasn't opposing the music. Was there an actual music, like that central thing in *The Magic Flute*, where all the boys at the beginning are attracted to the idea of playing some music? But only one of them eventually becomes a Mason and all that?

AS   Music was always a very strong background there. The radio was always on. I remember hearing things like Scottish country dance music on a Monday evening. I just suddenly made a connection there; when you were asking about the extended family. Regularly on a Monday evening these friends of the family would come to visit and they'd a boy about my age and we played together. And I knew if they weren't coming there'd be Scottish country dance music on the radio, and I'd know they weren't going to turn up. So ever since Scottish country dance music gives me a nasty feeling in the pit of my stomach, because it means, Gordon's not coming to play. (L)

IM So did you learn to play any music?

AS That came a wee bit later. But to go back to the radio, lots of children's songs I can sing along to to this day. But we must also have listened to Radio Luxembourg. I remember listening to dramatic serials on Radio Luxembourg, mainly Dan Dare, which was tremendously exciting and scary, lost on this alien planet, and there was a character called Whittaker, who'd become a baddie in the course of an episode. Having thought he was on our side he suddenly changed over and was possessed by the aliens – that was wonderful. So we must have been listening to Radio Luxembourg and must have been listening to the popular music of the time, which in the early fifties was pre-Rock'n'Roll.

When I went to secondary school I'd passed a bursary exam to get into Allan Glen's, which was a big deal, coming from the wee local Broomloan Road Primary School. I think I was thirty-eighth on the bursary list out of fifty who passed. I wrote about this in *The Magic Flute*. I think I did very badly in the Arithmetic paper: there were too many tricks and things I didn't know about. And I came home absolutely convinced I had failed, and was resigned to going to the local secondary school. But I must have done inordinately well in the English paper, so that over all I managed to scrape through.

IM I take it your parents were particularly keen that you should get on?

AS They were thrilled. By the time I actually sat the exam and passed it, my mother had died, but she'd known that I was trying for it, and ma feyther was proud as Punch. But one of the things that I did at this new school was start learning the flute. There was a school orchestra, and a lovely old man called Mr Dickson came round once a week to teach flute and oboe. I didn't work at it as hard as I should have: in retrospect I wish I had. At the end of the school day I just wanted to be out playing football with my friends. I didn't realise how much I wanted to play this music till later on. So I let it slide when I first started learning, which would be about second year at school, and I picked it up a wee bit later and actually managed to get into the orchestra, but I wasn't as good as the previous flautist had been – I was expected to be up at the same standard and wasn't. Rehearsals became a nightmare for me. I think I dramatised that in *The Magic Flute*, the sense of being completely lost in the score and not knowing where you were supposed to come in, what you were supposed to be doing. The mathematics of the music never appealed to me, and I never quite got the hang of fluent sight-reading. I was quite good at picking up tunes by ear, and I could play with a certain amount of feeling. But eventually these oppressive rehearsals got a bit too much for me, and I gave up altogether. And I didn't pick up the flute again until I was probably in my late twenties and felt inspired to learn again, and play some music, and I still play it to this day. Again, not brilliantly but well enough to keep myself happy.

IM   What about school apart from music?

AS   Primary school I think on the whole I enjoyed. I had a lot of pals, wee guys from the neighbourhood – this was Broomloan Road Primary School in Govan – and some very nice teachers who clearly saw that I was a bright wee bugger and could be encouraged. Especially I was good at composition. From Day One I wanted to be writing stories, and they nurtured that in me. I was also quite good at drawing, which probably I'd got from my mother. I would draw slightly unusual things: they would tell us to draw a figure composition and I would make it a building site with men digging in the foreground, and bulldozers in the background. And if I was drawing a war thing there would be a lot of detail, the barbed wire and the jagged trees and all of that. (L) So I was quite good at visualising a landscape in its entirety and rendering it on to the page.

There were two teachers in particular that I recall who encouraged me. One was a Miss Brown, who I think in her own way must have been quite militant. I remember the day after it was announced that Eden had bombed Suez, she came in in a fine rage, absolutely ranting and banging the desk – what right have we to do this kind of thing? We just sat there, hands on laps as you did, (L) and then she calmed down and got on with the Arithmetic lesson. It was she who first put the idea in my head of applying to sit this bursary to get me to Allan Glen's, probably a couple of years before I actually did it.

There was another teacher called Miss Daniels whose class I was in at the time I was ready to sit the exam, and she again encouraged me, made sure I got all the application forms in and gave me a wee book as a present when I passed the exam – *Moby Dick*, if I remember (L). Which I don't think I read immediately – maybe a few years later. But the intention was right, to ply me with great literature.

IM So, Alan goes to Allan Glen's. How does he react to all of that?

AS Now that was a different thing altogether. The primary school – it was big classes: there were forty, fifty of us in a class, and it must have been a nightmare for teachers to keep any kind of control. And of course they did it in an authoritarian way, strapping everything that stepped out of line. In the senior secondary school there were a lot of boys like me who'd passed the scholarship and were there on this bursary award, but there were a lot of boys who just went there because they could pay the fees – boys from a much more middle-class background than anything I'd ever encountered.

Again I made good friends. I made a very good friend on Day One. I ended up sitting beside this guy called Ronnie Weaver, and he was from a similar kind of background to me, and we just hit it off and were pals right through school and beyond. I settled very quickly into the things that I was good at – I was 'good' at English, and 'good' at Latin and 'good' at Art, and I could get by in the other subjects. I would have wee spells of inspiration when I did very well in the science subjects, Chemistry and Physics. I was never any more than just competent at Maths – I was never very comfortable with it. But the regime I found quite oppressive. The teachers wore traditional black, dusty gowns and set out to impose their will on us very early, and it was quite obvious a lot of them were just selecting someone to belt in the first couple of weeks, just to establish that that was the rule of law. Again, anyone that's ever crossed me is likely to have found themselves in *The Magic Flute* or one of the stories –

IM I was already going to ask you whether Ronnie survived recognisably at all into *The Magic Flute*, if he was a friend from Day One? Is he anywhere near any of the characters in *The Magic Flute*?

AS Probably not so much in *The Magic Flute* – There's a character is some of the short stories who's very much based on Ronnie, I think. I call him Doug, I think. There's one particular story called 'I'll be Han-Shan, You be Shih-Te' [*Stone Garden, pp 130–47*] about the two of us when we were about eighteen going off and camping at Loch Lomond. There are elements of Ronnie in some of the other characters in the adolescent stories, but not so much in *The Magic Flute*.

The corporal punishment thing; being belted for trivial things. I managed to escape this particular purge, but a music teacher had us trying to sight-read. Not proper sight-reading, but just in sol-fa – reading a line of music as doh, re, fah – and some poor sod said fa instead of fa-ah, and was dragged out and belted, and that was the way he went round the whole class – he must have belted about ten people. This was instilling in us a love of music! (L) There was a Latin teacher who was a bit like that, and a Physics teacher. This was just how they'd been brought up to impose their will on twenty or thirty boys and keep them in line.

IM   Did they impose their way of speaking as well?

AS   Yes indeed, but that had been there even in primary school – you were corrected if you used non-standard register in the classroom, which I suppose made for an interesting tension, because as soon as you were out the door, you would be right into that. In many ways a much richer way of expressing yourself, full expletives, the lot! (L). There was very much a language of the playground and a language of the classroom, but a lot of the more middle-class boys I was meeting at the secondary school I suppose had a different register anyway: they spoke more the standard way at home.

IM   And did you find you were less likely to make friends with them, or did voices and manners not make any difference when it came to making friends?

AS   Didn't seem to at all. I think the friends I made were from all sorts of different backgrounds. Football was always a great leveller. Rugby was the official preferred game at school, there wasn't a football team – it was rugby and cricket. I tried rugby. I went to one rugby session and that was enough. I could run fast, but not fast enough (L) to avoid these great hulking lads that wanted to smash me to the ground. I wrenched my knee in a tackle in the first session and that was it – I didn't want to go back. But I did enjoy playing football and was reasonably good at it. A few of us who were like-minded would play in the playground most days at lunchtime and at the end of the day.

IM   And all of this is all-male, isn't it?

AS Entirely. It was an all-boys school.

IM So again, coming from a home with no female influence any more, you were in a virtually all-male environment. Do you think that's a pity?

AS In retrospect, yes. It made me terribly shy in relation to girls. I was very, very insecure, I suppose until my late teens. Even about asking someone out: that whole male thing – it's made fun of a lot now, but it is a genuine dilemma, the terrible fear of rejection, when you're so insecure anyway about everything. To court that total rejection – the embarrassment of it. I think if there had been girls, just in the day-to-day environment in the school, it wouldn't have been such an awe-inspiring prospect, to actually go along and talk to one (L).

IM So it was taken fairly much for granted that you would go on to university or something of the sort?

AS Indeed yes. The school prided itself on preparing people for university. I suppose in retrospect my criticism would be that it was a bit too much of an exam factory. You were expected to pass and do well and there was a certain amount of grinding out results. I said something like that to the audience at a reading I did a number of years ago. I'd read a passage from *Sailmaker*, my play. I could have called it 'A Good Education': it's the character talking about the five or six years of his schooling in not very complimentary terms. Someone asked me about my own schooling and if that passage had reflected it, and I ranted on about the school as an exam factory and oppressive, the most grindingly awful five years of my life, and he came up afterwards and introduced himself as my old Chemistry teacher (L). Oops! But interestingly enough he had moved on from that school, and looking back he felt much the same way about it, and that was partly why he'd left.

The headmaster at the school Mr J B Somerville – he was known to the boys as 'Joe Boss': he was a terrifying prospect. He led the teachers in his black robe and he used to swoop round the school picking on any slightest irregularity in school uniform. If you wore white socks instead of the regulation grey, or a coloured pullover, or if your hair was over the top of your ears. And he wasn't averse to using the belt, if he was in that kind of mood. From about the age of fifteen, when Ronnie Weaver and I were starting to rebel a wee bit, and flex our wings and grow our hair long and listen to the Beatles, we were regularly falling foul of him. I remember Ronnie one day stitched a velvet collar onto his school blazer (L), and went round with his collar up all day in case Joe should come and see it. But we were regularly dragged out of dinner queues and marched into his office and given lines or some other punishment for these irregularities.

IM You mentioned the Beatles. There was a lot happening in the world of music. When do you think was your popular music awakening?

AS I remember listening to Luxembourg at a young age, and after the Rosemary Clooneys of this world, skiffle, rock and roll came in, in the late fifties, so I was listening to things like Lonnie Donegan, 'Rock Island line', that kind of thing –

IM Did you have a skiffle group?

AS No I didn't.

IM Alan! What was wrong with you? (L)

AS I know! Terrible! I should at least have had a tea–chest bass. I think it just never occurred to me. Maybe my friends couldn't afford even the basic guitars and things. But I did like the music, and the early rock and roll. I remember going to see the rock and roll films that were causing riots all over the place, what with slashing seats, and Bill Haley rocking around the clock. My particular favourite of them all was Little Richard. He seemed to have a rawness in him, an authenticity that the others seriously lacked. I used to keep relations entertained by singing things like 'Good golly, Miss Molly', complete with screams (L). I never cultivated the hair style, the curly quiff and slicked back at the sides, but I probably coveted it. I seem to remember when I was about thirteen or fourteen becoming a big fan of the Shadows. I loved that wailing guitar sound – aw, come on, I was a wee boy! (L) (I am responding here to Isobel's look of dismissal and disdain!) I went and sat through innumerable excruciating Cliff Richard films like *The Young Ones* and *Summer Holiday* – all of that just for five minutes of the Shadows playing in the middle. I was a real fan. I suppose nowadays people call these folk anoraks. I would buy things like *Rave* magazine to read about the Shadows and the Beatles, and cut pictures of them out and stick them up on my wall. And there were the girl singers. I remember Susan Maughan was one: Hayley Mills I was a big fan of: Marianne Faithfull, of course, and Jane Asher was a big favourite, although she wasn't a singer. Her face was often in these magazines. The bit of the room I had in Govan suddenly became transformed. With these colourful images on the wall.

IM   The bit of the room? You were sharing the room with your father?

AS   It was still just the room and kitchen, and the kitchen became very much a sitting room – that was where the fire was, and my dad slept in the bed there, and I slept in the other room which I never really thought of as my room, because we still shared it – the only two really comfortable armchairs were in there. So the kitchen was where we sat to eat and we'd maybe sit either side of the fire on slightly beat-up old armchairs but if we were really spreading out and relaxing we would go into the other room which was where my bed was. So I thought of one wall of it as being my bit (L) – that was where I stuck all these pictures, and that was behind the bed.

IM   And when did television happen?

AS   One of my aunties had a television set for the Coronation, which was in 1953, and it was a wee nine-inch set, and half the street were crowded in to her wee front room to watch this (L). We didn't get a television right away. I don't know if my parents couldn't afford it, or didn't think it was worth the effort. And I remember being quite jealous of my pals that had TV. We didn't get a TV until STV were up and running, I think I was eleven or twelve before we had a TV in the house. No – my mother was still alive, so I must have been ten. I was rushing home to see favourite TV programmes – mostly cowboy things, I have to say, the Range Rider, and the Lone Ranger, and Hopalong Cassidy, teatime fodder. So I would gallop home slapping my horse to get me there on time, (L) dismount outside the door and slide into my seat and watch these programmes before tea. I remember being very taken with the adverts. Any television I'd seen before that had just been BBC, but the adverts were great fun, and another source of songs and jingles – some of the ones that went in then are still there to this day – the Murray Mints advert, and Pepsodent – 'You'll wonder where the yellow went, /When you brush your teeth with Pepsodent!' (L)

IM   What did you think about going to university, aside from the fact that the school was a degree factory? Do you think you yourself wanted to go, or did you see it as in any way threatening to your own smaller culture?

AS   I think initially I just didn't question it: I just assumed that this was the next stage, and the school certainly did nothing to discourage that view. We were never given much in the way of advice at school as to what to choose to do at university; the emphasis in the school was on science and engineering subjects. It had been founded by an engineer, Allan Glen, and on average we got more science periods a week than the other schools, to the detriment of things like languages and art, so it was assumed that you would go on and do a science or engineering degree, either at Glasgow or Strathclyde/ I didn't want to do that, but I didn't quite know what else to do, so I ended up choosing Law, and started a Law degree at Glasgow. My father was well chuffed at this – I was going to be a lawyer! That sense of getting on, of getting a good job and getting out of the environment he'd grown up in. I'd not a clue what I was going to do. I was very young for my age – I was eighteen by the time I went to university, because I'd done a sixth year at school, but all that had taught me was how to become lazy and use my free periods to loll around the library (L) reading poetry books. That was actually when I really started writing, but I'll come back to that. In sixth year I became indolent, and started seeing myself as a poet (L). But the Law thing was a big mistake. I just wasn't temperamentally suited to it at all. There seemed to be a massive amount of sheer grinding memory work, which I didn't enjoy at all.

It came to a head in one particular exam, for Scottish Private Law, when there was a compulsory question on specific cases. It gave you maybe five or six famous court cases which had had a bearing on the development of Scottish Law in one way or another, and you had to say what the point at issue was in this case. This question was compulsory, you had to do it, and I didn't recognise any of the six cases. I thought right, I'm going to get zero for this question. And I was going to be pushing it to pass this subject anyway, so what's the point of sitting here trying to answer all the rest of the questions? So I folded up my paper and went to walk out, ten minutes into the exam. I walked from the back of the room, feet clonking on the floor in this big echoing hall, and of course folk see you doing this kind of thing, and stomp their feet and bang on the desk. I got all the way to the front and they turned me back. You have to stay for an hour: otherwise you could go out and give the paper to somebody else. So I'd to walk all the way back to my seat, thump, thump, thump, but I was determined I wasn't going to hand in a paper that they couldn't pass – I didn't see the point. That's the way my mind was working at the time (L). So I sat and doodled and stared into space and scribbled on the blotting paper, and when the bell went for the end of the hour I got up and walked out. I handed in a blank paper and went home. And of course I got nothing for that exam.

And I think that was effectively the end of my interest in completing a law degree. I remember my Adviser of Studies saying, you didn't do too well in the Private Law paper, did you, and I thought that was putting it mildly (L), I got nothing. Unless they'd given me maybe 5% for handing in class work on time. But I then investigated changing – it hadn't occurred to me I could change course, but someone suggested that I could change course. So I switched over to do an Arts course, and I did English and Philosophy instead.

I ended up dropping out of that as well, not so much because I wasn't interested, but the grant situation . . . I'd actually done two years of Law. And in order to finish an MA I was going to have to do two years. So I found myself having done one year of it, realising that I was going to have to find my own fees, and all. And that was coupled with the fact that I was feeling slightly oppressed by the whole business, and this was by now the late sixties and the whole hippy thing was about to take off, so there were other pressures on me. I just decided to take time out, as it were, from the university. I managed to work out the grant situation – I could finish a degree in one year, that's what it was. I couldn't have got funding for two more years, to finish an MA, but if I could squeeze the remaining subjects into one year I was going to be able to do it. I did that maybe four or five years later, after I'd dropped out and gone travelling, and really started taking myself seriously as a writer, because I figured that that was what I actually wanted to do and that was why I hadn't followed up these other career options – I was keeping my time free to create (L) – that was what I told myself.

So that was effectively the end of the university.

IM   Did you meet anyone at university, either as staff or as students, who made a big impact on you?

AS   I can't remember anyone from the Law degree times at all.

IM   I'm not surprised, really: it's not your kind of milieu!

AS   No! (L) When I switched over and did English, my tutor was Philip Hobsbaum. I was to come across him later. I think I must have got on the wrong side of him quite early on – I think he thought of me as just this effete hippy who was rather woolly-minded and vague in his approach to life in general. He did say some encouraging things about some poetry that he had me read at some kind of performance. I had by this stage got involved with one or two other writers who were around at the time – Tom McGrath the poet and playwright was very active at that time – he was about eight or nine years older than me, and had just come back from spending some time in London where he'd been the editor of a magazine called *International Times*, and was very involved in the whole counter-culture, hippy movement there. I had got together with another couple of friends and started a wee duplicated magazine called *Henry* which was publishing our own poetry and wee drawings and cartoons – this was our own version of the underground magazine. And we printed it up on a hand-cranked Roneo duplicator – this was in the days before photocopying was widely available. We painstakingly typed the material onto a waxed stencil which was wrapped round an inked drum and then cranked with this handle.

How I came to meet Tom was I'd heard he was back in town. I went and knocked his door and asked if he would give me something for the magazine. Tom being the generous soul he is not only gave me a piece of writing but he invited me in for lunch, and generally befriended me and encouraged me. And Tom's house became a focus of energy for a lot of us who were just starting out to write – I think that was where I first met Tom Leonard. Alasdair Gray dropped in there for one reason or another – Liz Lochhead was around. Another girl called Jean Milton who was writing a lot at the time, but I haven't seen much of her stuff since. All these folk got involved in my wee magazine and a few of us got together to do readings at the Edinburgh Festival Fringe. That led on to having stories published. It stems from that initial meeting with Tom.

IM   That would be about?

AS   1968.

IM   Ah! That year!

AS   Indeed. And at that time Philip Hobsbaum had his own kind of writers' group going, which included Tom Leonard, Jim Kelman, Liz Lochhead – not a bad wee grouping. But I never was drawn to that. I think the milieu that Tom was creating I found much more amenable. I suppose Philip's groups looked to me from the outside much more like a university tutorial: he would photocopy the material, and they would sit around and analyse it and discuss it, whereas at Tom's people were much more likely to be drunk or stoned or both and just read the stuff. Not that there wasn't criticism: I remember Tom shouting at me that something I had written was absolute crap, and I should tear it up. And Tom Leonard wasn't averse to words of criticism now and again if he thought the work warranted it (L). But it didn't feel like a tutorial. I suppose I got the impression that Philip's group had that orientation, so I was never drawn to it.

IM You mentioned people drunk and stoned: were you in on this culture at the time?

AS Yes indeed, I drank a lot when I came out of school – that was the thing you did. There was a pub called the Wee Hoose, somewhere near Charing Cross, and I remember regularly sitting there till closing time, and then we would roll out looking for a party somewhere to continue the bevvying.

IM Can I point out you were the person that said a couple of minutes ago that you were so hard up, you didn't know how you could manage another year at the university?

AS Aw, it's terrible, isn't it? But those were necessities! (L) The grant didn't go terribly far, I must say, and there was this fiction called parental contribution (L) – sorry, this is just doubling back. Based on what your parents were earning, they were supposed to donate a certain amount to your upkeep. Now my father was earning a pretty basic wage, but there must have been still an element of parental contribution assumed. It was more filial contribution to keep the old man going, bailing him out of one scrape or another that he managed to get himself into. But the pub on the Friday and Saturday night was part of the ritual thing. The drugs came in later. I found it difficult – I didn't smoke: I'd never smoked regular cigarettes. My father was a very heavy smoker, and I think I just took a scunner to it. So I found it difficult to smoke marijuana, but I'd occasionally eat a lump of it, and get mellowed out that way. Or someone would produce some cannabis tincture, which was legal at the time, apparently: you could get it on prescription, but I don't know where he managed to get hold of it. LSD was another matter altogether. Again it was probably 1968 I first sampled that, not knowing what on earth to expect. I'd read an awful lot about it – I read all these underground magazines, and folk like Tom had dabbled in this in London. The first time I tried it was with a friend called James MacKenzie in his flat somewhere in the West

End. And it was an astonishing experience. It was frightening in some ways, but . . . I remember reading this thing in Tom Wolfe's *The New Journalism* which was published in the early seventies, saying that if someone's writing about being drunk, chances are most of your audience will know what that feels like, so it's easy to convey – a few signals and they get the picture. But trying to write about an LSD experience, you've got less of an audience who'd know exactly what you're talking about.

I learned I'd had in fact a very limited sense of what 'I' was, and there was an awful lot more to me, both good and bad, than I had hitherto recognised.

IM   And you didn't have any kind of conscientious worries about drugs at that stage?

AS   No, not at all.

IM   And you weren't even like me, just absolutely terrified what they might do to you? (L)

AS   Surprisingly, no, I must have been either very brave or very foolhardy – a bit of both (L). I just wanted to know what all the fuss was about. And I never did get into it . . . Even after that first time I realised this was something you had to take very, very seriously, and it could easily tip one way or the other and lead to psychosis – and absolute madness! There were moments when I felt mad, I felt completely deranged. I think there's a common fear that you get in these experiences that you're going to get stranded out there and not find your way back to any kind of level, even keel. Even in spite of that I got an extra charge from it, or they were going out dancing and just wanted to . . . found enough exhilaration and some sense of insight into deeper things to make me want to try it again, but I never got to the stage when I was doing it regularly or doing it casually. I remember being shocked, meeting people in London at the time who would just drop some acid before going to the pictures, because they were going to see a horror film and wanted to get an extra buzz.

For me, from Day One, I regarded it as some kind of sacrament, that this was going to help me understand Life, the Universe and Everything. And whatever wee glimpses it afforded me into those areas of being made me want to try it a few more times. I think probably in all I took it five or six times over a two-year period. And then I realised the limitations of it, that this isn't going to do it. Whatever I think I've realised on these trips is not permanent; it's not grounded in any change in me. I'm still working with the same limitations, the same frailties. There's also the danger that you're actually causing damage to your cerebral cortex. So I'd reached the stage of thinking no, I'm not actually going to do this again: it's not leading anywhere. If I'm going to explore these areas of being, and try to discover the answers to these big philosophical questions, who are we, and what are we here for, and does life mean anything really, then there has to be another way of approaching that. And all along I'd been reading things about Eastern philosophy, Buddhism especially, and I'd been particularly drawn to Japanese Buddhism, Zen, and the clarity and simplicity of it. And the moments on these LSD trips that seemed to make some kind of sense sent me back to the clarity and simplicity and directness of Zen. But of course the more you read in these fields the more you realise that there's a discipline involved: it isn't an easy fix – you don't just drop a pill and suddenly everything is wonderful.

IM   It could hardly be more different, could it?

AS   That's right. So initially through reading books I began looking consciously for some kind of way, a path, a discipline that would help me tap those energies and begin to deal with answering those questions. I eventually found this man who was to become my teacher. In December 1970 I'd seen a poster around the university advertising a talk by this Indian teacher called Sri Chinmoy. The poster had a very striking picture of him, very austere-looking, very powerful and austere, not at all effete. This was no wilting hippy – there was a certain power in his face. But I didn't feel threatened by it. I'd been to see other teachers: I'd been to see a man called Rimpoche Chogyam Trungpa, and he was an interesting character: he'd escaped from Tibet, and founded the Samye Ling Tibetan Centre in the Borders, the Buddhist monastery which is thriving to this day. But he was a strange character, in that on the one hand he was espousing the side of spiritual discipline, and on the other hand he seemed to regularly get drunk and womanise with sixteen-year-old girls who came to him for advice. There was a hint of scandal about him anyway. I heard him give a talk at Glasgow University and found that what he had to say was interesting and impressive and intriguing at a cerebral level, but I didn't feel any charge or sense of empathy with him – I didn't think, I want to go and sit at this man's feet and learn how to meditate from him.

IM Do you think at that stage you were actually looking for somebody to sit at the feet of?

AS Without realising it, in retrospect. I thought I was just looking for some kind of guidance, someone who'd done this kind of thing before who could maybe suggest a direction that I could take, but I wasn't consciously looking for a teacher. I've since read some of Rimpoche Chogyam Trungpa's writings and found them quite lucid. He'd a very sharp mind and an ability to draw examples from different cultures – he's quite well read, and he could put things in a very lyrical, very poetic way. I think he was Allen Ginsberg's teacher for some time. He went to the States and was involved in something called the Naropa Institute and was quite influential on a whole lot of writers of that Beat generation in the States. I found him interesting and not much more. So when I saw this poster advertising that Sri Chinmoy was giving a talk, I went along in the same frame of mind, this will be at least interesting, and from what I'd read he was coming from a Hindu tradition, which was different from what I was used to. At the very least I'd get some inspiration from him, and he might be able to suggest some direction I could take. So I went along to hear him talk in the Catholic Chaplaincy at Glasgow University – the second of December 1970 (L), I remember it vividly – and I went along with my then girlfriend Maggie, who is now my wife, and has been since 1972–27 years this year! That is scary!

IM We should also mention at this stage that she has another name, because otherwise people may think you're a bigamist! (L)

AS That's right (L). Her given name was Margaret, and I knew her as Maggie, but at a certain stage in practising this meditation we took on other names which our teacher gave us, and her name is Janani. She came along with me – we'd been going out for a couple of months at the time, and she didn't know anything about meditation or Buddhism, but was just intrigued because I was going along. Tom McGrath was also there: in fact he had helped to promote the talk. The Philosophy Society at the University had approached him as someone who was in touch with other kinds of philosophy, so Tom had helped to distribute posters and leaflets, and he and I had talked about this image on the poster, how powerful and striking it was: the face looked very intriguing in all sorts of ways. So Tom was there with his wife Maureen.

I remember coming into the room with Janani, and we saw the guru Sri Chinmoy standing at the back of the hall, and he was wearing yellow robes, and he seemed to be scanning us, giving a wee half smile to everyone as they came in. My first thought was, God, what amazing presence he had: he just seemed to radiate a tremendous sense of well-being and physical health, apart from anything else: he seemed to glow. He looked very strong; he had a very powerful chest. His bearing was very impressive: he looked very grounded in himself. He came out and bowed to everyone, and he seemed to meditate in silence for a few minutes and then he started his talk. And it wasn't delivered like a discourse: he seemed to be in a meditative state: his eyes were half open and he was speaking very slowly and almost in an incantatory way, and his theme was duty and reward. Divine duty and supreme reward, not exactly a funky title (L). You really had to concentrate to follow what he was saying and follow the flow of his thought through sentence by sentence. Sometimes I would focus on what he was saying, and think, God, that was so accurate and so beautifully put, and while I was thinking that he'd moved on to something else. At other times I would completely lose the sense of what he was saying because I was so absorbed in just watching him. I was fascinated by what he seemed to be giving off. It almost became a radiance that he had. At one point I thought I could see this shimmer of gold light all around him, like an aura, and I immediately started dismissing it, but the image persisted. It's not terribly important in itself, it's an interesting phenomenon, but at least it was further indication that he wasn't just a normal run-of-the-mill guru who'd wandered off the street to give a talk.

This aura of gold light – there were one or two other folk who could see it as well, including the Catholic priest whose chaplaincy we were in, and I think he found it not quite decent that anyone should go round radiating gold light! (L) I also remember Professor Hirst from the Logic Department was there and I heard him at the back of the room saying, 'it's not exactly our kind of philosophy, is it?' (L) And I thought, no, and all the better for it, because I'd done Logic as part of my degree. At the end of his talk Sri Chinmoy said he would answer questions, and he fielded them very nicely, and seemed to take the questions very seriously and answer at great length. Eventually Tom McGrath asked him, how can we find out more about this meditation you're talking about? He said very courteously and sweetly, if anyone's interested, come and see me when the meeting's over. And then he looked at his watch and said, in fact, the meeting's over, so come and see me *now* (L).

And Janani remembers that 'now' as being tremendously resonant. During the questions and answers he must have indicated that there was a certain amount of discipline involved if you were practising his meditation, if you were accepting him as your teacher, as the authority in these matters. He wanted us not to smoke or drink or take drugs. I'd just come to the point where I thought the drugs weren't leading anywhere anyway, so I'd no problems with that. I thought the drinking might be a wee bit difficult socially, but I thought I'd give it a go. I wasn't sure; I was swithering, in spite of having been deeply moved by him, and seeing this gold light about him, and thought he was tremendously wise, there was still that hesitation. I looked at Tom McGrath, and he was having the same response, obviously, will we, won't we. Meanwhile Janani and Tom's wife had just gone straight out of the room after him, no hesitation at all. Whatever they'd seen in him, they wanted it. (L)

IM Was Janani less into drinking than you in the first place?

AS I think so, yes. But I think she'd genuinely seen so much in him . . .

IM Sure. I was just thinking that the male culture in Glasgow made it more of a thought for a man to give up.

AS Absolutely, and that's still the case. The best part of thirty years on I give talks on meditation, I give classes, and often people are getting a lot out of it but they're not willing to make those changes in their lives: the social thing is very set in place. So Tom and I just shrugged and thought, come on, let's give it a go, and I remember going into the room with him very much with a sense of, I'll give this a try. I can give this maybe six months and see how I'm getting on with it: if it's not leading anywhere I'll try something else – I'll keep looking. I suppose in the original lecture theatre there had probably been around a hundred people, and now there were half a dozen of us.

The half dozen of us had decided we wanted to give this a go. And he sat us down in a wee half circle in a wee ante room to the lecture theatre, and he asked us a wee bit about ourselves, what we did and so on. And he gave us some simple meditation instruction – very simple things that you could get in a text book. Told us to keep our backs straight, and just breathe slowly and evenly through the nose. And he wanted us to concentrate on a point in the centre of the chest,

which he was calling the heart-centre, and he told us to close our eyes
and imagine that we were breathing in and out, and to imagine a
flower at that centre in the heart. And he told the men to picture a
rose and the women to picture a lotus. Janani had never seen a lotus,
and she was a wee bit confused, but she thought it was something
like a waterlily, so she imagined a waterlily. (L)

At some point he said, I'll concentrate on each one of you
individually. I didn't know what that meant at all, but I just carried
on trying to go through the motions. We compared notes afterwards,
and everyone felt that we all sensed exactly when he was concentrating on us, and there was a very subtle change; and from being
something that was an effort it was suddenly just happening almost
spontaneously and then very easily. This image of the flower became
very vibrant, and there was a sense of expansiveness and a peace-
fulness, and just a sense of rightness. I thought, so that's meditation,
and how did he do that? (L) Over six feet of space he suddenly
communicated how you meditate. I've since read that that's very
much the way a real teacher does it. This communication of the
teaching is known as darshan, which I translated somewhere as 'the
silent teaching'. It's traditionally how a teacher communicates.
There's an old story about the Buddha giving what became known
as the Flower Sermon. He was in front of a whole gathering of people
and instead of giving a lecture which was what they'd come to hear,
he just held up a single flower. One of his followers, a man called
Maha Kashapa, who was sitting in the front row, responded by
smiling, and he said that in that moment he received everything that
he'd had to offer, and he said it's not communicated in words but in
profound silence. Sri Chinmoy himself has said something similar;
he said if you meet a genuine teacher (implying of course that there
are a lot who are not genuine (L), and that was very much the case in
the late sixties, early seventies), his silent gaze will teach you how to
meditate. So it's actually as simple and direct as that. Whatever he's
attained through his own meditation is an energy that can be
communicated directly, as far as you can be open to it. He's able
to awaken something that's there inside your own heart.

So we came out of this experience looking at each other and
smiling just like Maha Kashapa in the Buddha's story. He was just in
Glasgow for that one day to give the lecture, and he was going back
to London to give a talk there, and then he was heading back, as we

discovered, to New York, where he lived. I didn't see him for more than a year after that, but in the meantime the six of us got together once a week to try and meditate along the lines he'd indicated. A couple of weeks later we got some books in the post from New York, selections of his writings, aphorisms, simple meditation instructions, and we just took it from there. I've been doing it for the best part of thirty years. And the relationship with him is something that's grown and deepened and become very, very strong.

IM Does it matter when you don't see him for a long time?

AS In the long term, no, but at the same time seeing him is a tremendous inspiration: that's how it works. You're seeing someone who absolutely embodies what you're trying to achieve in your own life, and it's such a reassurance and an inspiration that he's still doing it and continues to generate that amazing energy. It's a wee bit like plugging into a source of energy, being around him physically, it's easier to feel the directness of it. But you feel it when you're away from him too. A couple of days ago he was trying to phone us from New York and we were out, and there was a message, but we worked out that at the exact time he was trying to phone us, we were sitting eating a curry in a place in Edinburgh, and Janani had said to me, God, I almost feel as if he was sitting here beside us, and I had suddenly felt an amazing peace: so he still communicates over distance.

IM Is the idea that you and Janani and the others all get to his level, or are you now a teacher, or do you become a teacher at some stage?

AS I do give meditation classes, but the way it seems to work, I'm just an intermediary to bring people: he is the real teacher. We're getting down to matters of belief now, but from my experience of him and what I've read, he seems to me a particularly exalted kind of teacher: he's not just even a run-of-the-mill guru (L). I think there are many teachers around who can help you and teach you to meditate and take you along the path towards what you're seeking, but he seems to me to be operating at a higher level than most people. He was given an Honorary Degree a couple of years ago from a Buddhist university in Sri Lanka. It was the first time the honour had been given to someone not from the Buddhist tradition, because he's Hindu. And the old monk who was making the award said Sri Chinmoy's a very special kind of teacher, and teachers of this order only come round every couple of thousand years. He was seeing the level that he's operating from. And I heard a Thai Buddhist monk who's a teacher in his own right and has hundreds of followers. He came to visit Sri Chinmoy in New York and he said he felt like a wee hill looking up at the Himalayas. These people are not noted for that kind of self-effacement when it comes to acknowledging other teachers (L). I don't imagine ever attaining that kind of level in my own life, but there's a certain amount of progress you can make.

IM He comes from a Hindu tradition: is he a Hindu?

AS No. It's not a teaching in that sense of a dogma, or a set of beliefs or a philosophy you have to take on board. In fact, initially I had some difficulty relating to the language he was using, because I had schooled myself in Zen Buddhism, which was very pared down and non-theistic, which was important for me. I'd come through this stage in my adolescence of becoming an atheist and rejecting anything to do with religion, having no truck with it, and then through the kind of hippy exploration I'd come back to some kind of sense of something that could be called God, or that kind of higher reality, but I still was very uncomfortable with the word God. So here was this Hindu teacher talking about a personal God, and about the whole pantheon of Hindu gods, but again not in a dogmatic way. He would also use the word Supreme, meaning the highest, the absolute. That didn't seem quite so personalised: I could relate to that a bit better, because it could refer to the highest in yourself. But eventually I just had to set all those reservations aside; because I felt so much in him personally; I thought he has what it is that I'm looking for: the semantics don't matter at this stage.

IM It's still interesting that you don't tend to use the word 'God' very much.

AS No, I still don't, it's true. And if he doesn't have a problem with that I don't either! (L) He does, quite openly. He produced a rather thick volume called 'God' (L). That's going for it! Very inspiring it is too. It's obviously not a simplistic notion: it's a wee word, but it's a very very complicated concept, and the way he writes about it is quite illuminating.

IM The six of you that started off together – is everybody still in there?

AS There are three of the six still doing it, which thirty years down the road isn't bad.

IM And would somebody who wasn't doing it any more feel guilty? I

come from a Scottish tradition, and think that's an important
question. (L)

AS   There isn't a simple answer to that, and I think it probably does
depend on the individual and what their background has been. Some
people just come in and do it for a few months, and they've gone
away learning a few things about how to meditate. Some people stay
with it for years and it becomes a very difficult decision if they have
to wrench themselves away. I've seen often not so much a sense of
guilt, but perhaps a lingering sadness that they're giving up something that's been so much a part of their lives.

The second part of this interview was also conducted in my room at
King's College, Old Aberdeen, on 18 May 2000.

IM   Today I want to talk to Alan particularly about his writing. I'll just
start by asking him how he came to know he wanted to write, and
what kind of thing he first did.

AS   The urge was there from a very early age. As soon as I could do
joined-up writing I wanted to be writing poems and stories, and
some of the teachers recognised this and encouraged me, even as far
back as primary school. I think it was the last year or two at
secondary school when I was 17, 18 that the notion of actually
being a writer started to take hold of me.

    I read a lot at that time, and I discovered Dylan Thomas and the
whole world of poetry, which was an absolute revelation to me. And
I didn't understand half of what Dylan Thomas was writing – he
himself called it 'ferocious and ununderstandable', and I was quite
happy to ferociously ununderstand it and go about ranting it (L). It
was wonderful, intoxicating stuff: if this was poetry I wanted more of
it. Reading his poetry led me on to read his prose, his short stories,
his one novel, *Adventures in the Skin Trade*. But I loved the stories:
they were like nothing I'd read before. They seemed to be about
ordinary, everyday life, and yet written with this heightened, poetic
vividness. Through reading books about him and the kind of things
he'd read, that led me on to reading Joyce and on to Chekhov, and I
gradually got a different sense of what a short story could be from
things I'd maybe read at school, or things I'd previously read for
enjoyment, which always seemed to turn around a surprise ending,
the twist in the tail (L), the Roald Dahl special. Although some of

those I still remember very vividly, particularly stories by Saki, H H Munro. I loved the elegance of those, and the otherness of the world he was describing, this effete Georgian upper-class universe, a million miles away from Govan in the sixties. That's probably why I was drawn into it and loved it so much.

IM It was specifically short stories you were liking, rather than longer fiction?

AS Indeed. Yes, for some reason I was drawn to that form. And I can't remember when the notion occurred to me that I could actually write stories myself, but I remember the first few poems I wrote, and they were also heavily influenced by Dylan Thomas. And I've told this story often, in schools when people ask you how did you start writing. I had got this notion that I wanted to write poetry, and I didn't know what to write about, and was feeling quite short-changed, compared with the likes of Dylan Thomas, who wrote about his summers in his Granny's farm in Wales. 'I was young and easy under the apple-boughs' – but I was looking out of my back window at Govan (L) circa 1965–6, which was one of the bleakest places on the planet. I just recently saw a photograph of one of those back courts where I used to play, in Alex Ferguson's autobiography, and it sent a chill down my spine, seeing the reality of it. I wrote about it in all those stories, and exorcised it, and wrote it out of my system, but to be confronted again with the reality of just how horrible and bleak it was – it really was ugly. And in the distance there was a wee boy up on a dyke, a midden, who could just as easily have been me. The photo was taken in 1945, a couple of years before I was born, but it hadn't changed.

Anyway, this was the landscape I was looking at out of my back window and it was like a moment of revelation. If it had been one of those Hollywood movies, this God-voice would have boomed out: 'This is what you've to write about!' I didn't know anything else, and I suddenly saw that there were things, when I looked closely at the landscape – it was a very interesting landscape, the scabby dugs snuffling about on the midden, and the kids playing in the stagnant puddles, and the wine-moppers sneaking through the back court, and so on. So I wrote a couple of wee poems, very heavily Thomas-esque, if there is such a word –

IM There is now.

AS And they were published in my school magazine, and I'd an English teacher, God rest him, Paddy Inglis, who died a few years back – this was at Allan Glen's school in Glasgow. And he thought these poems were rather wonderful, published them in the school magazine. And one of them was picked up by *The Scotsman* in their school magazine competition. It didn't win, but it was highly commended, and they published it. And Eddie Morgan was one of the judges, and it thrilled me to bits, that a real poet had read my stuff and liked it enough to give it a prize.

It was round about that time, as well as reading the poetry, I'd started moving into the short stories, and somewhere in there I thought I could actually write this kind of short story about exactly that kind of reality, the stuff I see out of the window, those lives, my growing up there, the people I knew. And that in itself was an important step, to realise that your own experience, your own biography, could be the material for a work of fiction as well. So I tried a story – I'd left school and gone on to university by that time – and I wrote a short story which I read out loud at a wee performance at the Edinburgh Festival Fringe. I'd met a few people at the university who were also writing – Tom McGrath had a kind of open house in his kitchen in Bank Street, where everybody and anybody who was writing used to drop in. That was where I first met Tom Leonard, Liz Lochhead, Alasdair Gray – a whole host of other folk who'd just drop in there and hang out.

A group of us had got together to do a week of readings and improvised theatre performances at the Festival Fringe.

IM Now we are talking *Magic Flute!* Did you hang words in trees?

AS We did indeed! The first year that we did this must have been 1968. And I had just written a story called 'Silver in the Lamplight' – a fine Gothic-sounding title – and I read it at this reading and this chap came up to me afterwards and said how much he liked it, and this was Bob Tait, who was at this time editing *Scottish International*. He liked the story; he wanted to publish it, and he was willing to pay me for the privilege – he paid me something like £18, which at the time was an awful lot of money (L) – I could live for a couple of weeks on that!

IM Can I interrupt to ask if 'Silver in the Lamplight' was a quotation from anything? Because titles seem to be quite important in your work.

AS No. They are, and they're often the first thing that comes to me, a

title will come and that will spark the whole idea. No: this just
emerged from the writing of the story, and it ended up being the last
line of the story, a sort of coda. I'd have called it something else if I'd
written it now: it seems a wee bit precious now, but I was twenty (L).
Bob was very keen on this story. It was just handwritten on A4 sheets
of paper, and he took it away and had it typed up and published it.
That was quite a thrill. He did a whole issue devoted to our group,
called The Other People – that was Tom McGrath's name for us.
There was an article by Tom, poems by one or two of the other
people in the group, and my story. And a photo of me, aged twenty,
all in black with shoulder-length hair, very Pre-Raphaelite, in a
garden in George Square (L) in Edinburgh. [*See Scottish International 8 November 1969, pp 27–32, 36.*]

IM   This is an irresistible question, though it's cheeky. Can one identify,
     if one knew them well enough, the characters in *The Magic Flute*? Is
     Bird Tom McGrath, for example, or based on, or connected to
     him? . . .

AS   That's an interesting one, and I think not. Part of the role that the
     character of Bird plays in *The Magic Flute* was the role actually
     played by Tom McGrath, but I think as characters they are quite
     different. There were elements in the Bird character of someone I
     had actually met at school – a musician who came from a middle-
     class home, with curly red hair and a sort of languid self-assurance
     about himself.

     By the time I'd got to *The Magic Flute*, although there were very
     strong autobiographical elements, it seemed to be working differ-
     ently, in that I had devised these characters, the four main char-
     acters, who were fictional constructs, but had elements of people that
     I knew – and elements of myself, especially in Tam and Brian.
     People often ask, which of these characters is you? And the answer's
     none of them, and all of them, really. But more of me is in Tam and
     Brian. I think Tam is the musician I would have liked to be. I do
     play the flute, but not as well as Tam does. I think I write better than
     Brian does – I'm the writer Brian would have liked to be, and Tam's
     the musician I would have liked to be (L). I invented these
     characters and was consciously putting them in situations that I'd
     been in, and allowing the fictional side of it to develop, rather than
     straight autobiography. That gave it a kind of flexibility, a sense of
     adventure for me, it wasn't set in stone what was going to happen to

these characters: they had lives of their own, and took these situations in different directions.

IM   But it is an interesting question, because both before *Magic Flute* and since, a lot of your writing has been, as far as I can tell, somewhat autobiographical, and very often back to the childhood. I'm sure you've written more about the boy and his mother and his father – you've gone back several times to your father, to the career he was deprived of, as a sailmaker, and the way he crumpled after your mother died. It's recognisable, when one does this artificial thing of re-reading Spence in a one-er (L), that the situation comes up many times. And you write about it in different modes: we've already mentioned poetry and short stories and novel, but there's also theatre, and there's a play about the father as well.

AS   *Sailmaker* – which I adapted and expanded from a short story of the same name. I wrote this originally as a short story, and my father actually read the story – perhaps even heard it read on radio, and was quite moved by it, and not in any way offended. He thought it was a very fair portrayal. A few years after that, I'd started writing plays out of necessity, originally. I'd become completely self-employed as a writer. I did the Writer in Residence post at Glasgow University '75–77. I came out of that, and suddenly the monthly wage was no longer there, and I'd got used to it (L). So I thought there must be ways I can make the writing pay. I started doing wee things like the occasional book review, and articles for *The Scotsman*, and then I got a phone call from someone at STV – a man called Robert Love, who'd just come back to Scotland and had taken over as drama producer at STV. The cynic in me now sees that this had a wee bit to do with STV applying for the renewal of their franchise, and having to be seen to show some commitment to native Scottish writing (L). He was looking for new drama talent, folk to write half-hour TV plays, and got my name from the Arts Council, and asked if I had any ideas for plays, and I said yes, yes, yes (L). I didn't have a single idea in my head, but I wanted to meet him and talk about this, because the money on offer was – at the time it was probably about £800 for half an hour, which was a lot of money at the tail end of the seventies: I could really live for quite a wee while on that.

So I had a look at some of my stories, and thought perhaps some of these would adapt as half-hour plays. The restrictions were that it all had to be shot in studio with a very small cast – budget considerations again! So I eventually homed in on a story called 'The Palace' from *Its Colours They Are Fine*. It was quite a long story, but I saw that the last section could be quite self-contained as a wee half-hour drama. I put this idea to Robert, and he liked it. I adapted it, and it was done very successfully. They even actually branched out and filmed a couple of shots outside, showing the Kibble Palace in the Botanic Gardens.

But I really had a stroke of luck with the casting. We had Paul Curran as the character of an old tramp, and the main character, who was modelled on my father, was played by Fulton Mackay. The two of them had worked together since the fifties, and just knew each others' ways inside out. They were such old pros, they were just a joy to work with. They really loved the material – they liked the play. And I learned a lot from them about how to communicate without words. Being STV, the thing had to be precisely twenty-four minutes or whatever, for the advert breaks, so there was some cutting required. And I remember at one point Fulton Mackay saying to me, that line there could go: I can communicate that just by the way I look at Paul. I wasn't at all convinced, but he said, we'll run that bit and I'll show you. He cut the line, gave him a wee look – and I bowed to his wisdom and his acting ability. But that was a real joy to work on: it had a very magical quality about it, quite a spiritual quality. And in fact when Fulton Mackay died a few years later, they showed that play as a tribute to him.

So then the same play was done on stage, at the Tron Theatre: they were having a series of lunchtime plays, again short ones. This fitted the bill perfectly – different cast, but it worked as a stage play as well. It was very simple. A park bench was the entire set. And a chap called Peter Liechtenfels who was at the time artistic director at the Traverse saw that and wanted to commission me to write a full-length play, so great, that means even more money: I can live for a year on this (L). Peter asked if I'd any ideas and I had two or three, one of which was to take the *Sailmaker* story and open it out, adapt it. But for some reason I wasn't too keen on that. I suspect I knew it was going to be painful to go as deeply into that relationship as I was going to have to do for a play. So I went along to Peter to discuss things with him, and I put the other couple of ideas on his desk, but he homed in right away on the fact that I was holding this one back. 'Tell me more about that one.' And he could sense my reluctance, and he very quickly worked out why I was reluctant, and he knew that the writing of this was going to be quite painful for me, but he was quite ruthless about it. He thought that it might make a good play because of the intensity of the emotion, and he insisted that that was the one he wanted to commission. So I went away and I wrote that. By this time my father had died, and I think it would have been difficult to write the play while he was still alive, because I was confronting the painful period in our relationship much more directly and honestly than I had in some of the stories. Maybe I couldn't have written it until after he had died.

Life is always throwing up these patterns and strange coincidences. When I was writing the television version of 'The Palace', which was effectively about my father at a certain stage in his life, I'd just finished typing up the last page – I'd an old manual typewriter at the time – wound the page out, put it down on my desk – the phone rang, and it was someone to tell me my father had just died: he'd had a heart attack and fallen down in the street. So that shook me a wee bit, the coincidence of me writing this thing that was trying to make sense of a certain time in his life coinciding with him actually dying. And during rehearsals for the television version of the play, Fulton Mackay was playing my father and there were times when it was chilling to me – I would look at him, and he was suddenly getting my father's mannerisms, it was bizarre. And where we were rehearsing the play – it was just a space in Glasgow's West End – I could look out the window and see the last house where my father had lived – it was just across the road. Fulton Mackay was asking me things about the character and trying to figure out what kind of job he might have done: 'I reckon he would be something like a storeman' – and that's exactly what he'd been for the last ten years of his life: he'd been a storeman in a factory and then in a Christian bookshop. So I'd obviously entered very deeply into the character of my father to create this stage character to the extent that Fulton Mackay could pick up on it. So the play was very much a kind of exorcism for me of the more painful aspects of my relationship with my father. I vividly remember sitting during rehearsals one time, and there's a scene between the boy and his father, and they're arguing, and I found myself getting completely exasperated at the boy, – God, why doesn't he leave the old guy alone? Can't he see he's doing his best? (L) I'd become so distanced from the material that I was just seeing it as artefact. Then there was one of those wee lights going on in my head – no, he can't see, and no, you couldn't see (L). And you were a mean wee sod to him at times. So all of that was very therapeutic.

IM And so, when you come to a distorted reflection of the same situation in *Way To Go*, for example, you're more reluctant about criticism because of the exorcism.

AS I think so, yes. And maybe freer to fictionalise the thing more.

IM And be funny.

AS Aye, exactly: I'm glad you found it funny (L). There are lighter touches of humour in the other stuff, and there are moments in *Sailmaker* when the audience always laugh out loud, but you're right – *Way To Go* is treating the material in a consciously comic or blackly comic mode. But the freedom is there to do that now.

IM I think what you've done is in a way contradict yourself quite splendidly. When I started asking you about this, it was all – you were doing it for the money, but the last wee bit you've been talking it's all been about how important your father was and how you felt about your father, which was the impression I'd got from my reading. Being so used to thinking of you as someone who's above or below or outwith mere matters of money.

AS I heard Alasdair Gray being interviewed in a dreadful radio interview, one of those live situations where he was retouching the mural he did many years ago in the Ubiquitous Chip restaurant in Glasgow, and he did this in exchange for a certain number of meals, and the interviewer said to him: 'So you were painting for food, were you?' And there was a slight pause: you could hear Alasdair's brain dealing with the banality of the question: 'I think we all work in order to eat – even you', he said (L). I was kind of half joking when I was saying the money was good, but I didn't have any other way of earning money, and I was genuinely making an effort to see if I could do it just from the writing, without having to fall back on other work.

IM You only didn't have any other way of earning a living because you didn't terribly want to become a nine-to-fiver.

AS Exactly, or pursue any kind of academic career.

IM Because of your desire to be writing and just having enough to get by on, that's my impression.

AS That's right. That's one thing the sixties did for me, I think, an ability to survive on a fairly meagre amount of money. Other things were more important than having the house in the suburbs and the car, and the 2.4 kids. That was a very conscious decision. It coincided with a sense of myself as a writer more than anything else.

IM   And the first of the Writer in Residences was in 1975. That must have been somebody fairly forward-looking, who gave you that job, because you hadn't published very much.

AS   That's right. I'd had a few stories in magazines, but I didn't have a full book out. *Its Colours They Are Fine* came out at the end of that residency, in '77. It was in the pipeline, and people knew it was coming. But that was remarkable: I was 27, went along for the interview, and I had not long graduated from Glasgow University, because – this may have been covered in the earlier part of the interview, I can't remember (L) – I had been to Glasgow University in two spells, one from '66 to '69, and then dropped out for a few years; finished off an Ordinary degree '73 to '74, and then got this Writer in Residence job in '75, so I'd only recently been a student there and saw the job advertised and thought, nothing to lose, may as well apply for it. Edwin Morgan and Tom McGrath gave me references, and I toddled along to the interview. As I was on my way into the interview Liz Lochhead was coming out. She'd just been interviewed for the job. Lorn Macintyre – a Glasgow novelist – he was waiting to go in after me. I think there had been three or four other people in the course of the afternoon, so I thought, I don't have a lot of chance here. And there were eight people around the table interviewing me – it really felt Kafka-esque. They were round three sides of you, so you'd be addressing someone and you could feel eyes boring into the side of you! But Edwin Morgan was actually on the interviewing panel, although he'd given me a reference: Alex Scott was on the panel: I've got a feeling Derick Thomson from the Gaelic Department was: there was a student representative, and one or two other University court types. And I felt I was grilled inside out for about half an hour, and I thought I'd done a very bad interview, because I got a wee bit heated at one point, and argued with Alex Scott about something (L), and thought I'd blown the whole thing. I came out feeling thoroughly depressed. Someone phoned me the next day to ask if I wanted the job! I was leaping in the air, kicking my heels together.

At the time I had taken on a job – I was living in Edinburgh by that time – I was doing a day job in the library at Napier College as a library assistant, and working in the evenings at a baked potato shop, just because we didn't have enough money. And neither of the jobs was enough by itself. I think Janani was doing her teacher training, so she was just subsisting on a student grant. So from having to do these two jobs to make ends meet, suddenly I was in this university post, enormously well paid for two years, and doing something that was really quite enjoyable and exciting.

IM   And was it enjoyable? I know these jobs are always trying to give you quite a lot of time to yourself to write, but also there's all the business of trying to help young writers, and organise conferences and all the rest of it: does all of that appeal?

AS   It does. The danger is that you can get too caught up in that side of it and not get enough of your own work done. I think for the first year in the job I was quite guilty of that. You're eager to please; you want to do the right thing, and also you're genuinely enthusiastic. I'd had different advice from folk who had done the job before. I remember speaking to George Bruce, who'd been a predecessor, and he was wonderfully generous and benign, and I got the feeling that he'd been very accessible and very available to students, and done a lot to help them. I spoke to another predecessor that I won't name and he basically told me that he just hid away and kept his head down, and if someone managed to beat a path to his door, so be it, he would deal with them (L). I think he was exaggerating slightly, but he definitely took it more in that direction than George did. Possibly because I was younger and closer in age to the students and was fired up with ideas about having readings and performances and all that kind of thing, I think I generated quite a bit of energy in the job, and I really did enjoy it. And I must have got enough of my own work done, because I managed to finish *Its Colours They Are Fine* and get it to the publishers during that two years. So there was obviously time enough for my own work. And I did organise readings – I remember I had Liz Lochhead, Tom Leonard, Alasdair Gray. Alasdair Gray came and read to I think nine people, including me. This was before *Lanark* appeared. John Purser came and read – I can't remember who else.

And I also pioneered these poetry videos. God knows what ever happened to these things, but I got Tom Leonard and Liz Lochhead to come into a studio and read some of their poems and then folk from the audio-visual department were trying to match the words to images on screen. And we tried to make it non-literal. As I remember it, there were actual words appearing on the screen, and fading into unrelated images.

IM   I was going to ask you about music. Do you listen to a lot of music now?

AS   I do, yes.

IM   And is it all Mozart?

AS   No! God help me, I listen to Radio One in the morning when I get up, especially when I'm staying in Aberdeen on my own. I have a wee routine: I get up and do some exercises and have the radio on – not too loud: if you don't have it too loud you can tune out all the babble and banter of the DJs. But I do find a lot of current rock and popular music still quite interesting and worth spending time on. But I also still listen to classical music, and Indian music and Japanese music – very eclectic tastes. No formal training in music whatsoever. I'd learned the basics of playing the flute when I was at school – bullied into the school orchestra at too young an age, and that put me off for many years. I came back to it years later just for my own enjoyment. I just picked up a flute one day and thought, I could actually get a lot out of this. Got one on hire purchase to pay up, and started learning initially just melodies composed by my meditation teacher, because he's written lots of devotional songs which are very sweet and simple melodies. I still mainly play those on the flute: occasionally I venture into other kinds of music.

IM   In *The Magic Flute* the popular music of the time when these young men were growing up seems terribly important.

AS   Absolutely, yes. I was writing about this for a website recently – *The Magic Flute* was included in a project by the Scottish Library Association to put books in schools, and they created a website with information about the different books, and I wrote a wee thing saying that it's almost like you're inhabiting your own video with its own soundtrack as you walk around, especially at that age. And the music of the time is very much a soundtrack to your life. I still find that the case. It was very noticeable then, that the music was so much a part of the changes that were happening: the music was part of this expansion, this sense of freedom, the revolution was in the air. I find music very affecting: it seems to touch me very deeply, whether it is rock music or classical.

IM   And the other things that a lot of the characters in *The Magic Flute* get up to is drug experiences. Is that you writing from your own experience?

AS Yes. We touched on this in an earlier part of the interview. [*See above, pp 175–7.*] I've never been heavily drawn into a drug scene. I don't want to sound like I'm recommending these experiences, because I think I realised at a very early age that it was quite a dangerous thing to mess with, and could very easily lead to psychosis. I saw enough people being messed up by it. At the time I was seeing it very much as a sacrament. I had read people like Timothy Leary and Richard Alpert and I thought that taking it in the right kind of context and with the right kind of preparation and the right care to your environment it could be something that actually was, to use the expression they used then, mind-expanding. [*Leary and Alpert were both Harvard professors of Psychology who wrote about achieving serious enlightenment through drugs. They became very popular among some of the younger generation, and both left their academic posts.*]

IM Several characters in *The Magic Flute* say that it is religious, or that it's 'Zen', and I'm wondering whether you wonder what the reader's going to make of that.

AS It was very much my attitude at the time. I moved beyond it very quickly. That period, especially '67 to '69, was quite an intense period. I went through four lifetimes at that time, from this wee boy from Govan studying Law to this Zen-interested hippy with shoulder-length hair. I realised very quickly that the drugs weren't going to do it. They could give a certain kind of experience, and I'm not sorry that I experienced things in that way because maybe I needed a kind of jolt out of my very narrow perceptions and my sense that life was as I perceived it – we think we know what reality is, we have it sussed, that how we perceive things actually is how they are. And these drugs gave such a jolt to that, and showed me that there were vast areas to our perception that I hadn't begun to tap yet, that you could perceive things very differently from the mundane everyday rational intellectual level at which we mostly operated. There were aspects to our minds that seemed able to incorporate a vastness, and to perceive the universe as something vast but which we could somehow be in touch with – we were part and parcel of that vastness, you could experience a kind of oneness (L) – it sounds so clichéd now, that's why I'm stumbling with words.

I heard a joke recently about the Dalai Lama ordering a hamburger. He was in New York and he passed a hamburger stall and he says to the hamburger stall owner, 'Make me one with everything' (L). But there is a sense in which we really are one with everything, and every religious urge or mystical urge or spiritual urge is about re-establishing that, that oneness with the vast universe, and with a benign loving presence that can be felt behind that. And I think these drugs gave a glimpse of that: in amongst all the chaotic stuff and the paranoia and the psychosis, there were moments of total expansion and a sense of that something other. But it's too violent. Someone described it once as like punching a hole in your consciousness – OK, you get through to the other side, but at what damage?

IM   Potentially irreversible damage . . .

AS   Often, yes. And my meditation teacher Sri Chinmoy – it was one of the first things he insisted on, that we all absolutely, categorically, from that moment stopped taking drugs, because he said they really do damage your system, they damage what he calls your subtle nerves, your spiritual faculties, your ability to tune into things in a very fine way. They really do damage that. So I'm very glad I met him. I think actually I met him just after I'd decided that for myself anyway. But I think it did leave a gap – I thought, I'm not going to do that any more, but how am I going to get in touch with that aspect of reality that I've glimpsed? And the meditation and my teacher, in his own very gentle way, seemed to be offering a path towards a much more integrated approach to those deeper realities. I had an interesting conversation with a friend in New York recently, a guy who's been doing this same meditation for exactly the same length of time as I have. (He met Sri Chinmoy one day before me, because Sri Chinmoy was in Dublin, where this guy was living. So he pulls rank on me, (L) he's been involved longer than me by one day.) But I had been voicing this notion, that maybe the drugs were an essential part of what we went through, and they were partly what led us to the spiritual path, and he said think of how many people you knew back then who were taking drugs and how many of them are following a spiritual path. There's you and there's me! (L). So it wasn't the drugs that got us out; it was a deep need that we had anyway, and we would have found our way to this way of life no matter what. The drugs were just something that we used on the way.

IM   I find this very interesting because earlier, you talked about the website and *The Magic Flute* going into school libraries. A book like *Magic Flute* hardly seems to me to have a message against taking drugs.

AS   I suppose I couldn't have written honestly if I'd taken the anti-drugs stance, because at the time I was writing it and trying to look honestly at my development through these years I had to take some kind of positive element from those drug experiences, even though ultimately I felt it wasn't a road I wanted to go down, and certainly wasn't a road I'd want to advise anyone else to go down. It would have been dishonest to have pretended otherwise.

IM   And I hasten to remind myself that the character of Paki Black and the children who are found dabbling in drugs at school are clearly not a good thing.

     And also what happens to Eddie was quite a shock to me. That's not a question of drugs, but of religious bigotry, thuggery, and drink. And Eddie just very suddenly and casually at the end of one chapter gets blown up.

AS   Some critics thought that was a bit too abrupt and too violent, and that I was evading dealing with the character of Eddie as he matured – what was he going to end up as? In the Special Unit at Barlinnie, becoming a sculptor, maybe? (L) But I decided right from the very outset that I wanted Eddie to end that way, and I wanted the violence of that absolute truncation, and the ending of all possibilities for him, because that's what the society we grew up in did, to folk like Eddie. His options were restricted from Day One, from the bullying father and the alcoholic mother and the big brother that cuffed him about the ear, and the absolute lack of understanding. I've known far too many Eddies, and dramatically it seemed to me the way to go, and I had that in mind right from the beginning, that he was going to disappear in the middle. Edwin Morgan wrote a wonderful poem years ago, the title of it escapes me, but it was about death, and it was unfinished, the last line just stopped in mid-line, and because it had such a powerful rhythm and metrical rhyme-scheme, you were going along with this movement of it, and it was such a shock to have that line cut off. [*See Edwin Morgan, Poems of Thirty Years, 'Interferences', vii, 'They put me in this bed, and said'.*] It was something like that I was trying to do in the novel by just stopping him literally dead in the middle of the book.

IM I think it works. Can I ask you also about *Space Invaders?*

AS *Sailmaker* had been a success at the Traverse, both in terms of
audience responses and critical reviews. One bad review from Joyce
Macmillan, and she was big enough, eight or nine years later when
the play was revived by TAG for Glasgow's Year of Culture to revise
her opinion of it, and say she got it wrong, and it was a play whose
time had come. Good on her! (L) She also had a couple of sly digs at
the earlier production, saying that must have been at fault. I didn't
think so: I thought it was a wonderful production.

But following on from that the Traverse wanted me to do another
full–length play. I had been doing a Writer in Residence post just for
one year in a school in Livingston, and I used to go running behind
the school every day at lunchtime. And those woods I used to run
through were the setting for an extraordinary incident that was
reported in the papers. A forestry worker came staggering out of
these woods one day with his clothes scorched, in a dazed, incoherent
state, and said he'd seen a flying saucer. There had been this ball
sitting in the clearing, and two smaller balls came out from that and
zapped him with some kind of electrical impulse, knocked him to the
ground and burned his clothes. So it was big news for a wee while
and all sorts of UFO experts were beating a path to Livingston and
interviewing this man in his house. I suppose I had filed the
information away, and was intrigued at the thought that I knew
the very spot: I used to run through that very clearing every day. So
the idea took root and I thought what must it have been like for just
an ordinary wee guy having his life totally turned upside down: how
would it have affected his relationships, his job situation, all that? So
I suggested this as possible material for a play to Peter Liechtenfels,
and he thought it was fine and commissioned it. And then I started
doing some research on flying saucers, and that was great fun, just
reading all these books about UFOs, and seeing how many similarities there were from sighting to sighting, and it was really
remarkable. There were certain patterns that just kept recurring,
whether it was in Broxburn or the Mojave Desert.

And I read a monograph by Jung on flying saucers – I was
astonished to hear that he'd written one. He was approaching it as
psychic phenomenon, and he took these recurring images as indication that it was a psychic experience occurring at some archetypal
level, some need that we had to have these experiences. So I was

intrigued at that notion as well. I was quite a few years embarked by that time on the practice of meditation and probably aware of being perceived as some kind of strange, weird character who was getting into all these esoteric areas of experience. The character in the play is called Andrew, and I suppose some of his efforts to articulate his need to understand the big picture about Life, the Universe and Everything were coming from my attempts to explain to people what I was about, with this meditation, and asking the big questions about life – why are we here, who are we, what's it all for.

That's effectively what Andrew's going through, through the invasion of these extraterrestrial elements. And you're never quite sure, I hope, by the end of the play whether it is something that has physically happened out there, or whether it is some kind of psychic or psychotic experience he's gone through. But either way he's purged by the end of it, and he's come to some kind of acceptance of his own life and his situation. Interestingly, after I'd read this monograph by Jung and used his ideas in the play, I heard that towards the end of his life Jung had actually revised his opinion and was convinced that there really was something out there, and that we were being visited by extraterrestrial life-forms (L). So there you go. I think in the play I hedged my bets sufficiently.

IM   And Jung wasn't really being an awful lot of help to Andrew.

AS   That's right, and he was being analysed by a Freudian psychiatrist who wasn't helping him much either. At the time I was quite interested in various forms of performance art as well: I had seen a couple of shows by a woman called Laurie Anderson, an American performance artist, who did these wonderful things, essentially monologues, and visual images on a screen. But the voices which Andrew is hearing in his head – they were embodied on stage – it was two actors playing the parts of these visiting forces, whatever they were. There's a certain word-play when these voices are speaking to him: it's like they're having a wee private joke to themselves, and teasing him, and poking at things that he knows and half-knows and thinks from his memories, and taking him back into memories from his adolescence and then from his childhood and memories from even earlier. But I think the technique of those voices, the wordplay, the repetitions, the patterns of words, were very much influenced by the kind of things that Laurie Anderson was doing, and other American performance artists were doing things like that. And I was doing my own version of it in a wee stage version of *Glasgow Zen*, which had live synthesiser music and back projections. This was the eighties, and so that whole synthesiser, techno thing was quite prominent and current, and that was what was being experimented with.

IM   And again your own interest in being part of a live theatrical experience is clear. While we're there, can we just talk a little about *Changed Days*? I think possibly that a cruel hostile critic might say about your work in general that while it's very penetrating, very moving, it sometimes seems to indulge in nostalgia for its own sake, and they might say that particularly about *Changed Days*. As you say at the beginning, it was a community play contributed by what the community said, and so you actually get conflicting attitudes because you're getting evidence from different people, but it's almost just let's indulge nostalgia.

AS   The brief, and there was a brief – this was a commissioned work – was to use this reminiscence material. The word reminiscence itself carries connotations of rose-tinted nostalgic looking back at the good old days. I was trying – some critics seemed to pick up on this – to set that up as a mode, let's have a singalong and talk about the old days: and constantly undercut that with the very harsh and brutal realities that these people did live through. So the play starts with the recreation of a community pageant in 1929, celebrating the history of Edinburgh from its inception. And that's cut across by the voice of the people saying OK, this is history as we're taught it and as we know it, but what was really happening in 1929, was twenty folk in a two-roomed tenement and cold water flats and rats and diphtheria and all of that. So that keeps coming in as a subtext – and then of course the characters with their irrepressible working-class bon-hommie have another sing-song. I think I was doing both things simultaneously; I was using that energy and playing on the nostalgia of the memories and the nostalgic expectations of the audiences to drive it along, and it did have great energy, like a music-hall production, but constantly bringing in this darker note.

IM   The darker note is very clear, but I suppose what I'm saying is that there is less 'message' that you would get from John McGrath using the same material. You could see John writing something really quite similar, except that there would be more of a push towards some end.

AS   Maybe I was just caught up in looking at the nostalgia business as well, because it ends with the recreation of a reminiscence group, and structurally looking back at what we've been doing and examining it. And I think it worked very well onstage. The very last sequence was pared down to just one woman on stage, just one character, and although the memories we used were the memories of many different people in Edinburgh, it focused in, as you were watching it on stage, it was as if you were watching the development of one family, these characters that you'd come to know. And in particular this one woman who'd been a child at the beginning of the play and was an old woman in the reminiscence group at the end of it. In the last scene she is left there with these ghost voices round about her which are lines from earlier in the play spanning fifty years. There's a wee throwaway gag at the end, but I think it becomes more than nostalgia. There's a sense of time passing and the transience of everything. I suppose for me it was almost a kind of Zen sense of time passing. And then the director John Carnegie wanted to do this song at the end, again a celebratory song about the Royal Mile, and we'd just been watching this stuff about the Royal Mile for a couple of hours, and the song itself is hugely ironic in context, and there's a very sudden cut to black and silence when you expect a big finale. It's just cut, and the theatre's in blackness.

IM   The problem I had reading it was that I don't know this song, and I don't know the music, and as I said earlier on music is terribly important in your work − but I didn't know this.

[Ever obliging, Alan here gave an impromptu chorus of the song, which more than proved his point, but IM pursued it more generally.]

A lot of the times I was reading your various books, I wondered whether younger people would be able to supply the music in their heads, and I felt privileged because I usually knew it, and it makes such a difference.

AS   This week I organised a reading by Kate Atkinson, and she was reading with a couple of younger writers, Sian Preece and Susie Maguire. I was making the point that Kate Atkinson and I are the same vintage − she's a couple of years younger, so I recognised so many of the cultural references, the Coronation, the music she was listening to in the sixties, and Susie was saying that it must be nice to be writing your generation, and she was conscious that they, her and Sian and other writers of that age, have their cultural references that they mention – a TV programme, or a particular pop song. All of that will get a response in the way things I refer to get a response. So maybe that's why I'm still desperately listening to Radio One (L) in a feeble effort to be current!

IM Tell me about the play that hasn't been printed, the Timex play which was called *On the Line*, and which was done in Dundee.

AS Yes, Dundee Rep [*1996*]. That was a very interesting project to work on. As with *Changed Days*, it was based on research material, largely interview material. Plus as much newspaper coverage, television coverage, as we could lay hands on. John Carnegie who directed *Changed Days* also directed this, and did a good deal of the research. He has a wonderful capacity for ordering information, John. The play was ostensibly about the Timex dispute. We did lots of interviews with people who'd been involved.

IM Remind me what happened at the Timex dispute.

AS The Timex management decided in 1992 to downsize, and already this had been happening over a number of years, just the nature of changing industry. And this latest round of cuts was going to be particularly brutal in its effect on the community. So the workforce got together and came up with a plan to have job-sharing, so only half the people needed to be laid off. The people involved were perfectly in agreement about it; it wasn't going to cost the company any more; it was going to solve their problem, keep people in work. The company said no, categorically. The workforce went out on strike and were sacked while they were out on strike, and a scab workforce brought in. The intention was obviously to run down the factory and close it. From the outset; it had been decreed at a much higher level, probably to do with money movements in the Philippines and the Hong Kong market. But the workforce mounted a picket line demonstration at the factory gates.

IM Which is where the title comes from.

AS And as with all my titles there are several layers of meaning, because they were putting themselves on the line, in all sorts of ways. It became a *cause célèbre*; there were folk coming to join the picket line from all over the place, and politicians turning up for photo opportunities. And Tommy Sheridan getting himself arrested and carted off to jail. It was headline news for quite a time. Eventually of course the factory was closed, as had been intended all along. But there was something in that struggle that had an echo of the great, heroic struggles of the past. It was a very complex situation, as all of these things are – industry *is* changing, and a lot of these companies can't keep things up at the level they once did. At one time Timex employed five thousand people, maybe seven thousand people in Dundee. And that had dwindled to a few hundred by the end, but it was still a very important employer. But it was the heavy-handedness of the management's position and the way they treated the work-force, refused at every stage to compromise or to find a solution because they didn't want a solution; they'd already decided.

So we interviewed hundreds of people, it felt like; strikers, one or two people from what they euphemistically called the replacement workforce, it was very brave of them to talk to us; middle management, but no one in any kind of authoritative position, and certainly no one from head office at Timex. I was in New York, and phoned up their head office, which was in Connecticut, just up the road, thinking I could go up and talk to someone. The people on the phone were very polite, very civil, but as soon as I mentioned Dundee, the whole manner changed. If you'd like to write to our PR department, sir . . . we got the bum's rush at every stage. Which was a shame, because it meant they didn't get a chance to put their side of the story: we had to just put their side of the story in published statements to the press, and media releases. Which weighted the material very much on the side of the striking workers. I think in spite of that I managed to get some kind of balanced picture of the whole dispute. We put it in historical context as well: we started with the formation of Timex in Dundee in 1947. And also philosophically look at notions of time, and what's time all about – that's my concerns coming in again. As with *Changed Days* there was a high energy knockabout, musical element to it. We'd music composed by Ricky Ross, who's from Dundee and a former singer with Deacon Blue. That was very dynamic, and got the audience going. But again the darker side was always there: these people's lives were being trampled on and there was a great deal of suffering.

Ultimately the hope was that by looking at this material we would begin to effect some kind of healing process in Dundee. That sounds very grandiose, and overly well-intentioned, but I think it actually did begin to happen. There was a group of young hotheaded strikers who called themselves the A Team, and they were going round doing things like putting bricks through scab workers' windows, and pouring acid on their cars, and beating people up as they came out of pubs – not very nice behaviour. And one of these guys actually came to the play and spoke to one of the actors afterwards and said for the first time in his life he actually understood what these people were going through, the people that just desperately needed a job. A woman who'd a couple of kids and was on her own was offered a job: she couldn't turn it down. For the first time he saw that there was actually more than one side to this story, and he came out of it actually chastened at the thought of his own behaviour.

IM   And as I remember, there was a very important local participation element in the production.

AS   Yes, we had a core group of ten professional actors, and then between thirty and forty local community actors, who worked at the Rep with the community wing there.

IM   That makes for a very exciting and community-healing sort of experience.

AS   It was wonderful. And a lot of those people had worked at Timex. People on stage effectively playing themselves. And the people we were portraying in the play were sitting in the audience on the first night. And we had to get it right – we couldn't hit a wrong note there (L). That was frightening. It was really intake of breath time when a character would come on and introduce himself. 'I'm John Kidd' – and John Kidd is sitting in the third row. But John Kidd came round and shook hands with the actor afterwards, and was thrilled at his portrayal of him.

IM   That must have been a huge help with what you're saying about the healing process, the participation.

AS   Tremendous. And theatrically it was so powerful. One evening I was there . . . There's a very dramatic scene where they're deciding whether or not to go out on strike, take this huge step, and there had been a canteen meeting, with shop stewards making various speeches for and against and we dramatised this meeting and had one actor after another and giving very fiery speeches, and what John Carnegie did was put some of the other actors in amongst the audience dressed in their overalls, so as someone would start making a speech he would be heckled from the audience. And you could see the audience startling at this, about to tell the person to be quiet and then realising this was OK, and then starting to join in, so by the time they were making the decision to go out on strike, the whole audience was up on their feet going 'Yes!' (L) It was hairs up on the back of the neck time – beyond theatre: these people were reliving something, exorcising something: it was very powerful.

IM Obviously it would be much less on paper, but are there any plans to print it?

AS It was rooted at the time. The project has had its day.

IM It's timeless in some senses. That situation is not going to stop.

AS Indeed yes. And I am working with John Carnegie again, and my latest project is an update of *The Three Estaitis*, David Lindsay's play, and funnily enough I mentioned the Timex script to him recently, but I was actually trying to track down a copy to give you. I've got papers in boxes all over the place, and John's very meticulous and has everything on computers. He has the finished text and I was saying it might be worth thinking about trying to publish it sometime, and he thought that was a wonderful idea – even just as a historical record.

IM Exactly. And if he does, can I suggest that they put in a couple of pages with, however simply, the tunes of the songs, so that future readers can do something to recreate the aural experience for themselves?

AS Yes. Every time I'm coming from Edinburgh to Aberdeen, as the train comes over the Tay, one of Ricky Ross's songs is in my head. 'Cold grey river slips down silver', and I hear it in my head, because that's what it's doing! (L)

IM And did he write the song, or did you?

AS We tried to collaborate, but I was writing poems instead of songs. That was an interesting experience for me. Basically I gave him rough ideas and titles, and sometimes wee refrains and chorus verses, and he expanded them and made something much, much more of them. He made songs out of them: he's a pro.

IM So now you have written two novels: do you still feel essentially a short story writer? Or are you becoming very flexible on genre? You do poetry: you've got poems coming out this summer. You do short stories; you do novels, you do plays which verge on theatrical events in performance. You've been contemplating a film about Thomas Glover, the 'Scottish samurai'.

AS I'm doing more than contemplating: I've finished a second draft screenplay now, and just heard that Scottish Screen are going to give me some development money to take that further. So there's more and more chance of that actually happening. It's such a huge project and the amounts of money involved are just beyond my comprehension, so I've no idea if it will ever . . .

IM But from your point of view the fascinating thing is you're not cowed in any way by any genre, quite happy to adapt or rewrite *The Three Estates*, for example. Tell me a bit about that.

AS Again that was commissioned. John Carnegie phoned me up some time last year, and put the project to me. It had been dreamed up by various people; John had got together with Angus Calder, Jean Urquhart who runs the Ceilidh Place at Ullapool – various folk got round the table at the Book Festival, probably over a jar or two, and thought, wouldn't it be wonderful to revive *The Three Estates*. It would be nice to make the language more accessible for a modern audience, and John Carnegie was roped into the discussion, and said, I know the very boy to do the job. Initially I was resistant, just because of work pressure, because the Glover film project was already under way, I was looking at adapting *Way To Go* as a television film, which is also in the pipeline. And thinking about maybe another couple of short stories, and do I have the time for all of this?

John can be very persuasive, and he satanically took me to a high place (L), and from Calton Hill he showed me Edinburgh spread out below, and he said, Imagine this – Festival time – laid out – pageant – the three estates are the audience: they're sitting there; there's eight hundred people up here watching this spectacle. He sold it to me. And of course when I read the play and saw how wonderful it was, and what great fun it was . . . Realising my time was short, he said, the contract is this: effectively you're being paid for twelve weeks. Of course I did a lot more than that, but I tried to limit it, and I worked really very hard – eight- or nine-hour days – for that three or four months. And of course the irony is that Edinburgh District Council, who were going to be funding that performance on Calton Hill, have pulled the plug on it – they've overspent for this financial year. They're saying apply again next year and maybe it'll happen. So that particular grandiose scheme isn't coming to fruition. It opens in Cupar some time in July [*3/7/00*] on the site of the original production in 1552 or whatever: it's now a council car park (L). But it's a perfect wee amphitheatre. It's surrounded by council buildings on three sides. Apparently the acoustic is fantastic: the actors love it, and weather permitting it'll be a glorious site. [*Keith Bruce's notice in The Herald, 4/7/00, was headed 'A Triumphant Condensing', and it called for longer life and fuller exposure of the play and the production*]

Alan Spence: Main Publications

ah! 50 haiku Janaka (haiku) Agni Press, Jamaica, N.Y. 11432 1975
Its Colours They Are Fine (short stories) Collins 1977
Glasgow Zen (poems) Print Studio Press, Glasgow 1981
Sailmaker (play). First performed at the Traverse Theatre Club, Edinburgh, 29 April 1982. Published by Hodder & Stoughton 1998
Space Invaders (play). First performed at the Traverse Theatre Club, Edinburgh, 9 June 1983. Published 1983 by Salamander Press, Edinburgh. Published by Hodder & Stoughton 1994
The Magic Flute (novel) Canongate 1990
Changed Days: Memories of an Edinburgh Community (play). First performed November 1988 at Muirhouse Parish Church Hall, Edinburgh. Published by Hodder & Stoughton 1991
Stone Garden and other stories (short stories) Phoenix House 1995
Way To Go (novel) Phoenix House 1998
Seasons of the Heart (haiku) Canongate 2000